Richard J. Foster
& Gayle D. Beebe

Longing for God

SEVEN PATHS OF

CHRISTIAN DEVOTION

IVP Books

An imprint of InterVarsity Press
Downers Grove, Illinois

InterVarsity Press
P.O. Box 1400, Downers Grove, IL 60515-1426
World Wide Web: www.ivpress.com
E-mail: email@ivpress.com

InterVarsity Press® is the book-publishing division of InterVarsity Christian Fellowship/USA®, a student movement active on campus at hundreds of universities, colleges and schools of nursing in the United States of America, and a member movement of the International Fellowship of Evangelical Students. For information about local and regional activities, write Public Relations Dept., InterVarsity Christian Fellowship/USA, 6400 Schroeder Rd., P.O. Box 7895, Madison, WI 53707-7895, or visit the IVCF website at <www.intervarsity.org>.

Scripture quotations, unless otherwise noted, are from the New Revised Standard Version of the Bible, copyright 1989 by the Division of Christian Education of the National Council of the Churches of Christ in the USA. Used by permission. All rights reserved.

Design: Cindy Kiple

Images: Eric Van Den Brulle/Getty Images

ISBN 978-0-8308-3514-0

Printed in the United States of America ∞

Library of Congress Cataloging-in-Publication Data

Foster, Richard J.
Longing for God: seven paths of Christian devotion / Richard J. Foster and Gayle D. Beebe.
    p. cm.
Includes bibliographical references and index.
ISBN 978-0-8308-3514-0 (cloth: alk. paper) — ISBN 978-0-8308-3527-0 (paper (large print): alk. paper)
1. Spiritual life—Christianity. I. Beebe, Gayle D. II. Title.
BV4501.3.F68 2009
242—dc22

2008046027

P	18	17	16	15	14	13	12	11	10	9	8	7	6	5	4	3	2	1
Y	24	23	22	21	20	19	18	17	16	15	14	13	12	11	10	09		

To my wife, Pam,

And to our children, Anna, Elizabeth and Richard.

"Seek and you will find, when you seek him with all your heart."

—Gayle

Contents

To stand within a tradition does not limit the
freedom of knowledge, but makes it possible.

HANS GEORG GADAMER,

TRUTH AND METHOD

Preface

THIS BOOK IS ABOUT THE MANY WAYS individuals and societies have become alive to God. Often these spiritual awakenings have created an inner longing for God's habitual presence that never ends. Thirty years ago this awakening occurred in me.

I was a freshman at George Fox College in Newberg, Oregon. Richard Foster was teaching at the college, pastoring the local Friends church and writing *Celebration of Discipline*. It was during a class led by Richard that I first read *Celebration* in mimeographed form. I had been in Christian circles all my life and yet I had never read nor experienced such a thorough ordering of how we could understand and make progress in our life with God. As you can imagine, it was a thrilling time. The discoveries I made during this critical period have guided me ever since and continue to this day.

After college I attended Princeton Theological Seminary, where I came under the remarkable influence of Dr. Diogenes Allen. At the time Dr. Allen was deep into his career as Stuart Professor of Philosophy. When I arrived at Princeton in the early 1980s, Dr. Allen was integrating philosophy, theology and church history in the most compelling synthesis I had ever seen. Here was an order and pattern that unveiled the depths of our life with God while providing the most robust evidence of the intellectual credibility of Christianity.

Together, these two have played an indispensable role in my own spiritual journey. Everything I now understand to be true about life with God was initially stimulated by their personal and intellectual influence. Because both men draw so deeply from the great saints of the church, it is important to follow their guiding insights as we seek to make progress in our own spiritual life.

Years ago, at the start of my spiritual journey, I began to read my Bible every day, practice rudimentary spiritual disciplines, and grow in my knowledge and understanding of this life. But I was challenged by my close friends who did not share my convictions. Their general spirit of indifference and occasional expression of hostility eventually triggered a five-year quest to determine the intellectual integrity of Christianity. I wanted to know for myself whether the faith could hold up in the marketplace of ideas. I was still haunted by the question, is it true? Is this life with God a charade or is it the very ground and substance of the universe?

To my joy, my quest was fulfilled. Knowing that our life with God was not only meaningful, but also true, satisfied a deep longing, and as I continued to read the literature introduced to me by Richard Foster and Diogenes Allen, my confidence in the Christian life strengthened. While in seminary, I realized it was the very essence of the Christian life to ask and pursue answers to the great questions that plague every honest seeker: What is the meaning of life? How can a loving God allow suffering? Why would a good God permit so much evil? Is there proof for the existence of God? Is Jesus the only way to God? If so, what is the role of other religions?

In 1992, Richard and I were reunited and began teaching a class together at a university in Southern California. During this time we developed a course titled "The History and Practice of Christian Spirituality." It is the interaction around the ideas and sessions from this course that form the foundation of this book.

Shortly after Christmas 2005, I was driving with my family when Richard called on my cell phone. He was watching (of all things) a football game while recovering from surgery. Eventually our conversation drifted to the topic of this book and we agreed to think further about it and pray. The next morning Richard called back to say he thought we should do it, and we immediately went to work.

It has taken us three years to complete our task. In the book we attempt to blend an understanding of the core texts with an interactive style that will help you use them in your own spiritual journey. As we have worked back and forth, I have found Richard's "Reflecting and Responding" sections especially meaningful. More than anything, we share a hope that this book will bring you closer to the heart of God.

Gayle Beebe

Introduction

Recovering the Seven Paths
of Christian Devotion

ACROSS TIME AND THROUGHOUT HISTORY, God's love has touched countless people. Often these encounters awaken a spiritual longing in us and we begin to seek this love more fully and to have it always present in our lives. No matter which approach or path we take, God's presence experienced in fleeting moments creates a longing for God's continual presence that never ends. But history reveals that our desire for this love is seldom fully satisfied.

And why does this longing seem so dormant today? In a word, distraction. In his *Confessions* Augustine states, "Our hearts are restless until they find their rest in thee." You see, although we need God, we at first do not desire him. We desire all sorts of other things—those necessary for life, to be sure, but also things we simply find attractive. And so it is only as God touches us with his love that we come to understand the nature of life in a new and profound way.

As with many things, our capacity to receive and respond to God's love needs to be developed. For example, even though we have the capacity to read and write, it takes a great deal of effort and assistance to cultivate that ability. Some people never learn to read and write because they never have the opportunity to learn. Likewise, there are countless millions who have the capacity to receive and respond to God's love but lack the proper opportunity to do so.

One key problem we face today is the fact that the cultural environment in Western civilization has become increasingly hostile to Christian faith. Our colleges and research institutions have set religion aside as a worn-out and irrelevant view of the world. When people experience a desire for God, the cultural environment does not encourage any consideration of God, let alone give that desire room to develop.

Searching for a Center of Value

As we move deeper into the new millennium, there is considerable speculation about what the rest of it will bring. Perhaps we will discover how the mind, brain and person are connected; maybe we will uncover the scientific explanation of the origin of life; or, and here is the greatest hope, we may even discover and agree on the ultimate goals to which we humans should commit our lives.

All of this speculation is filled with the hope that somehow we will rediscover a center of value that will provide the meaning, purpose and direction we so desperately need. At its heart, the search for a center of value reveals a growing desperation in Western civilization, and indeed the entire world.

Today there is a growing awareness, reflected in an important body of literature, that we have destroyed the main centers of meaning and value to such an extent that we are left with few resources to cultivate and sustain our common life.[1] At the same time a significant chorus of writers is seeking to recover the rich spiritual resources that once guided us morally, sustained us spiritually and satisfied our deep longing for God.[2] At the core of all these works is a concern with the process of spiritual formation.

Christian spiritual formation is a God-ordained process that shapes our entire person so that we take on the character and being of Christ himself. When we are open and responsive to this process, our outer life becomes an expression of this inner formation. Spiritual formation is concerned with the hidden dimension of every human life, the space God has given us to become the person we choose to be.

From this hidden space we make choices that utilize the resources of understanding, emotion and will available to us. It is here that we exercise our conscience before God and initiate relationships with our neighbors. It is in this hidden space that we are shaped, that our character is formed, and it is here where God encounters us and we choose to follow him.

How can this happen? How can we be shaped in such a way that our life becomes an expression of the spirit of Christ himself? We simply enter into a life with God, a conversational and redemptive relationship in which our own life becomes open to the influence of the Holy Spirit. The Spirit initiates life within us and guides us in a never-ending process of being formed into the likeness of Christ.

Many spiritual practices support this process: public and private worship, study, prayer, reading and memorizing Scripture, reflecting on God's activity in nature and history, and service to others. Other spiritual disciplines such as the practices of solitude, silence and fasting also facilitate spiritual formation. But these activities can also misfire and become burdensome, killing the very life we seek. All spiritual disciplines require care to produce growth and progress.

Properly employed, however, these disciplines help us attain increasing levels of spiritual maturity so that we respond to our life circumstances with the mind of Christ. Every one of us must work out this formation in a way that works best for us, but we make great headway when we draw on the wisdom of the paths others have pioneered.

Why This Book?

This book is written with two main purposes. The first is to explain the seven primary paths to God that have developed throughout Christian history. In brief they include:

- The spiritual life as the right ordering of our love for God
- The spiritual life as journey
- The spiritual life as the recovery of knowledge of God lost in the Fall
- The spiritual life as intimacy with Jesus Christ
- The spiritual life as the right ordering of our experiences of God
- The spiritual life as action and contemplation
- The spiritual life as divine ascent

The individual writers have been selected because of the way their witness to Christ has endured over time and guided people through the ages. These paths are described in detail in the following chapters.

The second purpose is much more personal: we want you to awaken and grow in your knowledge, understanding and commitment to God and to wrestle with the depth and riches these writers present. Contemporary books on spirituality tend toward one of two extremes: either they present the spiritual life in an analytic and detached way, or they portray it as a narrow range of distinct emotional experiences that are impossible to replicate. Both extremes fail to connect with the source of life. It is our goal to help you find the inexhaustible source of this life with God and to participate in its reality.

By presenting seven distinct paths, we are standing against the contemporary tendency to compress the wide variety of spiritual writings into an oversimplified, single orientation, a tendency from which the Christian faith has suffered greatly. In contrast, we stress that there are at least seven major paths to our life with God, all of them mediated by the person and work of Jesus Christ. No single path is the Christian path to the exclusion of the others.

At certain points one path may be especially helpful to us. Over the course of time, however, it is likely that we will experience all of them. This is as it should be. We are created to enter into life with God in multiple ways. As we continue the ongoing journey, over time we become formed into the image and likeness of Christ.

Each chapter describes a particular path embodied by certain classic spiritual writers who illuminate our understanding of the Christian life. No single approach is sufficient for every person because we differ in our needs, experiences, problems, temperament and place in life. We also draw from more than one approach throughout our own journey. For example, when we're thinking through Christianity's intellectual credibility, it is most important that we pursue the right ordering of our love for God and the recovery of knowledge of God lost in the Fall. But at other times, such as when we have had powerful encounters with God, we need to consider the right ordering of our experiences of God. Even though we might prefer one path over others, throughout the course of our life all seven become useful and relevant.

The title *Longing for God* alludes to Augustine's famous teaching that because we have been made to find fullness of life in God, all our activities in life, even our sinful ones, result from our longing for God. The paths in this book serve to orient us toward God so that we may satisfy this unquenchable longing rather than have it frustrated by inadequate or perverse sources.

So Great a Cloud of Witnesses

Many of us do not see a pattern to our life or understand the purpose behind our individual experiences. We walk most of our lives in the dark, without attaining nearly as much understanding as we would like, even when we do occasionally catch a glimpse of God's grand design. But we also have a privilege many in earlier times did not enjoy. We have the stories of the colorful personalities from the Old and New Testaments, including the story of Jesus himself. We know the stories of the great saints who lived throughout the two thousand years of Christian history. As the book of Hebrews records it, "we are surrounded by so great a cloud of witnesses" (Heb 12:1), an allusion to the cloud that led the people of Israel through the wilderness as a manifestation of the presence of God.

In this way we can move forward in our lives as a people of God, trusting that even though we do not always see why things happen or feel God's hand guiding and caring for us, we can still live by the promise of this future fulfillment. In studying the great biblical personalities, we, as God's children, develop a similar confidence in our own life with God.

In every age, great Christian saints have cultivated their life with God using the writings of Scripture, the theological reflections of others, the capacities of human reason, the cultural resources of the day and the spiritual disciplines. Through their reflections, the great saints witness to the work of the Holy Spirit and, when we study them, guide our spiritual life as well.

And so, above all, we hope that this book will captivate the hearts and minds of a new generation of believers. In doing so, we trust that it will enable this generation to seek and find "the life which is life indeed" (1 Tim 6:19 RSV).

PATH ONE

THE RIGHT ORDERING
OF OUR LOVE FOR GOD

I pray that you may have the power to comprehend . . .
the love of Christ that surpasses knowledge.

EPHESIANS 3:18-19

There is a crying need today for the right ordering of love. Our nature as human beings is to love and to seek love, but Eros, or romantic love, is overrunning our lives and making it impossible to find balance and satisfaction. Its unbridled lust, mindless greed and relentless pursuit of power is destroying our capacity to give and receive love. As a result, the law of love—the "royal law," as James calls it—is noticeably absent and desperately needed.

This is why God repeatedly calls us to his love. Scripture is filled with countless examples of this teaching. "Love your neighbor as yourself" (Lev 19:18), "Love the LORD your God with all your heart, and with all your soul, and with all your might" (Deut 6:5), and "He is good, for his steadfast love endures forever" (2 Chron 5:13)—these are just a few of the many passages on God's love.

To deepen our understanding, God repeatedly points us to Jesus as the most glorious embodiment of his love. Consider these teachings from Jesus' life: "You have heard that it was said, 'You shall love your neighbor and hate your enemy.' But I say to you, Love your enemies and pray for those who persecute you, so that you may be children of your Father in heaven" (Mt 5:43-45). "Then someone came to him and said, 'Teacher, what good deed must I do to have eternal life?' And he said . . . 'love your neighbor as yourself'" (Mt 19:16, 19). Elsewhere, Jesus sums up our life with God in these words: "'Love the Lord your God with all your heart, and with all your soul, and with all your mind.' This is the first and greatest commandment. And a second is like it: 'You shall love your neighbor as yourself'" (Mt 22:37-39).

The Nature of Love

Paul amplifies Jesus' teaching in 1 Corinthians 13, his highest and most famous treatment of love. Here and elsewhere he emphasizes the nature of *agapé* love, a term used more than a hundred times throughout Scripture. This emphasis reflects Paul and the early Christians' desire to contrast the self-giving love originating in God with the self-preserving love typified by Eros.

> Love is patient; love is kind; love is not envious or boastful or arrogant or rude. It does not insist on its own way; it is not irritable or resentful; it does not rejoice in wrongdoing, but rejoices in the truth. It bears all things, believes all things, hopes all things, endures all things. Love never ends. (1 Cor 13:4-8)

To get at the essence of Paul's teaching here, we could substitute the words "a self-centered person" for "love" and reverse the action. Here's how it would read: "A self-centered person is not patient; a self-centered person is not kind. A self-centered person is envious and boastful and arrogant and rude. A self-centered person insists on his or her own way, rejoices in wrongdoing and does not rejoice in truth. A self-centered person does not believe anything, hope in anything or endure anything. A self-centered person always fails."

What a dramatic contrast! This inversion simply yet dramatically illustrates that God's *agapé* love is beyond any capacity we possess as humans. We cannot on our own sustain the kind of perfect love that originates in God alone.

How then do we understand the nature and purposes of God's love? Whole theologies have been built trying to answer this question. God himself tells us simply that his nature is best known through pure love. God is *agapé* love and *agapé* love is God (1 Jn 4:16). There is no quicker or better way to understand God than to experience this divine love.

Because it is fundamental to human nature to love and seek love, the central purpose of our life with God is learning to love in such a way that all of our heart's longings—both natural and supernatural—are satisfied. Rightly loving God orders all the other loves common to human existence. We now turn to those who can aid us in the right ordering of our love for God.

Origen of Alexandria

The Quest for Perpetual Communion with God

If we examine the Scriptures we will find . . . that there are
forty-two stages in the departure of the children of Israel from Egypt;
and, further, the coming of our Lord into this world
is traced through forty-two generations.

COMMENTARY ON THE SONG OF SONGS

ONE OF THE EARLIEST PEOPLE TO EXEMPLIFY the right ordering of our love for God is Origen of Alexandria (185-254). Early in his life Origen established himself as a man of virtue, and he grew into a theologian of consequence who wrote on everything from first principles to hermeneutics to faith in God.[1] His use of Scripture and advances in biblical hermeneutics were original and legendary. Combining the philosophy of Philo and the rabbinical exegesis of Hillel with his own Christian faith in God, Origen led a fresh advance of the Alexandrian school of biblical exegesis.[2]

Origen left no question unanswered and was a tireless apologist for the Christian faith. He faced numerous challenges, including two theological investigations and a falling out with church authorities, but he persevered in making one of the most original and creative contributions in all of Christian spirituality.

Origen worked continuously to uncover the ordering principle of all reality. In this quest he identified the ultimate goal of human life as intimate and continual communion with God. It is not our will that should dominate life but our will participating with God's will in doing God's will on earth.

Forty-Two Stages

Throughout his writings Origen communicates a clear and compelling desire that Christians begin the process of ascent. He saw the spiritual life as progressing in stages, a perspective evident throughout his writings but especially strong in three important works: *On Prayer, Commentary on the Song of Songs*, and *Homily 27 on Numbers*.

In one telling scriptural interpretation, he compares the forty-two camps of the children of Israel in the wilderness (Num 33) with the forty-two stations we experience on our way to intimacy with God.[3] Just as the children of Israel struggled to make their way to the Promised Land, we must strive to know God if we are to progress in our spiritual life and recognize the unfolding of our eternal destiny. "These are the stages," Numbers 33:1 begins, "by which the Israelites went out of the land of Egypt." Origen weaves this historical account together with christological meaning, noting that in Matthew 1:1-18, the coming of our Lord and Savior is traced through forty-two generations.[4]

These stages, Origen says, also represent the soul's journey from earth to heaven. As we move from one stage to the next, we gain understanding and cultivate new virtues that strengthen us for the rest of the journey. Each stage also involves certain temptations. Yielding to these temptations disorients us from the path, but conquering them takes us ever closer to God.[5]

Origen highlights what we learn at each stage. For example, in the Egyptian wilderness of our life with God, we need knowledge of God's law, steadfast faith and the fruits of works well pleasing to God. We need the virtue that's cultivated by destroying pride, lust, unbridled desire and folly—this is what enables us to get out of Egypt.[6]

Every virtue is acquired through training and hard work.[7] And virtues lead us eventually to Helim, where twelve springs of water and seventy palm trees provide refreshment (Num 33:9-11). Origen's point is that if we endure temptation and cultivate virtue, we will enter pleasant places. But the end of the journey and the perfection of all things does not lie in these delights. The soul's arrival at Helim indicates a level of spiritual maturity that can discern the meaning of various spirits.[8] By this point it has mastered avarice, pride, anger, boasting, fear, inconstancy and timidity, and it recognizes that daily life is simply a stage for expressing its various spiritual states.[9]

When we finally arrive at our end, we can then turn around and encourage those coming after us, much as Plato advocates in his allegory of the cave.[10] When we have finished our journey and successfully negotiated all its temptations, we are ready for the final passage from earth to heaven. At this point we approach the river of God and enter the stream of his wisdom.

Ultimately, the forty-two stages identify how to begin, how to make progress and how to complete our life with God. They teach us a way to pattern our own spiritual life.

Three Levels

Although no summary can provide a complete account of how an individual thinks, general patterns emerge that assist us in our understanding. In completing his approach to God, Origen uses the neo-Platonic structure of the three levels to demonstrate how every aspect of our life with God is interrelated.[11] As a result, he offers one of the earliest forms of the right ordering of our loves in order to know God.

Table 1.1. Origen's Ordering

Level	Order	Book of the Bible	Principle of Judgment	Goal	Kind of Life
III	Spirit	Song of Solomon	*Apatheia*	Union	Contemplative
II	Soul	Ecclesiastes	Physics	Illumination	Active-Contemplative
I	Body	Proverbs	Ethics	Purgation	Active

On the lowest level, we find God through our five senses. Our focus is the body, and the book of Scripture that orients us here is Proverbs. We read Scripture literally and historically at this level, and we receive moral knowledge that produces ethical understanding if we are committed to a deeper life with God.[12]

On the second level, we find God through Scripture. The type of knowledge we receive is enlightened knowledge, and the human faculty that captures this knowledge is the soul, which includes the capacities found in our memory, intelligence and will. The key book of Scripture at this level is Ecclesiastes. Our reading is guided by grammatical interpretation, and our understanding is based on the natural sciences. As we study physical processes, we gain insight into the ways of God. The life that results is one of enlightenment based on a combination of active love and contemplative reflection.[13]

On the highest level, we find God through perpetual communion with him. The knowledge we receive here is "celestial knowledge," which we attain through the faculty of the spirit. Song of Solomon read on the spiritual level is of greatest importance, and our learning is guided by philosophy. Our spiritual goal is to attain *"apatheia,"* a passionless state completely absorbed in the Trinity and no longer controlled by desire. The goal at this level is to enter into union with God through contemplation, and the life that results is one of pure love and active charity.

When we order our lives properly, Origen tells us, our soul develops a proper love of God as we move from the tangible realities of the physical universe to the intangible realities of the spiritual realm. The greatest challenge we face is not lack of belief but the enormous gravity of our egocentric desires. The weight of these desires creates a force on human nature that is virtually impossible to escape. The only means of rescue is found in turning to God, beginning to imitate Christ and starting to progress from the lowest level of reality to the ultimate reality of perpetual divine communion.

Origen's farthest-reaching influence is the way he illustrates how our destiny is tied to the power of our desire. Unlike later Greek-influenced Christian thinkers, he does not see the life of faith as one of strict contemplation of the mysteries of God. For Origen, Christian faith begins and ends with our imitation of Jesus and the contemplation of God that results from this imitation. By imitating Christ, we ascend to a higher level than seeking to satisfy our temporal desires. But temporal desires are seductive. If we are not freed of their gravity, the divine love that should rule us becomes disordered and we attempt to attain it in ways that do not honor God.

Origen also emphasizes a forgotten truth: we need each other. The community of faith strengthens and sustains our life commitments.

Origen teaches that the mystical quest is always rooted to the life and teachings of the church. The church is not a tether that shackles the believer, but rather the body and bride of Christ living in dynamic relationship with the prevailing culture.

This flies in the face of contemporary spirituality, in which the dominant path in the twenty-first century is individualistic. Origen asserts that although faith always begins in us, it grows and develops through interaction with a broader community. There are no "community-less" Christians. Whether we find it in a group of two or three or a worldwide ministry of millions, we need a community to nurture and sustain us.

REFLECTING AND RESPONDING

Origen intrigues me endlessly. His learning was so very creative; one of the first efforts at a systematic theology was his *de principiis*. His literary output was enormous. While many of his works are lost to us, what we do have is sufficient to make us realize that he was a master of the written word. His popularity as a teacher and preacher was legendary; Mamaea, the mother of Emperor Alexander Severus, summoned him to Antioch to instruct her. And more.

Origin reminds me that we are never finished in the spiritual life. This life with God is always growing, always deepening, always thickening. How critical this is for the contemporary scene. Today, with few exceptions, we have no serious theology of spiritual growth. Many people are obsessively focused on heaven when they die, and most have simply given up on any substantial character formation into Christlikeness. But here is someone who keeps telling us that there is more: more love, more power, more insight, more joy, more peace. We can grow. We can learn. We can make progress forward. In short, Origen is inviting us into an ongoing, breathless experience of God's expansive—and ever-expanding—love.

I also note—and this is what I really love about Origen—his emphasis on intimate and continual communion with God. Here is someone way back in the third century telling me that the ultimate goal of life is to fall in love with Jesus over and over again. Nothing is more important. Nothing is more central. Nothing is more critical.

The key question in all of this, of course, is, How? How do we grow? How do we enter an intimate, ongoing communion with God? The answer is simple: with practice. We undertake experiments of everyday life in which we are learning to be with God. And the stuff of our day-to-day experience is the place where these experiments go on. This with-God life takes no time, yet it occupies all our time. When we go to work, we go to work with-God. At work we are learning how to bless those who curse us, how to weep with those who weep and rejoice with those who rejoice, how our very presence can be a joy to others. And the experiments are numerous and varied: "Today, Lord, teach me somehow to bless every person I meet. Show me the preciousness of each individual. Fill my mind with creative new ideas and show me how to break the horns of cruel dilemmas." The same is true for times at home with family and time with neighbors and friends. You get the idea, I am sure.

Dear Lord, in these next days would you help us learn from Origen about the right ordering of love? We live on the order of the body so much of the time. It isn't the distortions of human sexuality so much. No, for us it's the ease with which we view others based upon superficialities that have little to do with who they truly are. Or how much we worry about the way we come across to people. In our best moments, Lord, we really do want to live more fully on Origen's third level, the level of spirit.

May divine love become more real to us today . . . and every day. May we want to experience divine love more. May we want to seek out divine love more. May we want to love you more. Please, Lord, transform our "wanting." We would like to grow in love with you as well as fall in love with you. Show us the way. Amen.

Augustine of Hippo
Loving God with Our Body, Mind and Heart

What is God but he who made us.
What is man but that being which has both a body and a soul.
We are not God and we recognize that it is God who gives
to each of our senses its own place and function.
As we rise in stages towards the God who made us
we go beyond all the natural faculties of our senses and perceptions.

CONFESSIONS

No single figure in the history of the church has influenced Christianity more profoundly than Augustine (354-430). The themes and trajectories that occur throughout his writing are pivotal for our thinking and our living. Augustine's understanding of our life with God is complex, and we must review several works if we are to understand him adequately.

Like Origen's before him, Augustine's work centers on three levels of reality—body, mind and heart—and how these levels affect the ordering of our love for God. If we read, for example, his *Confessions*, we know of the disordering power of misplaced desire. If we read only his later theological treatises, we do not understand the human condition from which so much of his interest originally developed. Augustine's three levels depict the different orientations we take depending on our perception of what is most important. Augustine thoroughly examines these three levels and helps us see how they contribute to or distract us from our life with God.

For Augustine, the individual consists of a body and a soul (including memory, intelligence and will). God, who is above and outside creation, orders everything in the world properly. When we live in right relationship with him, he orders the levels of our body and soul so that we satisfy both types of needs properly. Augustine does not reject the needs of the body. He diminishes them, but he does not deny them. However, the needs of the body must be ordered by reason if we are to experience God's grace and redemption fully.

Likewise, the soul, which includes reason, is part of our innate nature. History is filled with civilizations and individuals who disrupted the proper order by advocating our ability to ascend to God on our own. This is a result of distorted reason. The right use of reason allows us to recognize our need for God. But reason alone cannot lead us to union with God. It can only show us that God is not present and help us recognize the depth of our need for God.

How We Know God

According to Augustine, God exists above all levels of human reality. He is known through Scripture, creation and the inward Teacher, Jesus Christ.[14] But because we do not know God initially, our efforts to make sense of life are haphazard and ineffective. Although we long for God, we do not realize it at first. All we can do is prepare for him by properly orienting one element of our earthly life: our will. Committing to knowing God and how he works means we must create habits that incline us to look for him. When we are taught how to look for God through reason and are protected through morality from distraction in our search, we can anticipate a visit from God.

Our capacity to reason sets us apart from the rest of creation. Because of it we can reflect on Christian truth and allow this reflection to influence our desires and activities. The objective of the right use of reason is to comprehend reality.

Augustine's interpretation of reality is that humans are estranged from God. On our own we cannot return to him. God, who sees our need and recognizes that we will never meet it on our own, sends Christ. But it is extremely difficult for us to recognize our own need because of three temptations: the love of power, the pervasiveness of lust and our inability to find contentment. These temptations keep us in turmoil, constantly churning, preoccupied with all of life yet unable to find lasting satisfaction. This condition allows our appetites to gain the upper hand. It disrupts normal human living. Ultimately, it places us in direct conflict with our true foundation, the love of God flowing outward in love of neighbor.

When our will is oriented to God, our judgments and motivations are based on love. Our concern is to gain wisdom, perfect holiness and realize happiness through loving God and our neighbor. When we live with a spirit of love, we naturally curb our desires. They just don't come to mind in the same way or with the same power. As the guiding motive of our life, love works with reason to allow us to comprehend reality accurately. According to Augustine, this opens the window of our understanding so that we see our need for God, how God provides for that need through Christ and how this divine drama plays out in history. Essentially, Augustine asserts, all of history reflects one of two things: either we love ourselves or we love God. Either we align our will with his or we are self-willed.

Augustine's identification of reason as the mediating link between God and our senses illustrates the importance he places on the power of the intellect. Reason reminds us that we are made in God's image. But reason can lead us astray. It has the power to produce comprehension, but it cannot produce any lasting happiness. When our reason is oriented by self-interest, we spend all our time satisfying the appetites and desires of the body. Yet it is also our reason that orients us to love God. And it is our love for God that properly aligns all of our human capacities.

The Nature of Faith

Augustine spends hundreds of pages showing us God's providential action in history. But he also helps us appreciate God's interest and involvement in our individual lives.[15] Specifically, he wants us to realize that it is God who initiates contact with us and not our own activity that leads us to God. That being the case, how do we understand our longing for God and its place in our experience of God's grace and redemption? Ultimately, Augustine concludes that we cannot manufacture God's initiative, but we can prepare for it by orienting our will to him.

Augustine also emphasizes that correct doctrine matters. This is not an emphasis we often encounter today, but for most of its history the church has recognized doctrine as the intellectual framework we need to understand our life with God.[16] Augustine teaches that we must move beyond a simple experience of God to a structured understanding of him.[17]

A quick scan of the contemporary theological landscape reminds us why. Most teaching today seeks to recover a vitality in the Christian life by emphasizing the love of God without equally stressing the need for knowledge of God. These trends bear a striking similarity to earlier movements that resulted in widespread ignorance and neglect of core Christian beliefs. In each previous case, the lack of knowledge of God eventually led to a lack of love for God.

Augustine teaches that proper doctrine brings faith to life. When we gain knowledge, our faith deepens and we understand life at a more fundamental level. The Bible invites us to come to the full wealth of our conviction (Col 2:2 NEB). This means that over time and through study we become convinced of the truth of the Christian life. In *The Enchiridion* and *The First Catechism,* Augustine identifies these principles through some of the most poignant and provocative teachings in Christian history.[18]

Augustine believes that by living the Christian faith, we will finally come to recognize it as true. In *The True Religion,* he identifies three reasons why he considers Christianity to be the one true faith: it offers the best understanding of human nature, it offers the best description of our plight in being alienated and cut off from God, and it offers the most realistic remedy for our plight as provided by God in Jesus Christ.

Ultimately, in order to recognize God's provision in Christ, we must also learn that we can do nothing to redeem ourselves. When we are unable to rise above our own self-love, we manufacture all kinds of diversions in an attempt to find a happiness that endures. But eventually we realize that nothing in this life provides the happiness and joy that come from God alone. The difficulty is that we reach this level of knowledge only if we persist in our love for God.

This leads us to our final discovery: that our only hope for enduring happiness is to discover the eternal peace of God, which harnesses and redirects the enduring restlessness of our spirit. Those of us who align our love and will with God's love and will realize the impact this has on our

Table 1.2. Augustine's Ordering

Level	Order	Faculty	Use of Scripture	Type of Knowledge of God	Disciplines/ Preparation	Goal	Distractions
III	Heart	Soul, supernatural knowledge	Scripture in conversation with itself	Jesus as inward Teacher	Gain wisdom, seek holiness	Happiness in love of God	Disordered loves
II	Mind	Natural knowing, memory, intelligence, will	Scripture in context	Reason aids in comprehension	Reflect on Christian witness and doctrine	Love of God through love of neighbor	Disordered thoughts
I	Body	Senses	Literal reading of Scripture	Created order manifests God	Engage in correct Christian practices	Love of neighbor	Love of power, pervasive lust, inability to be content

own life, as well as the cumulative impact on human history. The table "Augustine's Ordering" summarizes Augustine's understanding of the right ordering of our love for God.

REFLECTING AND RESPONDING

If anyone could understand the destructive nature of disordered love it was Augustine. Early in his life he had experienced enough of the "hissing cauldron of lust" to fill a good-sized book. Indeed, he did just that in his famous *Confessions*—the pioneer of the memoir genre. Descending into the "lower beauties" of sexual promiscuity, he wrote, "The enemy held my will and made a chain out of it and bound me with it. From a perverse will came lust, and slavery to lust became a habit, and the habit, being constantly yielded to, became a necessity."[19] Desperately longing for genuine love, Augustine had to confess, "I polluted . . . the stream of friendship with the foulness of lust, and clouded its purity with the dark hell of illicit desire."[20]

Augustine's famous conversion in that Milan garden came about because he realized that only Christ had the power to free him from the "whirlpools of vice" that so imprisoned him. And Christ did free him—perhaps a little too much! Wanting to make a clean break with the sexual promiscuity and professional arrogance that had dominated his life in Italy, Augustine left his mistress who had borne him a son, resigned his teaching post in Milan and returned to Thagaste, Africa, the city of his birth. From there he went on to establish the Augustinian monastic order and become the famous Bishop of Hippo.

Frankly, I wish Augustine had taken a different path. If he had married his mistress instead of leaving her, perhaps he could have given the world a whole new model of the holiness of human love. For me he diminished human love too much. I suppose I am projecting my modern sensibilities onto an ancient writer. Perhaps emotionally and psychologically he could not have done that. And historically it is nearly impossible to imagine it, since holiness in that day was so tied to monastic life. Still, I wish he and his mistress had married and been able to show us a more excellent way for the right ordering of love, at least on the human level.

Still, many valuable lessons emerge from the life and teachings of Augustine. I will mention three. The first is his keen understanding of both the importance of reason as well as its limitations. How important a teaching for our day. Mostly we see today only the extremes: either we embrace reason utterly or we reject it utterly. Not Augustine. He knew that reason rightly used can bring us to understand our need for God and lead us to right beliefs that provide the intellectual framework for structuring our life with God. At the same time he knew that reason can be severely distorted if not oriented around divine love. It is a wonderful balance we could learn from today.

Then, second, I am taken by Augustine's keen understanding of the role of the will in the spiritual life. He recognized the importance of the orientation of our will toward God as a way of preparing ourselves for a visitation by him. At the same time he rejected the idea of "free will," knowing instead that it is God who initiates and inclines us toward godliness. He understood better than perhaps anyone else before or since both the importance and the complexity of the human will.

And, finally, Augustine's understanding of Christ as the inward Teacher is so very intriguing. I wonder if his conversion experience in that Milan garden didn't play a part here. At a crucial moment he had heard the sing-song words of a child repeating, "Take it and read it. Take it and read it." He could not think of any child's game that would use those words and finally became "quite certain that I must interpret this as a divine command to me to open the book [the Bible] and read the first passage which I should come upon."[21] In dramatic fashion, Christ had become for Augustine the Prophet who would teach his people himself. This idea of Christ as the ever-living, inward Teacher is full of implications for our daily living, and Augustine was the first to give this idea real substance.

And, so, what does all this mean for our living? An answer is not hard to come by. We begin simply by asking Christ, our living Teacher, to guide us through our activities today. The same for tomorrow, and all the days that follow. We seek to orient our will toward his will, knowing that he is always there first, directing and guiding. We enlist the aid of reason's common sense toward our daily tasks, knowing that God guides us in this way.

And then what we hear and know to do, we do. Christ will never ask us to undertake anything he does not also give us the power to obey. And often the guidance is so simple . . . yet so profound: "Pay close attention to José today, he needs your affirmation." "Be still, rest, shalom." "Do not fear today's meeting, I will guide you." "Challenge the injustice at work and I will be beside you." Jesus, your inward Teacher, will be your strength and guide. Daily. Here. Now.

Dear Lord, we would like to learn from Augustine about the right ordering of love. It is a little hard because frankly Augustine overwhelms us—his towering intellect, his massive influence. . . . It is hard to know how to bring all that down to where we live. But we would like to try. We would so appreciate it if you would show us the way.

Augustine does describe his early life as "a whole frying-pan of wicked loves." That speaks to our condition. We're tempted often to distort love, if not outwardly then inwardly. We really do not know how to love rightly. One moment we are longing for "the good, the true, the beautiful," and the next moment we are "sinking down to the depths of the lower beauties," just like Augustine.

Perhaps we need a Milan garden kind of experience. It would probably scare us to death if that kind of thing happened to us! Besides, you seldom come by means of the fireworks of Sinai. More often it's the still small voice. Whichever way it is that you choose to come, "Come, Lord Jesus." In your time and in your way. Amen.

Bernard of Clairvaux

The Desire for God and the Ascent of Pure Love

I promise to tell you only what God will give me to say about loving him. This subject is more profitable than any other.

LOVING GOD

BETWEEN THE CLOSE OF AUGUSTINE'S LIFE and the opening of the Crusades, some of the most significant shifts in the history of Western civilization occurred. First, the fledgling Christian church was facing new opposition on virtually every major societal front. In the seventh century Mohammad initiated religious reforms that would culminate in the rise of Islam. He died shortly thereafter, in 632, but within eighty years of his death major Christian centers came to be dominated by this new faith. Damascus fell immediately in 634 and Jerusalem fell soon after in 638. By the end of the seventh century Carthage had become Muslim, and as the eighth century opened the Straits of Gibraltar and the vast lands on both sides of the mouth of the Mediterranean were Muslim as well.

Coinciding with these new religious and political movements was a dramatic urban reversal. Between 400 and 800, huge numbers of people left the cities and returned to the agrarian countryside. At the same time, theological concerns were developing over the nature of Christ, the role and importance of penance and the formalization of the Mass. These latter developments eventually led to the end of the use of vernacular languages in worship as the church, now centralized in Rome, instituted Latin as the standard language instead.

This social, political and cultural climate cut the nerve of spiritual development, which resulted in a dearth of spiritual writers during the Middle Ages. Despite these setbacks, however, God was preserving a remnant. Eventually a smattering of saints arose to rally the faithful and provide a compelling witness to Jesus Christ. One of these was Bernard of Clairvaux (1090-1153), a legendary spokesman of the faith and one of the great Christian saints between Augustine and Aquinas.

Bernard's influence is remarkable. His interests ranged from biblical studies and theology to literature and political thought.[22] Like Augustine before him, Bernard believed that we always love but we do not always love properly. Since love orders desire, the way we love directly influences how we attempt to satisfy our fundamental longings. Thus, what we desire to know shapes what we come to love, and what we love influences what we come to know.

Bernard is reported to have written numerous treatises that have been lost or destroyed, but the core of his spiritual writings is still intact. He lived during a period of great cultural renaissance in Western Europe. The twelfth century saw the rise of the troubadours and the emergence of courtly love. This context and Bernard's own inclinations combined to forge a love-mysticism theology unparalleled in Christian history.[23] His commitment to the right ordering of our love of God is best reflected in two distinct works: *The Steps of Humility and Pride* and *On Loving God*.

In *The Steps of Humility and Pride*, Bernard identifies twelve degrees of spiritual decline and twelve degrees of spiritual progress.

These steps—both of decline and of progress—are filled with insight into the human condition. The steps of decline begin with a contempt for our neighbor, lead to a contempt for those God places over us, and end in utter contempt for God and the complete alienation of our soul. Conversely, the steps of progress begin with learning to love our neighbor, migrate through gaining respect for those God places in authority over us and results in a full understanding of our life with God. The reason these insights are so vital for today is that so many people are making life-limiting moves simply because of the inability to embrace the God-given order and design for life.

Steps of Decline

The decline begins when our soul deteriorates through three major kinds of contempt, according to Bernard.[24] First, it deteriorates when we hold a spirit of contempt for our neighbor. Bernard divides this process into six

steps: curiosity about the affairs of others, light-mindedness, foolish merriment, boasting, trying to be different and arrogance. Each of these attitudes demonstrates a lack of love of neighbor.[25]

Bernard's Twelve Steps of Spiritual Demise

Loss of love of neighbor
1. Curiosity
2. Light-mindedness
3. Foolish merriment
4. Boasting
5. Trying to be different
6. Arrogance

Contempt for one's superiors
7. Presumption
8. Self-justification
9. Insincere confession
10. Rebellion

Contempt for God
11. Feeling free to sin and creating habitual patterns of sin
12. Showing utter disregard for the Ten Commandments

Considering these qualities in more depth, we begin with curiosity.
Curiosity about the affairs of others causes us to gossip. In other words, we
aren't interested in people because we want to help them, but only so we
can gain information to share with others. Continuing down the list,
light-mindedness reflects an inability to discern weighty matters from trivial
concerns. *Foolish merriment* is the pursuit of pleasure for the sole purpose of
being distracted from life. *Boasting* is a result of spending too much time
comparing ourselves to others and not enough time learning how to love
them. *Trying to be different* and *arrogance* reveal an excessive regard for ourselves.

Next, the soul deteriorates as it experiences contempt for superiors.
Here, *presumption, self-justification, insincere confession* and *rebellion* keep us
from submitting to earthly authorities. An unwillingness to submit to our

earthly authorities prevents us from submitting to God.

This provocative teaching goes to the heart of one of the greatest challenges we face in our life with God. We really do have trouble accepting the guidance of others. We presume to know enough to reject their input; we self-justify, explaining away our own misbehavior while condemning that of others. Ultimately, our spiritual life hinges on our ability to submit to powers and authorities outside ourselves. The extent to which we can master this ability directly influences the extent to which we can submit to God.

The final steps of the soul's descent reflect contempt for God. Here, *feeling free to sin, utterly disregarding the Ten Commandments* and *developing habitual patterns of sin without remorse* demonstrate contempt for God's law. This lack of regard for God spells ruin for the human soul.

Bernard's overarching concern is to help us recognize that when we fail to love our neighbor we ultimately fail to love God. There is no way to avoid it. We cannot express a pure love of God and ignore loving our neighbor. It is simply impossible.

Steps of Progress

By contrast, the twelve degrees of spiritual progress, or steps of humility, begin with a love of God and end in love of neighbor.

Bernard's Twelve Steps of Spiritual Progress

1. Love of God
2. Watchfulness against sin
3. Submission to superiors
4. Patience in the face of accusation
5. Honesty in confessing our sins
6. Refraining from taking the initiative to remove our sin
7. Humility in the face of others
8. Refusing to assert any special rights
9. Refraining from speaking unless asked
10. Reluctance to laugh
11. Restrained speech
12. Limited expectations

Ascending to a state of perpetual humility begins in stages one and two with a constant watchfulness against sin. As we exercise moral constraint, spiritual progress begins. Stages three through seven demonstrate how to submit to our superiors through patience in the face of accusation, honesty in confessing our sin and taking the initiative to remove any manifestation of evil. In these stages, we exhibit a respect for the authorities who provide guidance for our spiritual life.

The final phase of ascent leads us to a full love of neighbor. In these levels we are humble in the face of others, refuse to assert any special rights, refrain from speaking unless asked, are reluctant to laugh, exercise restrained speech and limit our expectations. Clearly, the steps of spiritual progress reverse the steps of spiritual decline.

This list reminds us of the early influence of Stoicism on Christianity. Bernard is challenging us to shackle any hint of individual desire or ambition. We are not only to rechannel these personal desires but eventually to completely stamp them out. The only desires that matter are the ones that emanate from a love of God.

These steps of progress and decline illustrate the ways we come to abide in God and the ways in which we turn away from him. The pivotal point in all of our motivation is love. To amplify this point, Bernard emphasizes the power of God's love and the incredible foundation we build when we love him.

Table 1.3. Bernard's Ordering

Level	Loves	Faculties	Actions	Spiritual Activity	Biblical Example
III	Spiritual	Wisdom	Contemplation	Union	Mary
II	Rational	Intellect	Active love, devotion	Illumination	Lazarus
I	Carnal	Desire of flesh	Confession	Purgation	Martha

Learning to Love Properly

In his landmark work *On Loving God,* Bernard outlines our fourfold ascent to a perfect love of God.[26] There are three degrees of love that correspond to the three levels of knowledge and a fourth degree that is rarely realized but gives us a glimpse of the eternal, uncreated love that we will enjoy in heaven.

First, Bernard begins with self-love. Part of human nature since the Fall has been the unrelenting capacity we have to love ourselves. But as Bernard notes and modern psychology confirms, this incessant egocentrism stifles moral progress and spiritual growth. Eventually, we awaken to our own mortality, and this awakening breaks the power of egocentrism.

Still, this awakening is not free of egocentrism altogether. The second stage is when we learn to love God for our own sake. At this point, we realize we will die so we seek eternal life through God. The primary motivation is self-preservation, not love of God, but we take this important step when we realize our ultimate destiny.

But then we begin to realize that God loves others as much as he loves us. This leads to the third stage and is a breakthrough. Here we learn to love God for God's sake. Thanksgiving for who God is and what God does supersedes our own desire for self-preservation. The breaking of the power of egocentrism results in seeing the world in its true light. Other people and other things are no longer evaluated by their ability to satisfy our own desires. Now, because God is seen as a center of the universe distinct from ourselves, others are seen as centers of value distinct from ourselves as well.[27]

The fourth and final stage, the one it seems can only be realized at the end of life, is coming to love ourselves in the way we are loved by God. This is difficult since the spirit of stage four is easily confused with the motivation of stage two. Coming to love ourselves the way God does is very different from coming to love God simply for self-preservation. Stage two is concerned with self-preservation; stage four is concerned with ubiquitous love.[28]

REFLECTING AND RESPONDING

Growing up I always had a great love for Bernard simply because of the hymn attributed to him, "Jesus, the Very Thought of Thee." I was especially taken by lines three and four:

O hope of every contrite heart, O joy of all the meek,
To those who fall, how kind Thou art! How good to those who seek!
But what to those who find? Ah, this. No tongue or pen can show;
The love of Jesus, what it is. None but His loved ones know.

This hymn had all the themes of divine love, or so I thought. Then as my education expanded I learned that Bernard was a great champion of the Second Crusade in 1149. My young mind simply could not put these two together—this great hymn of love and the savagery of the Crusades. And while I have since learned more about the nuances of the historical, cultural and political realities of the twelfth century, I still cannot put the two together. No doubt all of us deal with deep inconsistencies in the moral life.

I always loved the motto of Bernard, "To know Jesus and Jesus crucified." For me it was a motto that seemed to transcend the divisions of Catholic and Protestant and Orthodox. I still think it does. I always felt that his mystical devotion was well-stated, positive and based solely on love of God. Then, too, it was an intently practical mysticism, supremely reflected in the common sense counsel of his *Steps of Humility and Pride*. It always seemed so wise to me to see that we grow in humility by first learning to love God and that this will inevitably lead us to love our neighbor. And as we view our neighbor as better than ourselves, we do indeed enter humility of heart. We deteriorate into pride in exactly the opposite direction; we begin first to disregard our neighbor and this inevitably leads us to disregard God. This happens because we come to think of ourselves as the C.E.O. of the universe. So I find his practicality appealing.

Bernard's great work, *On Loving God*, however, was a different story. Oh, I know it is psychologically sound and theologically profound, but I have always had a hard time "getting it." Maybe my problem is that I can never arrive at the fourth degree of love (love of self for God's sake) by anything even close to actual experience. I can understand it in an intellectual way, but it is like a distant horizon in my actual living. Loving myself in the same way that God loves me! I'm sorry, but that is a long way off. Even the third degree of love (love of God for God's sake) only seems to come around now and again. Don't get me wrong; I have had experiences of loving God . . . but there always seems to be a mixture of motives. To love God purely because God is who God is—well, like I say, such experiences are rare indeed. No doubt, all it means is that I simply have a long way to go in this matter of the right ordering of love.

Lord, we are a real mixture of motives when it comes to loving you. And when it comes to loving, period. Would you please purify the stream of our loving, at least to the extent that we can stand it? Thank you. Amen.

Blaise Pascal

The Right Ordering of Body, Mind and Heart

The infinite distance between body and mind symbolizes the
infinitely more infinite distance between mind and charity,
for charity is supernatural. . . . There are three orders differing in kind. . . .
[This is why] the heart has its reasons which reason cannot know.

PENSÉES

THE ABSOLUTE BEST EMBODIMENT OF THE right ordering of our love for God is Blaise Pascal (1623-1662), a brilliant philosopher, scientist and social critic who appropriated much of Augustine's thought into his own age. Pascal's central concern was to demonstrate how the orientation of our will determines the outcome of our life. Against the background of the disastrous religious decline that followed the Thirty Years' War (1618-1648), Pascal argued that the Christian faith was not contrary to reason but worthy of reverence and respect.

If we think this idea does not sit well today, it certainly did not sit well in mid-seventeenth-century Europe. The entire continent had witnessed the brutality, chaos and terror caused by factional fighting among Christians. How could Christianity be reasonable, let alone deserve reverence and respect? Why should people want it to play a role in the reconstruction of Europe? What would it produce in the future since its effect in the present had been so disastrous? (Sounds strangely familiar, doesn't it?)

These and other questions propelled Pascal to address the nature of truth, primarily through his pivotal *Pensées.*[29] The Christian faith is true, he said, because it offers the best understanding of human nature: why we are the way we are and what we can do to remedy our condition. The Christian faith neither glamorizes our strengths nor ignores our weaknesses. It identifies both as a part of human nature, but then demonstrates that we will find mastery over our nature only through Jesus Christ. For Pascal, we must rise above our human condition to escape our plight.

The Right Use of Reason

In the *Pensées*, Pascal defines the human condition using three words: boredom, inconstancy and anxiety. Unless we recognize this state, the questions to which Christian truth responds do not make sense. Although Christianity is true, its truth is relevant only when we address our true condition.[30]

Pascal also describes how our imagination distracts us from an accurate view of our own reality. Because Western society believes reason is supreme, it is difficult for people to see its limitations and how easily it is diverted from what is real.[31] Pascal mounts a vigorous challenge to Descartes's *Cogito ergo sum* ("I think, therefore I am"). No single phrase has done more to challenge God's revelation than this famous maxim and the confidence it expresses in human reason, especially in the new scientific method that marked the seventeenth century. Pascal helps us see that we are not creatures ruled exclusively by reason but are in fact equally influenced by instincts and habits—many of which are highly irrational.[32]

In Pascal's day, as is true now, it was intellectually popular to be a skeptic. Yet throughout the *Pensées*, Pascal shows that the person who remains a skeptic has not considered all the evidence for belief in God. The problem with skepticism is that we never make a decision. But life requires decisions. We must decide how we will live and what we will do; we must answer the question of how our life will be invested. In always doubting we fail to recognize when we must exercise judgment.

Pascal is perhaps best known for his "wager" argument, in which he compares coming to Christian belief with placing a bet. This argument states that if we cannot prove the existence of God, it is still better to believe in him than to bet he does not exist and find out we were wrong. Pascal wrote this work to encourage people disposed to skepticism to at least consider the possibility of God's reality.[33] He believed that we could experience and know this reality, but it would not follow the lines of "proofs for the existence of God" that were crafted during the Middle Ages. These proofs did not address the inherently religious question of truth, which deals with why we need God and what our life would be like if we never discovered him.

For Pascal, the inherently religious question of truth is addressed by six key questions. "What religion," he asks, "will teach us our true good, our duties, the weaknesses which lead us astray, the cause of these weaknesses, the treatment that can cure them, and the means of obtaining such treatment?"[34] These six questions combine to form a powerful tool for evaluating any truth system. Through them we can arrive at the answers that guide every legitimate religious quest.

Both "Great and Wretched"

Pascal made a fascinating study of the paradox of how human beings are both "great and wretched." This is a defining contribution of Pascal to all religious thought. Throughout history various writers have either elevated or debased human nature. Take, for example, the contrasting ideas of Plato and Freud. Plato argues that the highest form of human nature is reason, and that reason works to make our passions subservient in order to reach our true end. Freud, by contrast, argues that reason is not supreme but is the handmaiden of passions. In fact, if it were not for reason directing passion to some measure of socially acceptable expression, passion would destroy our life and inevitably unravel civilization.

This contrast is exactly Pascal's point. Where, other than in the Christian faith, do we find a depiction of humanity that includes both sides of our nature and then instructs us on how to rise above our nature to find meaning and purpose? This, according to Pascal, is the genius of Christian thinking. We cannot emphasize our greatness or our wretchedness to the exclusion of the other or ignore our need for a remedy. Additionally, it is too trite simply to say that this is why everyone needs Jesus. The need for the remedy provided by Jesus must be demonstrated before the remedy provided by Jesus can be received.[35]

In a section of the *Pensées* which poses one of the most penetrating critiques of human nature ever penned, Pascal addresses the ways in which we divert ourselves from what is real. Pascal explores the psychology of motivation, the reasons we concoct to keep from thinking of God and the causes behind our many diversions. His insights are a marvelous extension of Augustine's idea that all sin is ultimately an attempt to fill our need for God with everything but God.[36] Ultimately Pascal confronts the extremes to which human beings will go to avoid thinking about the nature and reality of God.

Examples of diversion abound in our society as we continue to witness the unbridled lust for wealth, power and prestige. The enormous energy we consume pursuing "the good life" leaves us feeling completely depleted of any life at all. Our culture is riddled with the tragedies of people who have succumbed to debilitating and destructive addictions. From video games to sexual compulsions to drugs and much more, we see the toll exacted by our inability to face our human condition honestly.

A beautiful but troubling example of this is captured in John Steinbeck's *Cannery Row*. The novel is set along the Northern California coast just south of San Francisco. Its central character, Doc, is a biologist who turns his training into a legitimate business catching and selling marine life to various enterprises. The book itself is a wonderful portrait of the humanity of the people our society often pushes to life's margins.

In one scene Doc is pondering the nature of life and observes, "What doth it profit a man to gain the whole world and return to his mansion with a gastric ulcer, a blown prostate and bifocals?"[37] What a poignant consideration of our destiny. Are we simply pursuing possessions that ruin our health without ever improving our soul? Or are we pursuing a life built on lasting values that capture the deeper life of the spirit? This is exactly what Pascal wants us to confront: the troubling diversions we cultivate to keep from considering the reality of God, the nature of our life and our need for a remedy that God alone provides.

The Three Orders: Body, Mind and Heart

Having laid this preliminary groundwork, Pascal now takes up his central teaching on the spiritual life: the right ordering of our love for God. Deeply influenced by the Jansenist movement and its recovery of Augustine's teaching, Pascal outlines how we ascend through the three orders of reality (body, mind and heart) to find a life of humility and holiness in the unchanging presence of God.[38] He writes:

The infinite distance between body and mind symbolizes the infinitely more infinite distance between mind and charity, for charity is supernatural. All the splendour of greatness lacks luster for those engaged in pursuits of the mind. The greatness of intellectual people is not visible to kings, rich men, or captains, who are all great in a carnal sense. The greatness of wisdom, which is nothing if it does not come from God, is not visible to carnal or intellectual people. There are three orders differing in kind.[39]

Table 1.4. Pascal's Ordering

Level	Order	Faculty	Principle of Judgment	Objective of Importance	Kind of Life
III	Heart	Will	Charity	Holiness, wisdom	Humility
II	Mind	Intellect	Comprehension	Knowledge	Pride
I	Body	Senses	Appetites	Power and consumption	Unbridled desire

The body, as the lowest order, is governed by desire, Pascal says. These desires lead to a life of unbridled lust and activity, with no sustaining principle other than conspicuous consumption and the acquisition of power and resources to keep this consumption going.

It is easy to find examples of this kind of life. Consider a story from Scripture: the parable of the prodigal son. The troubling point of this account is the son's willingness to give up a life of responsibility and meaning to pursue wanton pleasure. The only measure of his life is his ability to indulge his desires whenever and however he wants. There is no boundary to his appetites. Fortunately, he eventually runs out of money and is forced to rethink his situation. His thoughts turn to his home, his previous life with his loving father, and so he returns. The story is a wonderful illustration of the reception we receive when we return to God, who is the true home of the human soul.

Or consider the people of today who are consumed with their physical appearance. They spend thousands of dollars and hundreds of hours doing everything they can to look beautiful. But a simple disease or a freak accident can take their beauty in an instant. What then remains? Virtually nothing; their life has been built on something fleeting. When the surface features they have cultivated fade or are taken away, there is no longer any meaning to their life.

Any life lived on the order of the body alone will end in emptiness. We simply cannot sustain meaning when the only measure of life is endless experience. The order of the body inevitably collapses under its own weight.

Pascal's next order of reality is the mind. Although higher than the body and its master, the mind is still natural and unable to bring us into direct contact with God. However, the mind does prepare us for contact with God. Through the right use of reason we can recognize false belief systems and understand how they fail to bring about the meaning, purpose and fullness we seek. Pascal shows that the order of the mind cannot prove the existence of God or even produce a revelation of God, but it makes us aware of our need for God, his provision in Jesus Christ and our need to yield to this provision if we are to discover the life we long for and seek.

Social observers often refer to our society today as a "knowledge society." By this they mean we have placed a high premium on what can be known. But this establishes a vexing dilemma. The problem with living on the order of the mind is that if we do not rise above it, we develop arrogance in our knowledge and know-how.

We have all met people who are incredibly bright—and know it. They enjoy displaying their masterful intellect and relish every opportunity to be the center of attention. Pascal suggests that people who live on the order of the mind and do not learn to use reason properly inevitably develop a pride that blinds them to areas where they are ignorant or ill-informed, including their need for God. This blindness must be penetrated by humility if we are to ascend to the highest order, the order of the heart, where God reaches us not through our desires or intellect but through the allegiance of our will.

On the order of the heart, we orient our will to the will of God. This enables us to order the intellectual concerns of the mind and satisfy the physical needs of the body properly. That is to say, to be oriented to God is to allow each order—our body, mind and heart—to find its proper expression. To elevate either the body or the mind over the heart is to ensure the dissolution of our life. We must use the mind and we must satisfy the body, but left on our own without the completing influence of the heart, we can never create a life with God.

Each element of Pascal's system reflects his overwhelming interest in motivating people who no longer consider God to be real to consider again the questions of truth. Each aspect of his approach is a request that they contemplate the relevance and truth of Christian faith. This is the ultimate destiny of human life.

What is riveting about Pascal is how he anticipated postmodernism. He could see a time when absolutes would be negotiated. Pascal recognized that a time would come when science would be our enemy, not our friend. He could see, even in the seventeenth century, that people were losing confidence in the reality of God and the necessity of embracing truth. He recognized that people are led astray by insidious philosophies with ruinous results. Pascal's effectiveness as a spiritual writer is rooted in the way he forces us to consider our own dilemmas and offers to guide us toward a meaningful life anchored to God. He is not preachy, telling us how to think, but instead asks us to consider the questions at the foundation of every search for truth and works to galvanize our longing for God.

The profound thinkers who address the right ordering of our love for God have guided Christians in every age—and they continue to guide us today. By considering how we can order our love for God properly, we better understand how all of our loves and desires help us find the life with God we seek.

REFLECTING AND RESPONDING

On November 23, 1654, from about 10:30 p.m. until 12:30 a.m., Blaise Pascal had an experience of the transforming love of God that changed the entire direction of his life. He had been reading the seventeenth chapter of John's Gospel, where Jesus prays before giving himself over to be crucified. As he read, suddenly the room was filled with the flaming presence of Christ as perfect Love. The word written in the book was confirmed by the Word present in the Son.

On parchment paper Pascal wrote out a terse stenographic account of what happened. At the top he etched a cross surrounded by rays. He sewed the parchment sheet inside the lining of his coat and it was only after his death that the document was discovered. And what was written there?

Fire

God of Abraham, God of Isaac, God of Jacob, not of the philosophers and scholars.

Certitude. Certitude. Feeling. Joy. Peace. God of Jesus Christ.

Forgetfulness of the world and of everything, except God.

Joy, joy, joy, tears of joy.

Jesus Christ

I have separated myself from Him: I have fled from Him, denied Him, crucified Him.

Let me never be separated from Him.

We keep hold of Him only by the ways taught in the Gospel.

Renunciation, total and sweet.

Total submission to Jesus Christ and to my director.

Eternally in joy for a day's training on earth.

Amen.[40]

This experience, which Pascal called his "second conversion," led him to abandon nearly everything. He sold his coach and horses, his fine furniture and silverware, and gave the money to the poor. Never again would he sign his name to his own writings, nor would he let his name be mentioned in praise. He left Paris and went to live among a Christian renewal group, the Jansenists, as a "solitary." Rather dramatic, you say. Yes, it was . . . and is.

Pascal's analysis of how human beings avoid God by means of constant distraction is brilliant. At one point he observes that our problems would be solved if we could learn to sit quietly in our room alone. What a challenge for us postmoderns with all our gadgets of distraction. "How do we do that?" you may ask. Well, we "just do it." That is all.

I am also taken by Pascal's insight that human beings are both glorious and wretched. We are glorious because we are created in the image of God; we are wretched because of our fall from grace. Today people want to tilt in one direction or the other: all gloriousness or all wretchedness. But we are both. This insight helps us immensely in dealing with people.

When another person seems all glorious we are not deceived—wretchedness is just around the corner. Conversely, if we see only wretchedness we know there is gloriousness in this person. God's good image may be eclipsed but it is not gone. And it is given to us to call it forth.

The head pains that eventually took Pascal's life at age thirty-nine ultimately grew so severe that he was unable to continue any mental exercise. One of the last things he wrote was a prayer asking God to use his illness for a good end:

> Lord, whose Spirit is so good and so gentle . . . grant that I may conform to Thy will, just as I am, that, being sick as I am, I may glorify Thee in my sufferings. . . . Unite my will with Thine and my sufferings with those that Thou hast suffered; grant that mine may become Thine. Unite me with Thee. . . . And thus, having some small part in Thy suffering, I shall be filled wholly by Thee with the glory which it has brought to Thee, the glory in which Thou dost dwell with the Father and the Holy Spirit, forever and ever. Amen.[41]

O Lord, Pascal's prayer is so magnanimous it takes our breath away. Perhaps we had better start more slowly. So for this week we ask that you will show us how to like people a little more. Normally we would say "love," but we fool ourselves too often with that word. "Of course I love people," we say to ourselves. So perhaps learning to "like" people a little more is a good starting point.

Are there people at work we don't like very much? Help us, Lord, to like them more and more, and maybe someday we will discover to our surprise that we do genuinely love them. And perhaps through learning to love them more we will come to love you more. This we pray in the good name of Jesus. Amen.

THE SPIRITUAL LIFE
AS JOURNEY

*Now the LORD said to Abram, "Go from your country and your kindred
and your father's house to the land that I will show you.
I will make of you a great nation, and I will bless you, and make your
name great." . . . So Abram went, as the LORD had told him.*

GENESIS 12:1-4

I was first drawn to the individuals featured in this chapter while sorting
out the various dimensions of my own spiritual journey. Questions and
challenges that come to every honest seeker had come to me and I needed
help. As I pursued these answers, whole new vistas of understanding unfolded before me.

I discovered that we are all on a journey in life. Hopefully, a journey
toward the heart of God. A journey into the subterranean chambers of the
soul. A journey into the spiritual unknown. At times all of us stumble and
fall along the way. Still, we are able to rise again—scarred, perhaps, but
wiser for the experience—and continue on. Most critical for this journey
is knowing that we are headed in a Godward direction.

To see the spiritual life as journey is to recognize that every step we
take in life requires reflection and discernment if we are to see God's role

in it. As we think our way along this journey, it is like following a path up a steep mountain. Occasionally we feel winded and need to stop—or even lose our footing and need to recover—but then suddenly we discover a whole new level of understanding we never knew existed.

Most of us are drawn to this journey by the massive challenges we face along the way. Will my life turn out well or poorly? If evil and suffering befall me, will I have the fortitude to withstand it? How can I become the kind of person who enters into meaningful, long-lasting relationships? Is there obvious purpose to my life and work? And, as I pursue God and set significant goals for my life, will I have the spiritual resources to keep from being derailed from the very life I seek?

These questions require answers. As we seek them, we realize that every approach to our life with God includes elements of a spiritual journey. We see this in the assumptions we make—that our spiritual journey should lead us from evil to good, from falsehood to truth and from self-centeredness to servanthood. As we pursue these answers, different expressions guide us.

Finding Our Lives in God's Great Story

Learning to look for God requires discipline and insight. Our individual personal experiences make sense only when placed in the context of our life with God. When we see our life in the broader perspective of God's active engagement with us, we enter the grand story of Scripture.

Every one of us requires frameworks of meaning to make sense of the world. These are often thought of as "plausibility structures," a term originally coined to explain the way individual facts of science fit into a meaningful whole.[1] The goal of Scripture is to teach us to see the way our life fits into God's great story. It is to come to see our life from God's perspective.

From the time of Adam and Eve in the early chapters of Genesis to the dramatic creation of a new heaven and a new earth in Revelation 22, the pages of Scripture are filled with the unfolding revelation of God's love and interaction with his people. As we review the entire breadth of Scripture, we see that it teaches us to recognize the tremendous clash between various understandings of a successful life.[2]

Success or failure in the eyes of society is measured in terms of wealth, power, prestige and personal achievement. But success in our spiritual life is measured in terms of our ability to understand and address our own spiritual condition as well as the spiritual needs of others. Yet there is almost nothing in our contemporary culture that directs us this way.

We can be successful by all the conventional measures of society and still be chronically unhappy. We are unhappy because the life we lead is unbalanced and we cannot give ourselves to the priorities and relationships that form the foundation of a meaningful life. We give ourselves instead to misplaced priorities and superficial relationships because we believe that if we just earn a little more money or gain a little more respect, we will achieve the inner peace we long for and seek.

To discover a life of balance is to find the true source of our happiness in God. It is to know that our life must connect with God if we are to engage in the activities that bring ultimate meaning to our existence. It is to submit to a process that takes time and develops across the span of our life, a process first captured in the early days of monasticism.

The Remarkable Alternative of Monasticism

Following the writings of Scripture and other key developments in the first three centuries of the early church, the spiritual awakening of the fourth century began with some of the most intense religious and military conflicts in the history of Western civilization. Wars within and against the Roman Empire, a crumbling infrastructure and rampant moral decay all opened the way for Constantine to conquer the Roman Empire. With his conquest, Christianity became the official religion of the state, and by the end of the century, the ideal of martyrdom as the ultimate act of Christian devotion had been eclipsed. In its place arose monasticism, a movement that would govern Christian spirituality for the next nine hundred years.

Evagrius of Ponticus

From Deadly Thoughts to Godly Virtues

If you are a theologian, you truly pray.
If you truly pray, you are a theologian.

CHAPTERS ON PRAYER

EVAGRIUS (345-399) WAS A LEGEND IN HIS OWN TIME. He helped forward the idea of monasticism as the highest expression of our love and devotion to God.[3] Mentored by the Cappadocian fathers (Basil the Great, Gregory of Nazianzus and Gregory of Nyssa) while living in and around Constantinople, he seemed destined for high churchly office. But temptation overran him. The details are vague, but we do know that while serving God he fell passionately in love with a married woman. Questions abound as to whether the relationship was ever consummated, but Evagrius fled to Jerusalem, eventually settling in the Egyptian desert and never returning to Constantinople.

In the measured judgment of many leading thinkers, it was in the desert that Evagrius developed the earliest and best understanding of the developmental nature of Christian spirituality. Having sabotaged a brilliant career by his own indiscretion, Evagrius began an excavation of the human soul that endures to this day. Heavily influenced by Origen, he displays some of the keenest insights into the psychology of spiritual devotion ever written. Beyond his capacity to systematize human thought and emotion, his even greater contribution is his sensitivity to human nature—especially his identification of the eight deadly thoughts that agitate our mind and ruin our life.

Challenges in Our Life with God

Evagrius's most important work, *Monichikos*, outlines the structure of the spiritual life and identifies the various challenges we confront as we develop our life with God. Later, under Gregory the Great (540-604), his eight deadly thoughts would be compressed into the seven deadly sins. We are still drawn to these ancient texts today because Evagrius shows such a deep understanding of human motivation. Here is a conceptual framework of his highly complex thought.

Table 2.1. Evagrius's Ordering of the Spiritual Life

Levels	Three Books of *Monichikos*	Human Action	Faculty of Judgment	Type of Spiritual Action	Goal
Highest	*Kephalia Gnostica*	Contemplation of God—*Theologike*	Nous *(imago Dei)*	Pure contemplation of God	Know God

Intermediate: from natural contemplation to knowledge of the *logikoi*, the eight deadly thoughts. If we are derailed by the eight deadly thoughts, we are unable to ascend to the highest level of pure contemplation of God. Evagrius believes this is where the demons assail our minds in order to prevent us from rising to pure contemplation of God.

Middle	*Gnostikos*	contemplation—*physike*	Psyche (soul)	Action and contemplation	Know the nature of earthly things

Intermediate: development of *apatheia* for bodily appetites in order to ascend to natural contemplation. It is on this level that Evagrius introduces the eight deadly thoughts. It is also here that we see for the first time the necessity of mastering the eight deadly thoughts if we are to avoid constraining our body (soma), thereby keeping us from moving to the next level in our life with God.

Lowest	*Praktikos*	ascetic living—*praktike*	Soma (body)	Action	Know the virtues of human behavior

The Soul's Return to God

The three books of the *Monichikos* outline the structure of the soul's return to God and provide a guide for ascending from the lowest levels of our earthly existence to the majestic heights of our life with God. Occasionally,

Evagrius is criticized for being too Platonic, a charge that could be leveled against almost every early Greek Christian (see appendix A). But his understanding of the mind's return to God is completely within the framework of Christian theology and Scripture because of his belief that the "nous"[4] is the faculty we possess that is made in the image of God (the *imago Dei*).

The first book, the *Praktikos*, consists of one hundred chapters on ascetic life and discipline. It outlines the process by which we harness the body in order to properly orient the active life to God. Here, we develop virtue that redirects our emotions and passions to that which is good. We repent from a life oriented against God and learn how to see ourselves as creatures within the broader purposes of God's love.

It is on this level that we discover Evagrius's most original contribution to our understanding of the spiritual life as journey: the eight deadly thoughts and the eight godly virtues, which together determine our spiritual destiny. If we succumb to any or all of the deadly thoughts, we create a roadblock that makes pure contemplation of God impossible. If we overcome these deadly thoughts by cultivating the eight godly virtues, we can transition to the highest level described in book three, *Kephalia Gnostica*, where we enjoy pure knowledge of God through prayer.

The second book, *Gnostikos*, consists of fifty chapters. It teaches us how to look for God in the created order, to cultivate a love of earthly realities by seeking God among human things. It is here that we refine our love of neighbor in order to ascend to a pure love of God. It is also on this level that our mind gains insight into the deeper nature of the universe. As we learn to love our neighbor, we also learn to love God. Because of our human limitations we almost never learn to love God before we learn to love our neighbor.

At the third and highest level, we enjoy pure contemplation of God. We enter into the vigor and strength of the fully animated divine "nous," the Divine mind. We come to understand that our capacity to know God directly reflects the *imago Dei*, the image of God innate in each one of us.

The Deadly Thoughts and Godly Virtues

The key concept in Evagrius's spiritual theology is that our ability to know and love God is tied directly to our ability to cultivate godly virtue. This cultivation proceeds by stages. Unless we face an untimely demise,

Evagrius believes that each of us will be assailed by all eight deadly thoughts. The question is how we will react to the gravitational pull of each deadly thought when it arrives. The eight deadly thoughts are:

- Gluttony (*gastrimargia*)
- Anger (*orge*)
- Greed or avarice (*philargyia*)
- Envy or vainglory (*xenodoxia*)
- Pride (*hyperphania*)
- Lust or impurity (*porneia*)
- Indifference or impatient discouragement (*akedia* or *acedia*—sloth)
- Melancholy or depression (*lype*)[5]

Evagrius's greatest concern is the disorienting effect of these deadly thoughts. They can throw us off course and impede our pursuit of life with God, preventing us from attaining this life as our ultimate destiny. We eventually learn that successful resolution of one deadly thought provides the momentum to negotiate those that follow. And although each deadly thought arrives at a particular moment in our spiritual journey, its lingering spiritual effects can last a lifetime. Ultimately, each deadly thought is interdependent with all of the rest. Although we face the deadly thoughts individually, their power is cumulative if left unresolved.

We overcome the disorientation of the eight deadly thoughts only through the orienting effects of the eight godly virtues, which correspond directly to the deadly thoughts:

- Temperance (overcomes gluttony)
- Mildness (overcomes anger)
- Generosity (overcomes greed and avarice)
- Happiness (overcomes envy)
- Humility (overcomes pride)
- Chastity (overcomes lust and impurity)
- Diligence (overcomes indifference and impatient discouragement)
- Wisdom (overcomes melancholy and depression)

These virtues develop as we conquer the deadly thoughts arising from our interactions with other people and social institutions. The virtues, like the deadly thoughts, are cumulative. Positive resolution at one level leads to positive resolution at subsequent levels. Just as the deadly thoughts create disorientation, the moral virtues create an orientation that helps us make progress in our spiritual journey.

Gluttony overcome by temperance. Gluttony is the insatiable desire to take things in, to consume and to attempt to satisfy desire through gorging. In the ancient world the monks often feared they would run out of food. "The thought of gluttony," Evagrius begins, "tempts the monk to give up his ascetic efforts in short order. It brings to mind concern for his stomach, spleen and liver. He remembers other brothers who have come to disgraceful end."[6]

Although associated primarily with food, gluttony can lead to any number of activities that reflect a loss of confidence in God's provision. Today, for example, we often fear loss of a job, and the deadly thought of gluttony can take root as compulsive overwork.

The virtue of temperance recognizes that there will always be more to come and that God will provide. It is based on a capacity for trust and a hope in a future that does not presently exist. Trusting and depending on God allows us to believe that our future needs will be met and that we do not need to hoard now, so long as we follow God.

Anger overcome by mildness. Christians have never known exactly what to do with anger. Anger arises from a sense of violation—a violation of self, of agreements, of principles. It also arises when we feel a threat to our social status or a desire to control other people's lives. Evagrius writes, "The most fierce passion is anger. In fact it is defined as a boiling and stirring up of wrath against one who has given injury. It tends to lead to a preoccupation with the one with whom we are angry. It ruins our health—both physical and mental."[7]

Mildness, on the other hand, is the capacity for self-restraint. Whether a principle has been violated or we simply feel a great frustration with ourselves or our situation, we can respond with mildness because we have confidence in God. When we center our life on God, our need to gain the world's acclaim evaporates. We no longer clamor to climb the corporate ladder or be noticed. We find that God totally satisfies our need to be valued and recognized.

Greed overcome by generosity. Greed essentially has no limit. It is boundless in its grasping for money or fame and its need to fill others' minds with ourselves. It leads to a lack of respect for the needs of others because our own needs overrun all normal boundaries and limits. Evagrius sees it this way: "Avarice suggests to the mind a lengthy old age, an inability to perform manual labor at some future date, and famines that are sure to come. It sees sickness that will visit us, the pinch of poverty, and the great shame that comes from accepting the necessities of life from others."[8]

The godly virtue of generosity overcomes greed by recognizing that our greatest good is found in sharing with others in community. It celebrates the contributions of others because we are content in the value and place of our own contribution. We no longer possess an insatiable desire for fame and money because we see God's provision as sufficient.

Envy or vainglory overcome by happiness. Envy awakens in us when we feel inadequate about our own gifts and abilities and begin to resent the gifts and abilities of others. It is motivated by a fear of losing our place. What if someone else has better gifts than I do? Will I still be able to accomplish my own dreams and ambitions? Envy ultimately prevents us from seeing our own gifts and celebrating the role we have to play in the social networks and organizations where we find our greater meaning.

As Evagrius shows, envy takes on an especially unique twist. Of all the deadly thoughts, he sees envy as "the most subtle as it readily grows up in the souls of those who are seeking virtue because even this desire for virtue can be motivated by the desire to earn the praise of man."[9]

Happiness, on the other hand, arises from a celebration of the mutual contribution that we make together, as well as the contributions made by others with gifts and abilities that differ from our own. Happiness is a result of recognizing our own competencies and celebrating the skills and abilities of others. True happiness is possible only when our egocentrism is controlled and our ability to be other-centered is fully developed.

Pride overcome by humility. Pride is a result of a disproportionate sense of our own contribution, manifesting in an inordinate belief in our own importance. Like envy, pride is unable to recognize the contributions of others because this very recognition threatens the view we want to hold of ourselves. Evagrius observes, "Pride is the cause of the most damaging fall for the soul. It induces the monk to deny that God is his helper and to consider that he himself is the cause of virtuous actions."[10]

Humility, on the other hand, is a result of seeing ourselves properly. It involves recognizing that our gifts and abilities need to be developed further. It understands that others have gifts and abilities as well. Humility allows us to see our role in the greater purposes of God's design without feeling threatened by the achievements of others.

Lust or impurity overcome by chastity. Lust ruins lives. It impels us to lust after bodies and attacks those who strive to practice chastity.[11] Lust results from egocentrism and the belief that the person after whom we lust exists only to satisfy our unbridled desires. Evagrius was acutely aware of the disordering effect of lust, perhaps because of his own transgression. Whatever the circumstances, he knew that lust can overrun a person and cause that person to lose all sense of self.

Chastity, on the other hand, works to properly balance love with the capacity to be loved. Chastity honors and cares for the person we choose to love. It indicates a fidelity to promises made that allow expressions of love to endure.

Indifference overcome by diligence. Indifference and impatient discouragement are a result of believing that the daily affairs of life don't matter. They reflect a belief that what we are currently doing has no outcome worthy of respect. We succumb to them when we lose confidence that the way we spend our life matters.

In contrast, the godly virtue of diligence reflects the perseverance that helps us get through tough times. It is believing that the ultimate purpose of our life rests in the hands of God. It is continuing to engage in the affairs of life because we believe God will eventually reverse our fortune. It is maintaining confidence in the providence of God even when there is no immediate evidence to justify such confidence.

Melancholy overcome by wisdom. Melancholy and depression arise from the belief that our very existence does not matter. This deadly thought indicates a complete loss of confidence in the goodness of the world and our place within it. It concludes that the priorities by which we have structured our life will have no lingering effect after we are gone. "It tends to come up at times because of the deprivation of our desires," Evagrius observes, "while on other occasions it accompanies anger. It arises from the deprivation of the things we desire most."[12]

Wisdom, on the other hand, is the ability to recognize the role our life plays in the greater affairs of the world. It is contentment with our individual contribution and recognizing that our priorities will affect the next generation and beyond. It is celebration of the past and anticipation of the future without being overly concerned about our particular involvement. It is to enjoy our legacy without feeling we must tidy it up before we are gone.

Evagrius believes that we must resolve the tension of each deadly thought by cultivating the corresponding godly virtue. This cultivation helps us on our spiritual journey as we progress through each stage of life and orients us to God. If we do not cultivate the godly virtues, we will never attain a sense of purpose and meaning in life. Evagrius does not teach that the goal of life is to know about God but to know God. This knowledge can occur only when the part of us that is made in the image of God, our "nous," joins with the mind of God through prayer.

Ultimately, Evagrius's work answers our enduring question: why go higher in our life with God? Since the whole purpose of the spiritual life is to help us find meaning, happiness and contentment, why must it be such hard work? As with each of these writers, Evagrius helps us see that our insatiable longings will find enduring satisfaction only on the highest level of knowing God.[13]

The Ultimate Goal

Evagrius defines our ultimate goal as *apatheia,* the state in which every thought, desire and action is properly ordered. In this state, the passions of our soul (envy, pride, melancholy, greed, anger) are overcome by love of God and neighbor, and the passions of our flesh (gluttony, lust, indifference) are overcome by self-discipline. We are brought into *apatheia* by the mercy of Christ.[14] Evagrius writes, "The proof of apatheia is had when the spirit begins to see its own light, when it remains in a state of tranquility in the presence of images it has during sleep and when it maintains its calm as it beholds the affairs of life." *Apatheia* is, in essence, being able to discern and respond appropriately to any physical, mental or spiritual stimulation.[15]

Elsewhere Evagrius notes, "To achieve apatheia is to achieve a full and harmonious integration of the emotional and spiritual life under the direct influence of God's divine love. It creates a state of deep calm based on obedience to the commandments of God and the practice of virtue."[16] In other words, a state of *apatheia* is the only way to experience the pure contemplation of God.

REFLECTING AND RESPONDING

The debt we owe Evagrius of Ponticus is enormous. He gave us a full-blown developmental understanding of life with God. It is hard for us, many centuries later, to recognize what an astonishing step forward Evagrius provided us. We live on the other side of the divide where it is commonplace to ridicule all the excesses of the seven deadly sins—the ultimate summation of Evagrius's eight deadly thoughts. Today we simply ignore this advance in virtue ethics as an antiquated relic of a darker period, failing to realize that the morally dark period is our own, not theirs.

Evagrius knew by bitter personal experience how utterly disastrous these thoughts could be. He understood that these thoughts, uncontrolled and uncorrected, could, very simply, destroy a life. It is why he called them "deadly thoughts." We simply cannot get around the reality of this insight: gluttony and anger and greed and envy and pride and lust and indifference and melancholy truly are ruinous to the life.

Right here we see the genius of Evagrius. He was well trained in how the mind works. He knew that deadly thoughts could be overcome, but not in a vacuum—they could be replaced only by godly virtues. The emptying of the mind of evil must, of necessity, involve the filling of it with good. And so we learn to take in virtues of temperance and mildness and generosity and happiness and humility and chastity and diligence and wisdom.

It is interesting that while all of the deadly thoughts and godly virtues are highly specific in their reference, they have interconnected effects throughout the moral life. For example, the deadly thought of lust is most often specifically aimed at unbridled sexual passions, and yet it can be seen in all runaway desires. Conversely chastity, which is often specifically aimed at fidelity and honor in sexual relations, in a broad sense means the loving control of all the passions by the grace of God. So a moral victory in one area of life has secondary effects on other areas of life. Likewise, a defeat reverberates throughout the moral life. The moral life is interconnected and interrelated. Always.

There is another thing Evagrius understood well. And here we are getting at a central issue in the transformation of the human personality. Anything that is drawn before the mind, whether of good or evil, does not disappear immediately. No, it lingers in the mind, and the scent of it stains the atmosphere of consciousness, even the unconscious, as we now know. This is why vices begin in the mind. And why they are so deadly.

On the other hand, the godly virtues have much the same effect. Well, not exactly. The stain of deadly thoughts seems so strong, so blatant, so loud, if you will. The godly virtues seem so weak, so unobtrusive, so quiet. Anyone who has worked intimately with people sucked into the vortex of deadly thoughts and the way those thoughts result in deadly actions knows their destructive power. Our oldest son, Joel, is a psychologist in the U.S. Air Force. He often works with the most traumatized of individuals, individuals from modern warfare's killing fields. Places where evil seems to have reached new definitions of horror. The destructiveness of evil in these places seems, at times, overwhelming.

Godly virtues appear tame by comparison. And yet I wonder if they don't have a power that is unseen to us. Surely they partake of that life from God that will never perish. Perhaps the godly virtues are actually the stronger. I remember George Fox describing how he saw a great ocean of darkness and death, but that it was overcome by a greater ocean of life and light. Now I know that this remains mostly a statement of hope and of faith. Still, is it not true that the power of God's light is strong, strong to the point of overcoming evil with good? This I hope, and this I believe. And the mind is the first and, in many ways, the most central arena of this battlefield in the moral life.

One final thought. When we look at Evagrius's list we clearly see the progression. Gluttony is the most basic of the passions and temperance the most basic of the virtues—indeed, temperance is listed as one of the cardinal virtues. Then when we come to melancholy or depression and its corresponding virtue, wisdom, surely we have come onto higher ground. All of that to say, there is a progression in the moral life. We do not take occasional joggers and put them in a marathon race, and we do not do that in the spiritual life either. We learn to grow step by incremental step. This is a reality with which Evagrius was well acquainted.

Dear Lord, all these deadly thoughts seem so . . . well, so deadly. Anger especially. Lord, so many people today seem to have such seething anger. Oh, we keep it well hidden under a veneer of pleasantries, but it is there nonetheless.

Someday our anger will surface like a volcanic explosion, and what will happen then? What, Lord, is the remedy for today's anger? Shall we vent it, or seek counseling, or what? Perhaps it is best simply to wait upon you for divine healing. And yet, that feels like avoidance more than anything else. So where do we turn? Wise Jesus, we're asking to know the way forward. Please, show us the way forward. Amen.

George Herbert

Weaving Life into a Meaningful Whole

If as a Flower doth spread and die,
Thou wouldst extend me to some good,
Before I were by frost's extremity
Nipt in the bud.

THE TEMPLE

THE SIXTEENTH CENTURY CLOSED WITH Christendom battling internal strife, which spilled over into political conflicts between emerging nation-states. As the trauma of the sixteenth century ebbed and flowed, the seeds of radical change were taking root in Western Europe. The elements of the Counter-Reformation—the division of Catholic lands among Protestant warlords and vicious fights among Protestants themselves—revealed the smoldering crisis that was brewing as the curtain fell on the sixteenth century. As it rose on the seventeenth, discontent and turmoil raged across Europe. England and Europe became embroiled in civil and national conflicts that would escalate into the Thirty Years' War.

Along with the political turmoil came social, philosophical and religious upheaval as well. These conflicts joined with the new science to undermine cultural and spiritual confidence in Christianity. As political allies became enemies and centuries of settled life crumbled under the weight of civil unrest, a continent's confidence in Christianity collapsed as well. The corruption of the clergy, the nominal religion of kings and the quest for new empires all conspired to unleash an avalanche of unbelief.

Most significant in this emerging period was the final and complete collapse of the Ptolemaic-Aristotelian worldview. Through the work of Copernicus and Galileo, science identified the sun as the center of the universe. There were other forces at work as well, but assumptions like ignorance as the cause of society's problems and science as the solution of all social ills helped shape what history has come to know as the "modern mentality."[17]

Stepping into this period of controversy and dissent was George Herbert (1593-1633), the brilliant English poet and pastor who articulated a poetic and passionate understanding of the spiritual life in his classic work *The Temple*. In this masterpiece Herbert shows how we begin in unbelief outside the church, come to initial belief, grow in our maturity in this belief and finally realize full intimacy with God. Herbert's genius lies in his wonderful ability to take the disparate parts of our life and weave them into a meaningful whole.

The Flow of Our Spiritual Life

To read Herbert is to gain a sense of how poetry can help us understand our life with God as journey. So often we expect our books to state their positions and then proceed clearly. Herbert's work is different. It moves between the obvious and the subtle—which reflects the way our very life progresses. Through his erratic poetic style Herbert portrays for us the ups and downs, the highs and lows, the heart-stopping advances and crushing defeats of the spiritual life.

Preparing to enter. The Temple is the record of Herbert's own struggle to make sense of life with God. It begins with two poems that form the "church porch." Both the words and the structure of these poems reflect Herbert's understanding of the motion of God as he communicates his ways and will to us. The church porch is where we prepare to enter life with God. On the porch we face two clear choices: to enter a life that leads to God or to pursue a life that ends in despair.

Herbert establishes a high moral tone that recognizes the gravity of vice while pursuing the elevating energy of virtue. If we undergo moral rehabilitation and develop virtue while on the church porch, this virtuous life frees us to enter "the temple," where we discover the attendant blessings God intends for those who choose a life with him.[18]

Steps in our journey. Each of The Temple's 165 poems highlights a step in our spiritual journey that brings us closer to the meaning and purpose promised in a life with Christ. The poems begin with an expression of the longing to make life a living sacrifice to God. Listen to the words of the opening poem, "The Altar," itself shaped like the ancient altar of the Anglican Church.

A broken A L T A R, Lord thy servant rears,
Made of a heart, and cemented with tears:
Whose parts are as thy hand did frame;
No workman's tool hath touched the same.

> A   heart   alone
> Is   such   a   stone
> As   nothing   but
> Thy power doth cut
> Wherefore each part
> Of   my   hard   heart
> Meets in this frame,
> To praise thy name.

That if I chance to hold my peace
These stones to praise thee may not cease.
Oh let thy blessed sacrifice be mine,
And sanctify this A L T A R to be thine.

This poem describes the starting point for our entire Christian pilgrimage. The spiritual life begins with the decision to make Christ's sacrifice real and present in our own life. *The Temple* ends with buoyant optimism that when Jesus, as Love, fills our soul, we find rest.[19] In between, the vicissitudes of life ravage us, providing moments of exhilarating insight woven together with long periods of melancholy and despair.

The role of suffering. Herbert is especially attentive to the problem of human suffering. Often suffering either opens us to God or causes us to turn away. Herbert invites us to allow our experiences of anguish and brokenness to bring us closer to God, realizing that it is through suffering that we become aware of a whole other dimension of spiritual truth. It is through suffering and the realization that nothing on earth can relieve it that we turn to God. Listen to these haunting yet hope-filled words from Herbert in "Affliction (III)":

My heart did heave, and there came forth, Oh God!
By that I knew that thou wast in the grief,
To guide and govern it to my relief,
   Making a scepter of the rod:
   Hadst thou not had thy part,
Sure the unruly sigh had broke my heart.

But since thy breath gave me both life and shape,
Thou knowest my tallies; and when there's assign'd
So much breath to a sigh, what's then behind?
   Or if some years with it escape;
   The sigh then only is
A gale to bring me sooner to my bliss.

Thy life on earth was grief, and thou art still
Constant unto it, making it to be
A point of honor, now to grieve in me,
   And in my members suffer ill.
   They who lament one cross,
Thou dying daily, praise thee to thy loss.[20]

How Beauty Calls Us to God

Herbert is also keenly aware of the way in which the temporal mediates the eternal. He sees this in the beauty of creation, calling often upon subtle, indirect imagery rather than overt description. Even the role of the preacher as the mediating link between earth and heaven, a role Herbert highly prizes, is valuable only to the extent that the preacher lifts our attention from the temporal to the eternal plane. One notable example is captured in the uplifting poem "Church Music." Herbert uses this poem to demonstrate how music brings joy to the soul and helps us forget our sorrows.[21]

Elsewhere Herbert implies that poetry is the language of God and the closest form of communication to direct prayer. This is especially true when he describes the mission of the church. In "The British Church," Herbert writes,

I joy, dear Mother, when I view
Thy perfect lineaments, and hue
   Both sweet and bright.

Beauty in thee takes up her place,
And dates her letters from thy face,
 When she doth write.

A fine aspect in fit array,
Neither too mean, nor yet too gay,
 Shows who is best.[22]

Herbert goes on to describe the variety within the mother church and
the beauty of each distinction, capturing the role of aesthetic sensibility in
our life with God. His work is highly reminiscent of Plato, who observed
that "beauty is the only spiritual essence we love instinctively by our nature." Herbert believed that beauty, second only to Scripture, elevates us
to God.

The Four Pillars of Our Christian Faith

Herbert was a man of the church. His robust confidence in the church is
anchored in his belief that there are no "churchless Christians." Everyone
needs a community of faith for their life with God to grow and prosper.
It is the church that strengthens the four pillars on which our life with
God rests. These pillars are Scripture, prayer, the sacraments and the ordered life of the church year.

Scripture is primary, as Herbert prefers the special revelation of
God's Word to the general revelation of creation. He is especially interested in exploring both the unity and diversity of Scripture and how
the canon holds together to convey both specific and general meanings
for our life with God. Consider this notable example from "The Holy
Scriptures (II)":

Oh that I knew how all thy lights combine,
And the configurations of their glory!
Seeing not only how each verse doth shine,
But all the constellations of the story.

This verse marks that, and both do make a motion
Unto a third, that ten leaves off doth lie:
Then as dispersed herbs do watch a potion,
These three make up some Christian's destiny.

Such are thy secrets, which my life makes good,
And comments on thee: for in ev'ry thing
Thy words do find me out, and parallels bring,
And in another make me understood.

Stars are poor books, and oftentimes do miss:
This book of stars lights to eternal bliss.[23]

Together, Scripture, prayer, the sacraments and the ordered life of the church year form the context for our life with God. Everywhere Herbert radiates a boundless enthusiasm for a sacramental view of life, a view that sees the touch of eternity in time, leading us to look for God in the affairs of everyday life.

As *The Temple* gains momentum, a vibrant optimism breaks out in "Praise (III)," suggesting that we reach points where a settled confidence in God's goodness stabilizes our life. To make this progress, however, we must undergo necessary growth and pruning. The poem "Paradise" speaks in both words and structure to this process:

I bless thee, Lord, because I	GROW
Among thy trees, which in a	ROW
To thee both fruit and order	OW
What open force, or hidden	CHARM
Can blast my fruit, or bring me	HARM,
While the enclosure is thine	ARM?
Enclose me still for fear I	START,
But to me rather sharp and	TART,
Then let me want thy hand and	ART.
When thou dost greater judgments	SPARE,
And with thy knife but prune and	PARE,
Ev'n fruitful trees more fruitful	ARE.
Such sharpness shows the sweetest	FRIEND,
Such cuttings rather heal than	REND,
And such beginnings touch their	END.[24]

This poem helps us realize that the goal of our journey with God is to bring us to a desired end. "The Pilgrimage" especially amplifies this theme when it identifies the obstacles we face on the way to our ultimate destiny. Along the way, the pilgrim is led into all manner of trial and temptation. His resistance to these trials and temptations brings him at last to death, which ushers him into paradise in heaven.[25]

Herbert is quite attentive to the rhythms of life. He celebrates the way the church year and church history establish both a linear and circular pattern for individual life as well as the corporate life of the community. This, too, is part of the spiritual life as journey.

The Double Motion of Our Journey with God

Herbert's theme of "double motion" is portrayed most dramatically in his brilliant poem "Colossians 3:3." His central assumption here is that spiritual formation is necessary because we are not fully formed when born but must develop over time. This poem is the centerpiece of Herbert's approach to our life with God and, as in many of his others, both the words and the structure convey his meaning. The double nature of our life with God entails both the seen and the unseen, the temporal and the eternal, the sacred and the mundane.

> **My** words and thoughts do both express this notion,
> That **Life** hath with the sun a double motion,
> The first **Is** straight and our diurnal friend,
> The other **Hid** and doth obliquely bend,
> One life is wrapt **In** flesh and tends to earth,
> The other winds towards **Him** whose happy birth
> Taught me to live here so, **That** still one eye
> Should aim and shoot at that which **Is** on high:
> Quitting with daily labor all   **My** pleasure,
> To gain at harvest an eternal   **Treasure**.[26]

In this poem Herbert introduces the idea that the Christian life is lived on two levels. Both the words he chooses and the pattern he constructs illustrate the way our life is conformed to the image of Christ over time. On the horizontal level, we mark our life by various experiences. But on the vertical level, which is hidden, our spiritual life is being conformed to the image of Christ over time. Hidden in the language of Herbert's poem are the words from Colossians 3:3: "My life is hid in him that is my treasure." This is the double motion of the Christian life.

On the horizontal plane, our daily life does not always seem to have meaning. Yet Herbert suggests that these activities are the very activities where we encounter God. We cannot always see meaning, control our moods or even sustain a consistent understanding of God. Nevertheless, Herbert helps us see that throughout our mundane days, God's Spirit is guiding our spirit. On the hidden vertical plane, decisions are being made, choices executed, allegiances cast and motives evaluated. It is on this level that we are becoming like Christ and being conformed to his image over time.

The significance of *The Temple* is Herbert's exploration of the range and scope of the Christian life through his use of metaphor. He teaches Christian doctrine indirectly and shows how it can provide the order and structure we need to be guided to God. Even though doctrine alone cannot bring us to God, it can help us understand the nature and destiny of the Christian journey.

REFLECTING AND RESPONDING

George Herbert astonishes me. To begin with, he wrote an incredibly wise and profound prose piece, *The Country Parson*. If we are trying to understand the work of spiritual formation in a local congregational setting and the place and role of "pastor" within it, there simply is no better place to turn. Frankly, *The Country Parson* trumps all the twentieth- and twenty-first-century works on the same subject. Herbert understands the spiritual formation work of the pastor because he lived it completely and knew how to explain it to ordinary pastors seeking to bring the wisdom of God to ordinary people.

But, of course, there is more. Smack in the midst of all the ordinariness of parish life—births and deaths, broken marriages and anxious parents, pastoral visits by the score and cups of tea beyond numbering—Herbert is writing the most astonishing poetry. His poetry, which takes us on an extended journey through everyday parish life, was published after his death. It causes me to wonder how much the people of his parish knew of his poetry, brilliant and beautiful beyond the telling. Did it crop up in his homilies? Did he read it to small groups in homes? Perhaps. My guess, however, is that the people Herbert ministered to day in and day out had no idea of the poetic treasure in their midst.

Herbert's poetry says two things to me right off. First, it says that God loves beauty. Today we tend to forget those great transcendentals—the good, the true, the beautiful—which guided so much of ancient civilization. And beauty especially we could use in greater measure in our day. Poetry—good poetry, true poetry—is beauty incarnated into language. Please understand, I struggle with poetry. Even the reading of it is hard, not to mention the writing of it. I must read thoughtfully and repeatedly. Understanding comes only with time and patience, but when it does come . . . well, I'm astonished.

The second thing Herbert's poetry says to me is that word choice is genuinely important. We live in a day of cheap sentences where words are prostituted for the purpose of propaganda. Text-messaging dominates the verbal landscape. "Any old word will do," we think, as we keep up a steady stream of monosyllabic prattle. No, any old word will not do. Mark Twain once observed that the difference between the right word and the almost right word is like the difference between lightning and a lightning bug. It is important that our word choice move from flat, lifeless and black-and-white to become animated with love and terror and pity and pain and wonder and all the other glorious emotions that make our lives dangerous and great and bearable. It was the great Welsh poet Dylan Thomas who said, "Out of words come the gusts and grunts and hiccups and heehaws of the common fun of the earth." Herbert's poetry reminds me of these realities.

I am very much taken with Herbert's idea that all of life's experiences have in them a "double motion." Outwardly we are carrying on the tasks of our day: scrubbing floors, talking with clients, working at our computer. Yet underneath, deeper down, our life is hid with Christ in God. And it is here in the innermost sanctuary of the soul that the real, substantive work of spiritual formation goes on. How hard it is for us to value this inward reality, which remains out of sight to all but the most spiritually sensitive. The outward is always clamoring and demanding. The inward is silent and never draws attention to itself. If we satisfy the outward we receive acclaim. If we satisfy the inward we receive nothing. Well, nothing outwardly—inwardly we experience a life of righteousness, peace and joy in the Holy Spirit. We must, however, remember that this is a "double" motion. It isn't as if the outward is bad and the inward good. Oh, no! It is that the inward is central and the outward flows out of the inward. As we give attention to that which is central, the outward tasks of life become more like a reflex action to the prior initiation of the heart. A double motion.

Finally, I am intrigued by Herbert's four pillars of life: Scripture, prayer, the sacraments and the ordered life of the church year. Each is valuable and each is important; together they form a bulwark against the chaos of modern life. It is one way we have of ordering the spiritual life, and a helpful one at that. Still, for my blood it feels à little too cut and dried. I've never found life quite that fixed, quite that settled. I sense the need for more. The immediacy of the Spirit to guide and empower, perhaps. Something else, maybe. I'm not sure. At least Herbert gives us something worth pondering . . . and living.

O Holy One of Israel, you spoke with glorious beauty through the poetic drama of the prophets of old. And the psalmists too. We're thankful. So much of life today is drab and flat. Sometimes we long for a sizzling metaphor just to liven things up a bit.

Thank you, Lord, for the singers and the artists and the poets of the world. No doubt they help prepare us for heaven where the music of the spheres will be multiplied beyond all human imagining. O may we love beauty in all its multifaceted expressions. This we pray in the name of the One who is utter beauty and goodness. Amen.

John Bunyan

The Pilgrim's Path to God

And thus it was: I, writing of the Way, fell suddenly into
an allegory about their journey, and the way to glory,
in more than twenty things, which I set down.

PREFACE TO *THE PILGRIM'S PROGRESS*

JOHN BUNYAN'S LIFE SPANNED A TUMULTUOUS period of history. He was born in 1628 in England, and when he died in 1688, France's Glorious Revolution was well under way. Bunyan underwent severe persecution and hardship, spending nearly twelve years of his life in jail. During these periods of isolation, his mind turned to his life with God and he began to reflect on how we make progress in our spiritual journey. Out of these reflections he penned one of our greatest spiritual masterpieces, *The Pilgrim's Progress*. Its timeless appeal is captured in its portrayal of the eternal longing of every human heart for God. It also provides one of the best depictions of the tremendous trials and tribulations that ravage every follower of Jesus as we embark on our journey with him.

Bunyan's life overlapped briefly with that of George Herbert. But his religious identity was tied to the dissenting groups and breakaway factions that dominated England during the second half of the seventeenth century. He was touched deeply by the religious revolutions sweeping England and personally suffered many of their attendant injustices. As a member of a dissenting group, Bunyan often found himself out of step with the ruling government. Hence his years in jail. *The Pilgrim's Progress* was written during one of his imprisonments.

Entering the "Life"

Bunyan's great work begins with the protagonist, Christian, setting off to relieve himself of the burdens that so deeply afflict him. These burdens are rooted in a fear of death and the judgment that awaits him in the life to come. Early in the story, Bunyan emphasizes that we must enter the Christian life for it to begin to make sense. He notes how difficult it is to begin this life because we are beset by afflictions and diversions. But as we undergo preparation, the journey becomes more visible.

Each step of Christian's journey illuminates a deeper dimension of our own spiritual life. Bunyan shows that truth and understanding of God's ways come to us over time, beginning with a recognition of our need for redemption. The successful resolution of each stage in our pilgrimage determines the degree to which we come to a fullness of our Christian faith.

A central point of *The Pilgrim's Progress* is that we do not know all of the twists and turns we will meet along the way. As we travel, we seek and find guidance for that part of the journey. And often the knowledge comes just in time for us to make an obedient response. As we progress, we face new temptations, all of which threaten to disorient us just as those previous temptations did. In this way we come to rely on God for guidance and provision. It is through his mercy and providence that we find the right solution at the right time to meet the dilemma that confronts us.

Christian must overcome different temptations if he is to find the joy and meaning of Christ's way of life. We, like Christian, must forsake our own inclination to self-reliance and learn from God. Early on we are tempted to work out our own salvation. Additional temptations come when we encounter unexpected setbacks or acute suffering in life. At these times we suffer not so much a loss of belief in God, but a loss of confidence that the Christian life is true.

Facing Multiple Temptations

Bunyan's illustration of the numerous temptations we face in our journey with God is unparalleled. We are tempted to abandon the pursuit of God's love. We are tempted to settle into a moral religion. We are tempted to self-deception and hypocrisy. We are tempted to be scornful and critical of others. We are even tempted to believe that we have committed such heinous evil that we stand beyond the limits of God's ability to forgive.

In each case, Bunyan wants us to understand the power of the temptation so we can rely on God to marshal the strength to resist it. In overcoming temptation we forsake our inclination to self-reliance. We overcome the way in which hardships so often disorient us from our life with God. And in the final analysis, we overcome our temptation to base the meaning of life on a moralistic form of religion.

As Christian progresses in the spiritual journey, the temptations become more subtle and destructive. One tempter likes to talk theology but makes no progress in his Christian life. A second engages in endless conversations about the difficulties of life without ever resolving them. A third tempter challenges Christian to prove that what he has learned on his journey is in fact true. This conversation recalls the original temptation of Adam and Eve in the garden, when the serpent leads them to forget what God has taught them. In the same way, we can end up losing the perspective that comes from accumulated wisdom and experience in our Christian journey.

Because of the turmoil and unrest that marked much of Bunyan's life, he continually draws from the touchstones of Protestant orthodoxy: the supremacy of Scripture, the suspicion of claims of individual authority based on spiritual experiences, and the quest to assure our selection as the elect of God. He also draws heavily on Foxe's *Book of Martyrs*, which portrays the grand sweep of history as part of the larger purposes of God's providence.[27]

Ultimately, *The Pilgrim's Progress* reveals that life is a journey. It recognizes that we are never finished fighting the good fight and acknowledges that we fight not only against flesh and blood, but also against principalities and spiritual powers. It further reveals that our responses to temptations along this journey help determine the outcome of our life with God. As a result, Christian serves as a model for understanding how the decisions we make, the choices we embrace, the challenges we overcome and the opportunities we face all contribute to the significance we find in our life with God.

REFLECTING AND RESPONDING

I owe a special debt to John Bunyan and his allegorical masterpiece, *The Pilgrim's Progress*. I was fresh out of seminary serving as pastor to my first congregation. The people were most patient and kind to me as I was finding my way in pastoring and my voice in preaching.

As you might imagine, being the pastor of a small congregation meant that I had to be prepared to do almost anything, from printing the weekly newsletter to emptying the trash to visiting the sick. One of the tasks that fell to me was delivering the children's sermon each Sunday just before the little ones made their way to their own service. This was a delightful assignment, really; I loved the challenge of speaking to children with adults listening in just to see if I could keep both interested and engaged.

Exactly how it happened I do not remember now, but somehow I began telling the stories of *The Pilgrim's Progress* in serial form. I knew that there was something here for the youngest to the oldest, for the most tentative believer to the most mature Christian. What a joy to tell these little ones about Christian and the many people he met on his journey: Faithful, Obstinate, Pliable, Mr. Worldly-Wise, Talkative, Little-Faith, Faint-Heart and so many others. I especially found the folk in the town of Fair-Speech of interest: my Lord Turn-About, my Lord Time-Server, Mr. Smooth-Man, Mr. Facing-Bothways and the parson of the town, Mr. Two-Tongues. I must not forget to mention the many adventures Christian had in places such as Vanity Fair, By-Path Meadow, Doubting Castle, the Delectable Mountains and more.

The trick was to tell the story so that each week Christian was left hanging by a thread and the children would need to come back next week to find out what happened to him. With sincere apologies to John Bunyan, I suppose I embellished the stories just a bit in order to keep the suspense at a high level. Actually, my changes were minor, for Bunyan himself had a real flair for the dramatic.

I think the children found it all great fun and high adventure. The one thing that I did not expect, though, was the interest and anticipation of the adults. Every now and then some mother would call or some father would drop by the office saying he or she had to be out of town next Sunday and please could I tell them what happens in the next episode— just to keep abreast of the story, you understand!

Well, I rather imagine that those brief children's sermons had more lasting effect for good on our little congregation than all the erudite sermons I worked so hard to prepare and deliver. That is the power of *The Pilgrim's Progress.*

In terms of spiritual formation and, most particularly, the idea of the spiritual life as journey, allow me to highlight several key themes. The first is the importance and significance of conversion. The journey makes no sense without this decisive turning. Christian must make a clear decision to turn away from the City of Destruction and to Christ, and pass through the Strait Gate and experience the great burden of sin falling off of his back. No half measures here. A real turning and a real journeying toward the Celestial City. So for us.

Then, too, I am impressed with the stress Bunyan places on struggle in the spiritual journey. He made much of the grace of God throughout his life (at one point he wrote a book titled *Grace Abounding to the Chief of Sinners*), but he never saw grace as opposed to struggle, only as opposed to earning. Christian struggles through the Slough of Despond and struggles to enter the Strait Gate and struggles up the Hill of Difficulty and struggles to overcome Apollyon. At times he stumbles and falls, and he must struggle to overcome these setbacks.

This story of genuine struggle is much like the Old Testament story of Jacob wrestling with the angel at Peniel and receiving a new name: Israel—"the one who struggles" (Gen 32). Struggle, you see, is true to the realities of a good world gone bad. It was true for Jacob; it was true for Bunyan; it is true for us.

One final thought. For Bunyan the spiritual journey is never over until it is truly over. When Christian and Hopeful are within a hair's breadth of reaching the Celestial City, they are nearly overcome by Flatterer and Atheist. You would think that after all they had gone through and all they had learned they would not be taken in, but they were. Escaping the traps of Flatterer and Atheist they come to the crossing of the River, passing from this life into greater Life. Christian finds the crossing exceedingly difficult, and without Hopeful there to help him out it appears he might not complete his journey.

But they do cross over, and as Christian and Hopeful enter the gates of the Celestial City they see Ignorance, who had been with them from time to time on their journey. Ignorance marches right up to the gates of the Celestial City but is refused. Indeed, he is bound hand and foot and carried through the air and shoved into a door in the side of the hill. Bunyan's conclusion of the matter: "Then I saw that there was a way to Hell, even from the very gates of Heaven, as well as from the City of Destruction."[28] Our pilgrim journey, you see, is never over until it is over.

Lord, we too are on a pilgrim journey. Today the journey feels filled with grace and mercy. We know that the journey will bring hard days as well, but today it is filled with your light and life, and we thank you. Thank you for loving us and guiding us. Thank you for giving us patience with our children. Thank you for the strength to face the challenges of life with courage and compassion. Thank you. Amen.

Thomas Merton
Finding Our Home with God

Look at your own life.
Perhaps the Book of Life, in the end, is the book one has lived.
If one has lived nothing, one is not in the Book of Life.

THE INTIMATE MERTON

THE ESSENCE OF THOMAS MERTON'S approach to our life with God is captured in his earliest work, *The Seven Storey Mountain*,[29] and in his favorite multivolume work, *The Journals,* where we see his intelligence, wit and charm roam across a vast sea of events, experiences and people. *The Seven Storey Mountain* is a beautiful and troubling vision of our longing for God. Intermingled with Merton's deep and probing insights is a description of the tragic loss of virtually every significant adult member of his immediate and extended family. It is a chronicle of the utter annihilation of our earliest and most prominent community—the family.

But Merton's story is also a glorious portrayal of our life in Christ that leads to our participation in God's greatest community—the church. Here Merton finds the love, comfort, nurture and support from which his vital creative energy springs. Ultimately, Merton is captivated by God's relentless love for the world. It is soothing in its message and powerful in its effect, propelling Merton to a life of service and sacrifice that captivated an entire generation.

It would be easy to categorize Merton as a conventional thinker in the tradition of action and contemplation, for he spends a great deal of time on the progression one must undergo from action to contemplation to active contemplation. But to categorize Merton as a single type is to miss the dynamic interplay that continued right up until his untimely death.[30]

Merton was born in 1915 to a New Zealander father and an American mother. His childhood and youth were spent shuttling between America, Europe and various outposts of the former British Empire. His overwhelming impulse was to determine how we can spend our life overcoming the sin and mortification that rack every human being. In *The Seven Storey Mountain*, he identifies the nine issues with which each one of us must wrestle—life, death, time, love, sorrow, fear, wisdom, suffering and eternity—then uses Dante's image of the multiple levels of purgatory we must overcome if we are to discover a pure relationship with God.

The entire book tells the captivating tale of one man's journey to God. But its timeless appeal is in Merton's passionate desire that each one of us develop a deeper desire to know and love God. Along the way we meet Merton's companions on the journey, including his close personal friends, his various academic interests and especially the books that had a formative and lingering effect on him.

Merton describes his interest in keeping a journal as simply the desire to write a book into which everything of his life might go. His sensitive treatment of his friends draws us into reflecting on our own friendships. His vast travels take us to exotic ports around the world. The images of the places he has visited and the people who inhabit them permanently mark him. His writings reflect an ongoing quest to find "patterns of experience" that connect us to God. His very life reflects one of the most robust engagements with God in all spiritual literature.

Merton's Expression of the Seven Paths

Merton's approach to the spiritual life easily covers all seven paths of Christian devotion. His somber reflection on his past sexual transgressions reminds us of Augustine. He knows the ordering power of God's love because he has known the disordering power of his own unbridled lust. Reflecting on the nature of love, Merton muses, "It is only love that gives us life, and without God's love we would cease to be."[31] Elsewhere he emphasizes how critical it is that we give everything to God: "There is only one thing to live for: to love God. And only one unhappiness: not to love God."[32] Ultimately his own inability to experience human intimacy awakens him to the need to find our ultimate intimacy in God.[33] Toward the end of his shortened life he begins to order his loves properly, seeing the connection between the human longing for intimacy and our need to understand the wisdom of God.[34]

The entire landscape of Merton's writing depicts the spiritual life as journey. One highlight is his entry on what to do when we have begun the spiritual life and have not reached an answer for our dilemma. Here is his response: "We are often confronted by questions that we cannot answer because the time for answering them has not yet come."[35] Merton recognizes the silence that we experience between the time when we enter the spiritual life and God's ultimate response at the end of our journey.

Elsewhere, Merton defends both the insights of his earlier writings and the reality that he has migrated beyond them. When challenged about the validity of some of the positions he had embraced earlier in works such as *The Seven Storey Mountain*, for example, he simply states, "The things I have said fairly well are things I needed to say: I stand by them."[36] Inevitably, his experiences in life help him realize that we must trust even when we don't understand.

The people who influenced Merton the most were his friends, both personal and literary. His literary friends were too numerous to count but included Augustine, St. John of the Cross, Meister Eckhart, the English mystics, Etienne Gilson, Aldous Huxley and many more. From his early days in France and England to his student days at Columbia and Cuba to his final trip to the Far East we see a man with an insatiable appetite for life. Every encounter is an opening to a deeper experience of life and every authentic experience of life is a deeper encounter with God. These travels become the cauldron for the pivotal experiences that change him.

Merton's evolving interest in nonviolence resulted from his engagement with the world. He migrated beyond the cloistered exclusivity of Roman Catholicism as a result of his encounter with the East. He recognized that the great questions of life open us to a higher and more illuminated understanding of the meaning and purpose of life. His intellectual curiosity and insatiable appetite to find patterns of meaning amidst seemingly arbitrary experiences guided every encounter and every conversation.

Merton's most explicit treatment of the spiritual life as journey is found in one of his final works, an essay titled "From Pilgrimage to Crusade."[37] The work itself is a beautiful and poignant historical treatment, but it moves beyond history to invite us into a reflection on our own personal journey. The Celtic innovations and the Irish nuances show a progressively deeper interior exploration of the spiritual life as journey and also invite us to see how our own external experiences open us to a deeper life with God.

Merton's works roam across vast amounts of spiritual literature, crafting a synthesis as unique as it is compelling. He addresses the role and importance of religious experiences. He searches far and wide to recover our knowledge of God lost in the Fall. He dedicates an entire work to the imitation of Christ. His journey to the East inspires a whole new dimension of divine ascent. Even the otherworldly theme of contemplation is tempered by his emphasis on daily work.

Merton ended his life pursuing an understanding of the similarities and differences between Eastern religions and the Christian faith. He was especially interested in the contrast and interplay of action and contemplation. Here is one example: "The spiritual life is not a life of quiet withdrawal, a hothouse growth of artificial ascetic practices beyond the reach of people living ordinary lives. It is in the ordinary duties and labors of life that can and should develop our spiritual union with God."[38]

Perpetual Quest

When we recognize Merton's love of literature, his attention to great literary and spiritual figures and even his debt to Dante, we begin to understand his great commitment to the spiritual life as journey. We do not remain the same. We are always moving. Merton's own spiritual and intellectual journey demonstrates a soul on the move. As he explored the knowledge and literature that energized him, a specific direction unfolded. There was purpose and intent to all his activities and to all of our activities as well. There is also an ultimate outcome for our journey when we experience an eternity with God.

In all, Merton wrote thirty-five books, each one designed to introduce us to a new resource or enhanced perspective that takes us deeper in our life with God. In addition, hundreds of other books have been written about his life and thought. Ultimately, Merton stands as one of the greatest twentieth-century embodiments of the spiritual life as journey. His life is a testimony to the power of God's love and grace to restore a damaged, misplaced soul to his eternal kingdom.

REFLECTING AND RESPONDING

On December 10, 1941, Thomas Merton, age twenty-six, stood outside the gates of the Abbey of Gethsemane in Kentucky and asked to enter. On December 10, 1968, twenty-seven years later to the day, he died tragically in Thailand. Merton was in Bangkok to address monks and theologians, and he spoke of the monastic vow of *conversation morum*, "conversion of life." It was, he said, the most essential of the vows, and the most mysterious. It meant a commitment to total inner transformation, a commitment to become a completely new person, a continuing pattern of death and new life.

Those words now have a prophetic echo to them, for Merton retired to his room to take a shower and was accidentally electrocuted by a faulty fan. As Merton was making his way out of the lecture hall he was asked about the need to convert people to Christ. Merton's reply gives us his last words: "What we are asked to do at present is not so much to speak of Christ as to let Him live in us so that people may find Him by feeling how He lives in us."[39]

Merton's first and most famous book, *The Seven Storey Mountain*, is a literary and spiritual tour de force. It is autobiography strikingly in the tradition of Augustine's *Confessions*. Indeed, it is the closest piece of writing I can think of to the *Confessions*, some of the phrases equaling that of the famous bishop of Hippo. Consider, for example, Merton's description of his impressions at age ten of the medieval city of St. Antonin in southern France, where the labyrinth of narrow streets all converge on the church so that its steeple dominates everything:

> Here . . . the very pattern of the place, of the houses and streets and of nature itself, the circling hills, the cliffs and trees, all focused my attention upon the one, important, central fact of the church and what it contained. Here, everywhere I went, I was forced, by the disposition of everything around me, to be always at least virtually conscious of the church. . . . The whole landscape, unified by the church and its heavenward spire, seemed

to say: This is the meaning of all created things: we have been made for no
other purpose than that men may use us in raising themselves to God, and
in proclaiming the glory of God. . . . Oh, what a thing it is, to live in a
place that is so constructed that you are forced, in spite of yourself, to be at
least a virtual contemplative![40]

It is, of course, an endlessly interesting and twisted journey before
Merton himself is transformed from being "a virtual contemplative" to
becoming an actual contemplative, a journey I must not spoil for you if
you have not read the story for yourself. Suffice it to say that with *The
Seven Story Mountain* Merton gives us a stunning piece of spiritual autobiography, perhaps the best of the twentieth century. He concludes with the
Latin *Sit finis libri, not finis quaerendi*, roughly translated as, "This may be
the end of the book, but it is not the end of the searching."

To be sure, searching was a hallmark of Merton's life. By the time of
the tragedy in Bangkok, he had become one of the twentieth century's
most articulate and thoughtful writers on the spiritual life. Searching, always searching. He quotes with appreciation the perceptive words of P. T.
Forsythe that "prayer is to religion what original research is to science."[41]
Merton most certainly did "original research" both in his praying and in
his writing. Indeed, his writing was an extension of his praying. He wrote
books, articles and poems. He wrote about meditation, about literature,
about war and peace. Praying and writing. Esther de Waal observes,
"Prayer was essential for this was the way [Merton] could know God most
fully. He was a writer because this was the way he could express himself
most fully."[42]

*Dear Lord Jesus Christ, we may have a hard time praying like Merton did, and
certainly we cannot write like him. Yet, here we are . . . just as we are. And today
we dare to believe that you receive us just the way we are. O Lord, please accept our
stumbling efforts to pray. Words do not come quickly or easily for us. We're so glad
you see past our words and into our hearts. We really do want our hearts to be pleasing to you. May the mute language of our hearts be acceptable in your sight, O
Lord, our rock and our redeemer. Amen.*

THE RECOVERY OF KNOWLEDGE
OF GOD LOST IN THE FALL

But the serpent said to the woman,
"You will not die; for God knows that when you eat of it
your eyes will be opened, and you will be like God, knowing good and evil."
So . . . she also gave some to her husband, who was with her, and he ate.
Then the eyes of both were opened, and they knew that they were naked.

GENESIS 3:4-7

Each one of us has a longing to know—to know right from wrong, to know the ultimate destiny of our life, to know how we can make a meaningful contribution with our gifts and abilities. We want to know where we were born, how we were raised and what we will do in the future. We want to know that we are part of something greater than ourselves. Ultimately, we want to know that we belong to God. This knowledge never comes about quickly or completely; it must develop over time as we deepen in understanding our life with God.

To understand this part of our Christian life, we need to consider the spiritual life as the recovery of knowledge of God lost in the Fall. This is the path that will stretch our intellects the most. To clarify our thinking, three legendary personalities will guide us: Thomas Aquinas, Martin Luther and John Calvin.

Despite the presence of faithful Christians, the two hundred years leading up to the thirteenth century saw growing corruption in the church
and increasing disdain from the prevailing society. These tensions started
to produce fault lines around settled understandings about life with God.
For nearly nine centuries Christians had believed that monasticism expressed the highest degree of love and devotion to God. But this understanding was about to change.

As the thirteenth century opened, new and vigorous approaches to life
with God emerged. Amid increasing pressure to break free of the monastic cloister, Francis of Assisi emerged and advocated the right to minister
freely and broadly in the world. His approach gained momentum as news
of dramatic results poured in. Several other significant movements also
began to unfold, including five that are especially noteworthy.

Five Key Developments

The first development was an increase in biblical literacy. Thirteenth-
century believers were becoming more interested in reading and understanding the Bible apart from the editorial additions of the monastics.
During the Middle Ages, monks would spend much of their day listening
to the "master" teacher and writing in the spaces between passages of
Scripture. These "glosses" became the texts from which they would then
preach and lead their congregations.

Over time, the glosses had become increasingly narrow in scope and
heavily influenced by philosophical movements of the day. Duns Scotus
and William of Occam, for example, emphasized a rational approach
known as nominalism that narrowed the active work of the Holy Spirit
and Scripture. As a reaction to these and other trends, people began to
seek a more robust role and purpose for Scripture. This in turn led to a
recovery of interest in earlier thinkers who focused on both the literal and
the allegorical senses of Scripture and diminished the influence of philosophers who had wandered off from the pages of Scripture to construct
their own systems of thought.

This same period also witnessed a rise of spiritual theology. As formal
theology became increasingly isolated and specialized, the general church
rebelled and began to doubt the validity of any system that did not result

in a deeper love for God. This reality is best expressed in the tension between the formal theology of Thomas Aquinas and the spiritual theology of Bonaventure. They lived and worked at the same time, at the same university, and they were two of the most remarkable thinkers in the history of the church. However, they differed greatly in their approach to and ultimate conclusions about our life with God.

A third and exciting development was the emergence of women as church teachers and advocates for life with God. Hildegaard of Bingen in the twelfth century and Mechthild of Magdeburg in the thirteenth were but two of the many women who exploded onto the scene, casting a long and impressive shadow across the face of Christian spirituality. Because of the obvious power of their words and the evident work of the Holy Spirit in their lives, they were empowered by the church to teach their new and provocative insights into the Christian life.

Another significant development was the modification of the goals of spiritual formation. Earlier, the focus had been on cultivating eternal contemplation of God, a focus that would continue for centuries, albeit in diminished form. In the thirteenth century, a twin track was added that recovered an earlier emphasis on personal communion with God. This spiritual approach was exemplified by the "Brothers of the Common Life," a movement whose best advocate, Thomas à Kempis, emerged in the fourteenth century. His classic text on the subject is *The Imitation of Christ*.[1]

A fifth and final shift was the growing interest in the education and training of the general public. This movement took on renewed seriousness as people committed to learn the deeper meanings of Scripture. But it carried broader implications as well. As the masses became literate, they availed themselves of the transforming power of Scripture in ways that forever changed the known world. They became more interested in self-governance. They espoused open air meetings, mass revivals and universal literacy. All of these developments contributed to the germination of the seeds of renewal and change that were blossoming across Europe.

Together, these five developments reflect a massive shift that changed the church. As more and more individuals developed their own understandings of God, the authority of the church began to shift from institution to individual, a shift that would culminate in the Protestant

Reformation. It was in this context that Thomas Aquinas emerged in the thirteenth century to write one of the greatest theological works ever penned, the *Summa Theologica*, a work that continues to influence the theological perspective of millions of Christians.

Thomas Aquinas

Learning to Love and Know God Fully

*To know that God exists in us in a general and
confused way is implanted in us by nature.*

SUMMA THEOLOGICA

THOMAS AQUINAS (1225-1274) WAS captivated by the work of Augustine
and Aristotle. In effect, much of his *Summa Theologica* is an integration of
the two men's thoughts blended with his own dramatic insights. Aristotle
gave to Aquinas the basic rubric within which he structured his entire
system. And Augustine connected him to orthodox Christianity.

According to Aquinas, everything in life is a potential state that is moving toward its actual state. That is to say, we all have a purpose and a destiny that we are moving toward. Only one path will lead us to our actual
end state, and it is critically important that we find the right path. But
how do we discover that this is our destiny, and what resources will guide
us along the way?

The Ultimate Goal

Aquinas's system provides an answer. For him, our ultimate destiny is a
state of happiness found in eternal contemplation of God. To gain this
state, every potential part of our nature must reach its actual end. With
precision and detail he outlines the necessary steps that lead to our ultimate destiny. Because the natural leads to the supernatural, the temporal
leads to the eternal and nature is completed by grace, Aquinas begins with
what we know and desire on a natural plane. What do our natural desires
and ambitions teach us about our eternal life with God?

In effect, Aquinas's system reflects an architect's master plan, which
coordinates the construction of the entire complex of buildings. A master

plan identifies the site and function of every necessary structure. Then, careful thought and attention determine the design of each building so that it contributes to the architect's overall purposes.

Since we are born incomplete, we realize that our mind and spirit must undergo formation. But to undergo this formation we must understand our ultimate goal in life and then determine how we will reach this goal. Early twentieth-century philosophers referred to this as "intentionality of consciousness," which develops according to how we spend our life energies—our thinking, our feeling, our desiring. These choices determine how we as humans grow and develop.[2] And this is the way Aquinas says we can achieve the end for which we were created.

The Results of the Fall

Before the Fall, Aquinas asserts, Adam and Eve lived in perfect communion with God. There was nothing that impeded their love and communication with him. But afterward, they lost the divine connection that had produced their automatic happiness. In its place grew an overwhelming longing, but no clear understanding, of how to satisfy it or look for its fulfillment in God.

As a result, our incessant longing for happiness is the indirect beginning of our life with God. Since every part of our spiritual knowledge arises from our natural knowledge, everything we desire naturally has an ultimate spiritual end. This helps us recognize how natural reason is not contrary to faith but is completed by it.

"To know that God exists in a general and confused way is implanted in us by nature," Aquinas begins.[3] He says that it is reason working with our will that creates the drive to discover God and grow in our knowledge of him. Unfortunately, sin distorts our reason, but we retain a sense of God through our longing for happiness. It is then our will desiring to find happiness and our reason sorting through all of our options for happiness that lead us toward God. Often this journey includes several missteps when our passions overrun our reason, distorting our judgment.

This problem has plagued us since the Fall. When Adam and Eve allowed their passions to overrun their reason, they set in motion a chain of events that has never stopped. Our original relationship to God was based on the submission of our will to God's will. When Adam and Eve disrupted this order, they sabotaged our natural human destiny.[4] And this disordering of our natural destiny caused us to lose our sense of God. As a result, we no longer seek him.

Despite this disordering, we retain the innate human capacities that distinguish us from the rest of creation, especially our reason. With our reason guiding us, we begin to seek the best life we can live, believing that our rational discoveries will lead to true happiness. In the process we discover that our will naturally desires to help us find what is true. Since the will is the motivating power that drives all of our desires and actions, it is essential that the will direct us to the truth and to the discovery of our contemplative life with God. The unfolding of this life with God in turn provides the happiness and stability we seek.

Natural Knowledge and Spiritual Knowledge

With our will motivating us to know happiness and our reason leading us to truth, we discover the building blocks of our life with God. Ultimately this leads us from knowledge of earthly things to things eternal.[5] Since our knowledge always begins with experiential understanding gained through our senses, Aquinas insists that we come to a vague knowledge of God by seeing his effects on our world. It is this recognition that helps us see that to love our neighbor is the starting point of learning to love God.

Natural knowledge alone is not enough, though.[6] Eventually, all that we can know by reason must be completed by the knowledge of God we obtain by faith. Thus the journey toward God begins when our will is aligned by reason to pursue him as the only enduring source of stability and peace.[7] Once our natural knowledge of God obtained by reason is completed by our revealed knowledge of God obtained by faith, we possess complete knowledge that leads to happiness. This means that nature does not destroy grace but is completed by it.[8]

With this recognition in mind, we can move from the potential knowledge that lies within us to the actualized knowledge only some obtain. It is a long and arduous process filled with pitfalls and mistakes. But for those who make the effort and recover the knowledge of God lost in the Fall, the reward is supreme.

We are strengthened in this process by cultivating the cardinal virtues (prudence, justice, fortitude and temperance) and the theological virtues (faith, hope and love). We gain the ability to exercise each virtue at the right time, for the right reason, in the right way and with the right outcome. Together, the cardinal and theological virtues order every part of our natural and supernatural life, producing the right type of satisfaction of all our natural and lawful desires.

Primary Acts and Secondary Effects

Spiritual formation is critical to our development, and for Aquinas, this process begins with justice. The virtue of justice produces the capacity to receive exactly what we are entitled to receive, and, under the virtue of justice, reason and will work most deliberately. Under justice Aquinas assigns the secondary virtue of religion. In Aquinas's system, religion is the highest moral virtue, holding a middle place between the cardinal and theological virtues. Religion and the practices that give rise to it form a bridge that interconnects all aspects of our human personality. It is here where the interior and exterior acts of religion meet, providing the connecting points between our natural and spiritual life.

The interior acts of religion are devotion and prayer. These acts develop the right motivations so that when we participate in the exterior acts of religion, they stimulate the right effects. Devotion pertains to the orientation and intentionality of our will. Prayer deals with the right and proper use of our reason as it governs the will. In considering devotion, Aquinas begins with five questions:

- What is devotion?
- To what virtue does it belong?
- Why?
- What are its causes?
- What are its effects?[9]

In answering these questions, he demonstrates that devotion is an act of the will in which we are prompted to worship and serve God. Aquinas emphasizes that devotion, as the first and principal act of religion, must be present in all acts of religion. If it is not, the act is not a true act of religion at all but an empty shell and useless expression.

In Aquinas's system, there are external and internal causes of devotion. The extrinsic cause is God himself. The intrinsic cause is contemplation, which results from our desire to find God and our discipline in seeking him. The effects of devotion are manifold, but they are principally expressed as a spirit of boundless contentment and joy.

Contemplation, like every other part of the *Summa*, is addressed through the format of provocative questions and structured responses. In question number 153, Aquinas raises eight queries on the nature of the contemplative life:

- Does the contemplative life pertain to the intellect alone?
- Do the moral virtues pertain to the contemplative life?
- Does the contemplative life consist in one action or in several?
- Does the consideration of any truth whatever pertain to the contemplative life?
- Can the contemplative life of man in his natural state lead him to the beatific vision of God?
- What are the movements of contemplation assigned by Dionysius?
- What pleasures accrue from a life of contemplation?
- How long should one contemplate?[10]

In responding to each question, Aquinas helps us see the reasonableness of our convictions. Our contemplative life needs to include both our intellect and our affections. The moral virtues not only pertain to the contemplative life but lay the very foundation that makes the contemplative life possible. The contemplative life helps us coordinate our pursuit of God. After providing specific directives on how this can occur, Aquinas discusses the way every truth pertains to contemplation, the way God works to complete our human reason in order to bring about a higher state of divine awareness, and the importance of Dionysius (see chap. 7) in helping us understand the pleasure and duration of contemplation itself.

Ultimately, Thomas defines our highest good as eternal contemplation of God resulting in perfect love. Our capacity for contemplation is the most dramatic way we differ from every other part of the created order. In order to contemplate, we must have a sound body, ordered passions achieved through moral virtues and prudence, and freedom from external disorders such as crumbling governments and decaying civilizations. If these physical realities that contribute to our stability are not present, then the desire and opportunity to contemplate God will not be present either.

Contemplation produces in each one of us the conviction that we should give ourselves to God in worship. The result is our realization of the goodness of God. Contemplation also helps us see how we are inadequate and thus awakens a keen sense of our need for God. Contemplation helps us appreciate the person and work of Jesus Christ. Through his example, we are inspired to imitate his life.

Finally, contemplation produces both a positive and a negative effect. Its principle positive effect is heartfelt joy. Its principle negative effect is spiritual sadness or regret when we are reminded of all the ways we have acted against our known awareness of God. Aquinas concludes by emphasizing that we are given varied levels of divine understanding. We are responsible to be faithful to the level of understanding we acquire and to work without ceasing to recover the knowledge of God lost in the Fall.

While devotion turns our will to God, prayer completes the commitment of our whole being to love and serve him. Prayer is an act of reason, so it comes under the influence of the will because the will moves all other human faculties.[11] It is the will that moves us to pray, just as it is the will that moves our intellect to worship God.

Aquinas's treatment of prayer is the longest question in the entire *Summa*, stretching to seventeen sections. Because prayer is a part of the virtue of justice, and justice is concerned with getting things in the right order and giving people their proper due, prayer helps direct our reason to the development of laws that ensure justice. To balance his thought, Aquinas emphasizes that we give our bodies to God through worship, our minds to God through prayer and our wills to God through devotion.

Mistakes That Defeat the Work of Prayer

Thomas discusses three common mistakes people make when they pray.

The first is to believe that the world operates independently of God. This belief causes us to become indifferent to God and, in extreme forms, to deny his providence.

The second error is to believe that everything is fixed. This belief causes us to wonder if we should even pray, since everything is predetermined. This mistake cuts the nerve of actively seeking God's will and inhibits us from developing the full knowledge of our convictions.

The third mistake is to believe that God changes his mind. This belief arises out of our temptation to interpret certain passages inadequately, or from our egocentric hope that God will soften the consequences we bring into our life by our own actions. Aquinas teaches that we must accept that God's will has an ultimate purpose. Once we settle this matter, we recognize that prayer is a secondary cause in which God invites us to join with him in accomplishing his purposes.

Through prayer we work to sort out what role we will play as secondary agents in God's primary purposes. Prayer is not telling God what we think, or simply thanking him for his provision of food and drink. Rather it is our active, intentional effort to understand what God is doing and how we can join him. Thus through prayer we become coparticipants with God. God's will sets everything in motion. Our will, directed by devotion and prayer, allows us to participate in his purposes. Together, prayer and devotion form our inner being. These two interior acts of religion are the way our will and intellect are given to God.[12]

REFLECTING AND RESPONDING

For someone who early in life received the nickname "dumb ox," Thomas Aquinas certainly produced a substantial body of literature in theology, philosophy, law and ethics. Some forty books, in fact. He developed perhaps the most thorough synthesis of Aristotelian philosophy and biblical theology. His most famous work, the *Summa Theologica*, is a systematic compendium on all the theological, philosophical and ethical topics debated in the medieval universities of his day, including what have become classic statements on natural law, virtue ethics and arguments for the existence of God.

But now I must give full disclosure: my understanding of the *Summa* is fragmentary at best. I am a layman in Aquinas studies, having never taken a single course on his writings. In my early years I made several attempts to grasp the *Summa* on my own—all pretty much in vain. But even then I was impressed by the fact that Aquinas devoted 175 pages to the role of "habit" in the moral life. I had never read anyone who gave such sustained attention to habit: what it is and why it is important and how it develops and functions. This was of keen interest to me, for habits play a key role in the development of virtue. Indeed, we can think of virtue as deeply ingrained habits we can rely on to make our lives function well. (Conversely, vice involves bad habits we can rely on to make our lives dysfunctional.)

This is, of course, a huge subject that can be followed with genuine profit, and it was Aquinas and his *Summa* that started my work along these lines. So even though I did not fully understand the *Summa*, I was helped by it. Since those early days, Gayle Beebe's lectures and writings have tutored me on Aquinas, and I am grateful . . . though I am sure there is still much I do not grasp.

We can always be grateful for the large place Aquinas gives to right reason in the spiritual life. By separating will and intellect—sin diverts will, not intellect, from its proper end—he could see human reason remaining operative despite the Fall. And here is the key: Aquinas never pitted faith in opposition to reason as is so common today. No, reason and faith work hand in hand, two ways of knowing, both valid and both necessary. Faith completes reason as reason gives the grounds for faith. Reason helps us sort through all the options for a good life, and faith enables us to commit ourselves to this life.

Another thing: Are you as taken as I am by the importance Aquinas places on prayer? Here we witness a massive intellect totally in the service of devotion. On a pastoral and practical level, I appreciate his dealing with a major mistake about prayer so many people make, a mistake that simply defeats the work of prayer. I refer to this notion that everything is fixed, that we live in a closed universe. When you go to a teacher or employer about some matter, and they invite you to sit down and share your concern, appearing interested and attentive, and later you learn that the decision was made before you even entered the room—you know how that makes you feel. Well, a lot of people have a similar feeling about prayer. If everything is set, then why pray? It is a good question.

But I say to you that ours is an open universe, not a closed universe. God has sovereignly chosen to invite us into this process of bringing about his will on the earth. Theologian John Goldingay has written, "It is a characteristic expression of the instinctive self-humbling of God to share with us the making of decisions in the world; and we do this by intercession."[13] Think of it. We are, as the apostle Paul puts it, colaborers with God, working together to determine the outcome of events.

And prayer was where Aquinas ended. On December 6, 1273, during the Feast of Saint Nicholas, he had a profound mystical experience of heaven and the surpassing glory of God, after which he declared, "All that I have written seems to me like straw compared to what has now been revealed to me." He died three months later. We know, of course, that the *Summa* is far more than straw, but it is instructive for our growth in grace to see that after all Aquinas's carefully framed argumentation about the validity and importance of reason, he has a mystical experience so overwhelming that it trumps reason.

Thomas Aquinas said on his deathbed, "I receive Thee, the price of my redemption, for Whose love I have watched, studied and labored. Thee have I preached; Thee have I taught. Never have I said anything against Thee: if anything was not well said, that is to be attributed to my ignorance."[14]

Dear Lord, we're so glad Thomas Aquinas is part of the Christian team! He was indeed the "angelic doctor." We certainly cannot match his intellectual power, but we can be grateful for it. Thank you, Lord, that all of Aquinas's thinking and all of his reasoning and all of his argumentation was in your service. In the name of the Father and of the Son and of the Holy Spirit. Amen.

Martin Luther

Growing in the Freedom of God's Love

Because there are still so many hindrances and temptations of the devil,
our new life in Christ should be one that continually develops and progresses.

THE LARGER CATECHISM

WHAT DO WE MEAN WHEN WE SAY we want assurance of our salvation? Is it that we are simply too self-centered to care about anyone else? Or could it be that we have an innate need to know that we are loved by God? It is this question that riveted the mind and energy of Martin Luther.

The torrent that became the great Reformation began as a series of small streams and estuaries. As these small movements and innovations gained momentum, they swept some of the strongest Christian personalities into their wake. Standing tall in the midst of these raging forces is the legendary figure of Martin Luther (1483-1546).

Like Aquinas before him, Martin Luther believed that the Fall of Adam and Eve fundamentally changed us. But his response to this change was completely different. If Aquinas' autobiography is irrelevant to understanding his writings, then almost everything about Luther's life is necessary for understanding his work, as well as his love and experience of God.

There are few personalities in history as colorful as Martin Luther. Born November 10, 1483, in a small Bavarian town in modern Germany, Luther was raised in a strict, austere religious environment. His father's remoteness, coupled with his mother's severe religious temperament, colored Luther's view and approach to life from an early age.

Luther trained initially as a lawyer, and his parents hoped he would pursue a career in government or social service. But another destiny was brewing. There is no other way to describe Luther during this time than as a cauldron of discontent. But this discontent opened him to the majesty of God's work and its mesmerizing effects, which drew him into the priesthood. Although this decision angered his father, Luther was satisfied in his new life and launched a quest that would result in some of the most remarkable spiritual insights ever recorded.

The Heart of the Gospel

In his writings, Luther's chief concern is that believers throw off the stifling effects of Catholic scholasticism. For him, the scholastic approach to life with God imposes the rigidity and formality of pagan philosophy and its meager attempt to build a stairway to heaven. In Luther's estimation, what was lost in the Fall of Adam and Eve was the capacity to respond naturally to God in love.

Instead of earning our salvation by moving up the scale of human love to a pure love of God, Luther sees God reaching down to restore and guide us. We do not recover our love of God incrementally. We experience God's love fully through the sacrifice of Jesus Christ. The immediate and evident effect of God's love is that we are able to love others. Loving God and loving our neighbor are the two sides of our experience of redemption. We cannot have one without the other.

While still a pious monk and despairing of his personal salvation, Luther finally discovered satisfaction for his longings when he stumbled on the central message of the gospel. It was his understanding of God's grace freely given, beyond any human effort, that set Luther free to enjoy the "medicine of immortality."

Believing that earlier Christian thinkers Dionysius and Bernard placed too great an emphasis on human initiative, Luther states that the central importance of our encounter with God is revealed in Scripture. He criticizes the idea of natural revelation that comes through the "book of creation" and the "book of experience." Earlier theologians and mystics emphasized finding God through his mediated presence. Luther, however, sees these overtures as diversions from the two most reliable sources of divine knowledge: the Holy Scriptures and the sacraments.

As a result, Luther places a dual emphasis on the work of Christ in redemption and the work of the Holy Spirit in our sanctification. We cannot ascend to God, the way others advocate. We can only respond to the promptings and leading of the Holy Spirit. For Luther, the whole tone and nature of the Christian life is the response of our spirit to the Spirit of God.

The Essence of Luther's Faith

Ultimately, Luther says, God is hidden. As a result we can know him only through faith. Faith, though, is not based on personal experience or creation but on total confidence in God's will as revealed in Scripture and confirmed by the sacraments. The key to faith for Luther is *anfechtung*, a state of hopelessness and helplessness. Only when we enter this state are we able to recognize our utter dependence on God and then respond to him in an appropriate act of faith.

This response of faith activates God's structure of salvation. Faith creates godliness. It drives out sin. It produces strength. It enlightens spiritual blindness. It guards against moral relapse and empowers the believer to perform good deeds in fulfilling God's command to love our neighbor. The commands of God are clear and, when we respond in faith, they become not an onerous responsibility but a liberating structure of mercy and grace.

Faith reveals the purposes of spiritual formation. It also shapes our inner life as Christians and molds us into the image of Christ. This inner formation leads to transformation and allows us to respond in active service and witness in the world. We do works of love and service not to earn our salvation but to respond to the living witness of God in our life.

Although Luther has been accused of deprecating the spiritual life and devaluing the work of sanctification, this is simply unfounded. Luther demonstrates a robust confidence in the power of faith to establish a relationship with God that leads us beyond our inclination to sin. If we try to become pious without faith, God is not allowed to work. If we act in pure faith, then God, through the work of Christ, relieves the burden of sin that weighs on our conscience. If we do not yield to God in faith, it is because we have a perpetual yearning to continue a life of sin.

Of significant influence in Luther's own development was his "Damascus road" experience. The time was 1514 and Luther had been through a bout of serious depression. Realizing that all of his efforts to perfect himself in the eyes of God fell short, he was suddenly overcome with a perceptual reorientation to the "righteousness of God." As a response to this overwhelming experience, Luther began to write. These writings changed the world. They also led to his confinement by religious and civil authorities in the castle tower at Wittenberg.

Yet this imprisonment did not break his spirit or deter him. Rather, it stimulated him to understand the ways and purposes of God. As a result, Luther was dramatically overcome one night by the sudden realization that "the just shall live by faith." The just are brought to an assurance of salvation not by what they do but by how they are liberated by God to serve in the world.

The Dual Agency of Word and Spirit

The tower experience forever marked Luther and became a powerful component of his new theology. Whereas Thomas Aquinas had focused on the first person of the Trinity and the power of God the Father, Luther now focused on the sacrifice of Christ and the ministry of the Holy Spirit. "All Christians," Luther says, "need the comfort and aid of the Holy Spirit."[15] This experience of the Holy Spirit is not discernible or discoverable by human reason but is revealed supernaturally from heaven itself through a proper understanding of the "theology of the cross."

The work of the Holy Spirit. The Holy Spirit creates the theater of action. The Spirit's work as sanctifier brings all of Christ's work as justifier to fruition in the believer's life. Because we are born not fully formed but must develop, the Holy Spirit provides the guidance we need as we anchor our life to God. "The goal of redemption," Luther states, "is the transformation of the believer who dies to sin in order to live for righteousness. The old man, the old Adam is replaced by the new man in Jesus Christ."[16] Ultimately, for Luther, the essence of the Christian life is love that comes from a pure heart, a good conscience and a sincere faith.

Because of his own profound experience of the Spirit leading and guiding him, Luther taught that the central, motivating force in all of Christian life was the active work of the Holy Spirit—but not the Holy Spirit acting on its own. As a constraint and guard against those who would set aside the law, Luther maintained a strong emphasis on the work of the

Holy Spirit that occurs most profoundly through reading Scripture. He advocates a creative balance: The Spirit's activity is best understood in conversation with Scripture.

Becoming God's tabernacle. This dual agency of Word and Spirit became a hallmark of Lutheran spirituality. "To study Scripture effectively," Luther writes, "one must read the Scriptures with the eyes of faith."[17] For Luther, it is impossible to understand the Scriptures without the aid and guidance of the Holy Spirit. "Believe me," Luther continues, "for I have had experience in this matter."

Ultimately, for Luther the "one who is spiritual is the Christian who has the spirit of Christ."[18] Luther's spirituality is concerned with the way the Spirit of God works to bring our human spirit to its natural fulfillment and maturity. God has created us for eternal fellowship with him in the communion of saints. Thus heaven is populated with people who have given their life fully and completely to Jesus Christ and dedicated themselves to realizing the meaning of this life in every dimension. It is this energizing influence of the Holy Spirit that awakens our human spirit and propels us to pursue our ultimate fulfillment and destiny.

Luther uses the structure of the Jewish tabernacle to demonstrate how the Spirit of God shapes our body, soul and spirit to become a dwelling place for God. Like the physical tabernacle of old, we become a dwelling place for the Spirit of God in the new and exciting world of post-law grace. Here Luther draws on his strong scholarly training to amplify his point. Utilizing the allegorical tradition of biblical interpretation, Luther presents his threefold progression of the spiritual life. Each of us consists of a spirit that is the holy of holies, a soul that is the place of seven candlesticks and a body that is the outer court open to the sky.

In the highest stage, the holy of holies, God dwells in the darkness of faith. This is the realm of human life that is not discernible by reason and not available by experience. It is here where we learn to believe what we can neither see nor prove. The second level, our soul, is where God manifests himself through reason, knowledge and understanding of all visible and bodily things. The third level, our body, is the outer court where we connect with all manner of experience and life.[19]

Although God intends for us to be thoroughly sanctified in every part, it is our spirit that is especially sensitive to overtures from God. Drawing on John 14—17, Luther shows us that it is God's full intention that we enjoy union with him through Jesus Christ. For it is here where the Holy Spirit provides us with the same opportunity to be present with Jesus as the first disciples.

The balance between extremes. Of course, anytime you place such a hearty and robust emphasis on the Holy Spirit, you open yourself up to potential abuse. Luther was especially resistant to the radicalism of Karlstadt, Munster and Zwickan, three Anabaptists who emphasized the superiority of the Spirit over Scripture. To their credit, these three leaders and the thousands who followed them were trying to break free of the ossified biblical interpretation of the nominalists and scholastics. But the result was a diminishing of the importance of the biblical text and an overemphasis on our reliance on the Holy Spirit.

Luther's concern is steadfastly anchored to his understanding of human nature and his interpretation of the Bible. Because God always reaches out to us first and foremost through our senses, he likewise comes to us first and foremost through the visual words and texts of Scripture. For Luther, the outward always precedes the inward, for this is God's order. But the Anabaptists, according to Luther, ruin God's order. They not only claim that the inward precedes the outward, but also insist that the outward is secondary at best and often unnecessary for gaining the spiritual insights we need to live a life pleasing to God.

Enjoying God's love. For Luther, the life-changing reality of regeneration is the starting point for our life with God.[20] It is here where faith begins and the early root system of the spiritual life develops.[21] Because of his own existential dilemmas and the way they awakened a longing for God's habitual presence, Luther realized that our ultimate need as Christians is the assurance that comes from knowing we are right with God. "For I am convinced that neither death, nor life, nor angels, nor rulers, nor things present, nor things to come, nor powers, nor height, nor depth, nor anything else in all creation, will be able to separate us from the love of God in Christ Jesus our Lord" (Rom 8:38-39). This passage is central to Luther's psychology of Christian belief. We come to this assurance by the outward reading of Scripture and the inward testimony of the Holy

Spirit. This is an inner confirmation that exceeds all reason, although it is reasonable.[22] It is discernible to the person who peers with the eyes of faith and can see the full meaning of the gospel.

It is this discernment that propels us forward. The spiritual life is active, not static. The Spirit leads us through progressive stages of understanding to deeper levels of love and holiness. Thus, although Luther never teaches that our works of holiness bring salvation, he does state that holiness reflects the progressive sanctification of every committed follower of Christ.[23]

In a seldom emphasized section of his theological works, Luther teaches that believers are given power to live and lead a new life of righteousness.[24] Every single one of us who responds with affirmation to God is given a new life through Jesus Christ. But not every one of us who is given this new life fully manifests its fruit. The difference lies in the level of dedication and response each one of us makes to the work of the Holy Spirit.

The Scandal of the Cross

For Luther, there is enough evidence for those who want to believe in God and enough mystery for those who want to turn away. But God clearly makes himself known to us through Scripture, through all of the world religions that reflect a longing for him and through the classical authors Paul quotes in Acts 17. We carry within ourselves a conceptual idea of God even if we have not yet understood this idea.[25] This general knowledge is not enough for salvation, since complete and confirming knowledge of God is taught only by the Holy Spirit through experience. But it is evident and it does provide every human with an opportunity to respond.

This is Luther's idea of the knowledge of God that must be recovered as a result of the Fall. We possess both superficial and proper knowledge of God. Superficial knowledge is available to everyone and is gained by reason. Proper knowledge of God comes only through the witness of the Spirit in the revelation of Scripture.

This discussion is undergirded by Luther's intense dislike for scholastic theology. Luther states that philosophical and scholastic speculation about God is simply human reason trying on its own to build a citadel of belief without the need for faith. But this denies the way God comes to us first through our senses so that we can recognize and receive him and then grants us deeper knowledge through faith in Jesus Christ.

Luther's whole enterprise culminates with his profound emphasis and original contribution on the "theology of the cross." For Luther, true theology—the only reliable approach for gaining knowledge of God—is found in the cross. There is no such thing as direct, unmediated revelation of God. In fact, Luther says we can see only the "rear end" of God; we cannot view him face to face. As a result, through the cross we come to understand that it is impossible to know anything of God apart from what is revealed by Jesus Christ. Because God is revealed only through the cross, we do not initially recognize him as God. The cross shatters our confidence that we can know anything about God apart from that which is revealed to us through the cross.

The cross, then, becomes the central symbol of Christianity and embodies the role of suffering in our knowledge of God. Part of this emphasis on suffering is tied to Luther's own acute suffering. But it moves beyond his experiences to reveal that all spiritual reality is based on physical reality and suffering. And suffering, as a part of our physical reality, opens us to spiritual realities in new and specific ways. This is why the spiritual disciplines matter so much. We cannot arrive at the fullness of our spiritual life in Christ without them. Thus reading Scripture, accepting the authority of Scripture, participating in baptism and the Eucharist, confessing our faith, obeying the Ten Commandments, engaging in corporate and individual prayer, practicing liturgical worship and much more all provide essential help in our life with God.

When discussing prayer specifically, Luther emphasizes three reasons why we should pray: God wants us to pray, God promises to hear our prayer, and prayer strengthens our resolve to resist temptation and the devil. In this emphasis on prayer, Luther steers away from what he saw as the rigidity and legalistic works-righteousness of so many prayer books. While emphasizing the central importance of the Lord's Prayer, Luther levels his most devastating blow against medieval practices when he suspends any invocation of the saints in prayer. Instead, he highlights the singular role of Jesus as our mediator with God.

Finally, it is by faith that we enter into God's grace. And it is by faith that we realize the effectiveness of God's grace through participating in the spiritual disciplines as aids to salvation. By participating in these aids to salvation, we build immunities against the devil's temptations. For all his emphasis on the fact that the just shall live by faith, Luther ultimately emphasizes the freedom of the Christian to make an authentic response to God through a life of love, service and prayer.

REFLECTING AND RESPONDING

Martin Luther was a robust personality, to say the least. From his ninety-five theses nailed to the door of the castle church in Wittenberg on October 31, 1517, to his resounding confession at the Diet of Worms: "My conscience is captive to the Word of God. . . . Here I stand, I can do no other." From his gripping translation of the Bible into German to his exceptional skill as a hymn writer. From his famous tower experience, perhaps in 1514, when he came to the dramatic insight that "the just shall live by faith" (*sola fide*) to his declaration at Leipzig in 1519 of the supreme authority of Scripture over all ecclesiastical authority (*sola scriptura*). From his "Sermon on the Mass," which teaches the priesthood of all believers, to "The Freedom of a Christian Man," which states that the Christian is both a free lord subject to none and also a servant subject to all. From his dissolution of monasteries and the ending of clerical celibacy to his marriage to the former nun Katherine of Bora and a satisfying domestic life with six children.

Three things especially strike me about Martin Luther. The first is his rare theological insight. He could see to the heart of theological questions and express himself with astonishing originality and force. This can be seen in what over time has come to be called the "five solas of the Reformation": *sola fide*, justification is by faith alone; *sola gratia*, salvation is by grace alone; *sola scriptura*, ultimate authority is in the Scripture alone; *solo Christo*, salvation is from Christ alone; and *soli Deo gloria*, everything is for the glory of God alone.

Luther's theology of the cross is perhaps the most vivid illustration of this. The cross stands right at the heart of his massive theological construct. For Luther, everything points to the cross and everything culminates in the cross. Jesus' death on the cross paid sin's debt, satisfied divine justice and reconciled us to God. The work of Christ on the cross makes our justification before God possible. Indeed, it is the linchpin for our salvation. No works of our own will suffice. It is faith alone, grace alone, Christ alone.

Luther was absolutely committed to Christ alone as the one who merits and mediates our salvation. In the language of theology, this is called the "penal substitutionary atonement." Christ bore the penalty for sin, for all sin—both past and future, both before baptism and after baptism—and there are no more acts we need to perform to satisfy God's justice, whether of ascetic mortification or active service. No punishment is left for us to bear because Christ bore it all. In his *Lectures on Galatians* Luther uses the word "satisfaction" repeatedly as a kind of shorthand for this idea of penal substitutionary atonement. On the cross Christ paid the penalty for sin and satisfied the justice of God once and for all.

This laser-point emphasis on the finished work of Christ on the cross has led some to define Luther's understanding of justification exclusively in forensic terms. Such a view excludes any essential connection to our sanctification, to our growth in grace, to our spiritual formation into the likeness of Christ. This, however, is a distortion of Luther's position. Exciting new research by a group of Finnish Lutheran scholars is showing Luther's more fully orbed theology. Tuomo Mannermaa's new book *Christ Present in Faith: Luther's View of Justification* devotes fully six chapters to "The Presence of Christ in Faith and the Holiness of Christians."[26] Mannermaa shows the clear connection Luther saw between justification and sanctification, between our right standing with God and our growth in character formation.

A second striking reality is Luther's extraordinarily grounded common touch with ordinary people. Think, for example, of his translation of the Bible into a superbly simple and idiomatic German. It proved to be enormously successful and just as influential a force in the German-speaking world as the King James Version would later become in the English sphere. The Luther Bible should be regarded as one of the most valuable contributions to the German church.

Or think of his letter to his barber, Peter Beskendorf, who had asked Luther for guidance on how to pray. In response Luther wrote him forty pages under the title *A Simple Way to Pray . . . for Master Peter the Barber*. I have always loved the humility of spirit in Luther's beginning instruction: "I will tell you as best I can what I do personally when I pray. May our dear Lord grant to you and to everyone to do it better than I! Amen."[27]

Or think of Luther's *Table Talk*, meal conversations with students and colleagues who were furiously scribbling notes as he spoke. Reading these excerpts it is easy to imagine Luther gripping his beer stein with its ten rings in honor of the Ten Commandments and holding forth on issues of grave concern to the Reforming movement. Here is one excerpt that underscores the importance of Scripture to the Reformers: "Oh! How great and glorious a thing it is to have before one the Word of God! With that we may at all times feel joyous and secure; we need never be in want of consolation, for we see before us, in all its brightness, the pure and right way."[28]

Finally, I am profoundly struck by Luther's skill as a hymn writer and his love of music and poetry generally, which gave special impetus to his liturgical reforms. As with the Bible he put worship into the common tongue, and he restored congregational singing to the people. Indeed, he consistently placed strong emphasis on the congregation actively engaging in worship rather than passively listening to the leader. Just think: Luther gave the people a vernacular Bible so that God might speak directly to them and a vernacular worship so that they might speak directly to God.

We are all moved by Luther's "A Mighty Fortress Is Our God." Many also know his Christmas hymn *Van Himmel hoch da komm ich her*, "From Heaven High to Earth I Come."[29] And much more. It is hard to overestimate the power of setting the hearts and minds of the common people aflame with music. Samuel Taylor Coleridge observed, "Luther did as much for the Reformation by his hymns as by his translation of the Bible. In Germany the hymns are known by heart by every peasant; they advise, they argue from the hymns, and every soul in the church praises God like a Christian, with words which are natural and yet sacred to his mind."[30]

O Christ, Gracious Savior, we thank you for your work of redemption on the cross. You took into yourself all the sins and all the sorrows of all the world. You ransomed us from sin and death and hell. You paid in full the price for our rebellion. You utterly and completely satisfied the justice of God. On Golgotha's hill you became the perfect example of self-sacrificing love. You delivered us from a life of fear and hatred. Thank you. Thank you for reaching down to us when we could not reach up to you. Thank you for your continual cleansing and redeeming love. Thank you for your free gift of salvation. Thank you for becoming the propitiation for our sins, and not for ours only, but also for the sins of the whole world. O Christ, your supreme sacrifice on Calvary has made your name precious beyond the telling. And it is in this name that we pray. Amen.

John Calvin

Knowing God and Knowing Ourselves

Knowledge of God and knowledge of man are inextricably linked;
one cannot be had without the other.

THE INSTITUTES OF THE CHRISTIAN RELIGION

No OTHER SINGLE BOOK FROM THE sixteenth century does more to define the nature of our life with God than *The Institutes of the Christian Religion*, a handbook on piety written by John Calvin (1509-1563). Massive in volume and compelling in impact, the *Institutes* set the agenda for Protestant theology and spirituality for the next three hundred years.

In the *Institutes*, Calvin begins with the same question as Thomas Aquinas and Martin Luther: How do we recover our knowledge of God? "Knowledge of God and knowledge of man are inextricably linked," Calvin begins. "One cannot be had without the other. But out of respect for God, let us begin with knowledge of God."

Calvin introduces this polarity to establish the foundation for his entire work. We cannot know God without knowing ourselves and we cannot know ourselves without knowing God. As with so many great Christian thinkers, Calvin frames this pursuit as a threefold process: first we gain knowledge of our salvation, then we grow in our knowledge and, finally, we determine the ultimate destiny of our spiritual life.

Three Primary Sources

According to Calvin, our knowledge of God comes from three primary sources. First, we enjoy an innate sense of God originating from being made in his likeness. Every human being is made in the image of God. This is God's divine stamp on each one of us. Unfortunately, this image is corrupted because of sin. Consequently, many of us ignore our innate sense of God and misunderstand his presence in our lives.

The same is true when we consider the second source, God's created universe. Everywhere the design of nature bears witness to God. His providential formation of the created order reflects his majesty. It also inclines the sensitive heart to seek the cause of this order and majesty. Calvin's confidence in the beauty, order and design of creation is striking. Just as he recognizes the miserable condition of creation and humanity, he also exudes an overriding confidence in the ultimate goodness of God and his redemptive plan.

The third and final way we recover knowledge of God is through Scripture. Scripture is God's divine word. It teaches us about God, reveals his plan of salvation and identifies his activity in creating and sustaining the world. Scripture helps us understand what our life is like without God and what awaits us as our destiny if we are joined with him. It helps us gain a deeper understanding of God's nature by reflecting on his activity in the created universe. Finally, Scripture teaches us God's providential activity in history and his specific activity in creating his people, first as the children of Israel and then as the New Testament church.

Inward Knowing

Once we realize we can know God through Scripture, Calvin demonstrates how we can cultivate confidence in the reliability of our knowledge. Here he introduces a principle that will become a hallmark of his work. It is neither human reason nor even the authority of the church that establishes the authority of Scripture, but the inward testimony of the Holy Spirit. This is the hinge of Calvin's entire system. The Holy Spirit's work confirms the reliability of Scripture, our knowledge of God, the provision and acceptance of salvation through Christ, the election of God, the ability of leaders to discern who should be ministers and the viability of our Christian faith.

This inward testimony of the Holy Spirit is how we recover knowledge of God lost in the Fall. This confirmation does not occur apart from Scripture but in conversation with it. In fact, in opposition to the religious enthusiasts who misunderstood this Augustinian principle, Calvin insists that we cannot know God properly without the Holy Spirit confirming our knowledge of God in the context of reading Scripture.

Like Augustine in *The Teacher*, Calvin provides an outstanding example of how we come to understand the inward work of the Holy Spirit. The work of the Holy Spirit and the inward confirmation by Christ's spirit are essentially the same thing. Christ as inward Teacher illuminates our understanding and convinces us of the certainty of our faith. This illumination allows us to know supernatural and eternal truth even while still constrained to our natural and temporal world.

Law and Grace

Also like Augustine, Calvin believes that Christ is not only the inward Teacher but the author of our faith. Becoming like Christ and realizing the fruits of our salvation are the twin focuses of his theology. His emphasis on the person and work of Christ originates in his recognition that humans need redemption, that our attempts to find redemption within God's law are futile, and that without Christ and his willingness to meet our needs, we cannot make up for our lack.

In considering the person and work of Christ, Calvin shows how Christ's work is necessary because of our estrangement from God. To overcome this estrangement, God initially provides the law and eventually gives the gospel. The two are related but not equal. Both play a role in the work of Jesus Christ as God's scheme of redemption is ultimately completed. But they are strikingly different.

The law was given to teach us God's moral imperatives for life. These are timeless principles that we are all obligated to follow. The gospel does not replace the law but works to complete it through Jesus Christ. Although the ceremonial and judicial aspects of the law have been set aside, the moral aspects continue. The importance of the law is that it educates us concerning God's expectations for us as humans. When we realize we cannot live up to the expectations of the law, it makes evident our need for Christ.

Calvin's treatment of the Ten Commandments as the law of God is some of the most exhilarating commentary ever written. He notes that the first four commandments teach us what it means to love God. To love God means loving only God. To love God means recognizing God as a spiritual essence and not an embodied idol. To love God means to speak wisely and accurately. And to love God means to stop, rest and reflect on his nature and activity. In this last action of Sabbath rest, we utilize our aids to salvation by taking the sacraments, participating in Christian worship and listening to Christian teaching.

Then the last six commandments show us how to love our neighbor. Civic order and peace begin in the family. Learning to live under God's authority in the order of the family helps us accept his order across all areas of life. To love our neighbor begins with learning to honor, love and obey our parents. It also includes honoring one another in marriage. Loving our neighbor means respecting the right to own property, speaking the truth and finding satisfaction with our station in life by not coveting what others possess. Finally, to love our neighbor includes not inflicting violence on innocent people.

In each category, Calvin recasts the way medieval thinkers presented the Christian life. His concern is that people move beyond the legalism of the Roman Catholic Church to understand the spiritual essence of the Ten Commandments embodied in the life and Spirit of Jesus. The ultimate importance of the Ten Commandments is that they capture God's grand expectations for all people and spell out the responsibilities each one of us bear personally.

As a result, we recognize our need for Christ as communicated in the Gospels. The Gospels teach us that Jesus was fully God and fully man. They accept Christ's participation in divine activity and his illumination of our divine understanding. They establish why we cannot satisfy God on our own and why Christ as fully human does satisfy God. Because Christ is fully God and fully man, he is perfect in obedience to God. He does not alter the law but fulfills it.

To understand Christ in both his person and work, we need earthly metaphors that communicate in ways we can accept and understand. Consequently Christ is depicted as prophet, priest and king. As prophet, he proclaims the truth and reality of God, our situation as humans and our need to respond individually and collectively to God. As priest, Christ mediates our salvation. As king, he governs universally. Each office reflects a particular aspect and activity.

These activities become callings for us as Christians as we engage our earthly work as well as contribute to God's work in the world. The inward work of the Holy Spirit depends on what Calvin calls the "effects of faith": repentance, Christian life in which we exhibit a love of God and a love of neighbor, justification leading to Christian liberty, and a life of prayer. The work of the Holy Spirit is particularly evident in Calvin's treatment of the life of prayer. In the longest single chapter in the entire work, Calvin devotes nearly one hundred pages to the primacy and importance of prayer. Prayer is the way we adjust all that we are and aspire to be to the ways and will of God. Prayer is neither a rote exercise nor an optional activity. It is absolutely essential if we are to understand the nature and reality of our life with God. Ultimately, the evidence of God's internal activity in the Christian believer is manifested as a holy life.

The Role of the Church

Finally, Calvin returns to a theme emphasized so often by earlier writers: the work of God, the significance of Jesus Christ and the ministry of the Holy Spirit is best known through the life of the Christian community. In the church, Christians learn to love both God and neighbor. This love is cultivated through the faithful exercise of the sacraments, the core responsibilities of the Christian life and active participation in civic affairs.

The church serves as the one institution placed in society by God to partner with the state in regulating sacred and secular matters. The church's ultimate aim is to bring people to faith in Christ, to see them grow in Christ, to preach God's word, to disseminate discipline, to prepare the leadership of God's people and to administer the sacraments. In this way, the church becomes the body of Christ, perpetuating the will and way of God in the world.

After Calvin, the Protestant Reformation broke into all manner of diverse expression. Some took the Reformation to radical extremes that threatened to undo Christianity. Others, such as the Puritans in England, sought to modify and systematize Calvin, turning his teaching into a rote system of religious authority. By the end of the sixteenth century, the Protestant Reformation was firmly entrenched. The Roman Catholic opposition continued and spawned new reform movements that continue to this day. Yet Calvin's legacy, communicated so effectively through his primer on Christian piety, lives on in the many expressions of the Reformed tradition that are spread around the world.

REFLECTING AND RESPONDING

From the standpoint of spiritual formation, John Calvin's *Institutes of the Christian Religion* is of genuine interest. In the title page he boldly declares that it contains "almost the whole sum of piety" and is "a work most worthy to be read by all persons zealous for piety." Well, he most certainly delivers.

Calvin's material on the Ten Commandments, for example, gives us much to work with for life formation. It fits perfectly into his overarching theme of knowledge of God and knowledge of ourselves. The first four commandments instruct us in our relationship to God, "to recognize and profess him as the only God, to love, honor and fear him above and before all else, to repose in him alone all our hopes and needs, and always to ask his help."[31] The remaining six commandments relate to our duties of love toward one another. As Calvin puts it,

> Our Lord sums up the law under two heads: we are to love God with all our heart, all our soul, and all our strength, and our neighbor as ourselves. Even though the whole law has been included under these two heads our Lord . . . has willed to proclaim more deeply and explicitly by ten commandments, about everything that pertains to honor, fear, and love of him, and all that has to do with love which, for his own sake, he enjoins upon us toward our neighbors.[32]

You notice the strong stress throughout his teaching here on love— love of God and love of neighbor. Indeed, in summary, Calvin writes, "It is easy to fathom the direction of all these things, namely, to teach love."[33] Hence, under Calvin's skillful pen the Ten Commandments move from being harsh, rigid laws to becoming perceptions into the royal law of love. I find that most instructive.

Then, too, we are instructed by the theme of God's sovereignty that weaves its way throughout the *Institutes*. We cannot fathom God on our own, Calvin says. The gulf between God and us is too vast. God is above all, the sovereign Lord of all. And it is this sovereign God who sovereignly reveals himself to humanity. God, out of divine love and mercy, takes the initiative; we cannot.

Now, all of this sovereignty language does not play well in contemporary society. It strikes us as an insult. After all, don't we have the ability to take the initiative to frame our own future? Aren't we in charge of our own destiny? Can't we become anyone we want, do anything we want, go anywhere we want? Independence and autonomy are the watchwords of our day, not dependence and submission. And this is precisely why we need to hear Calvin's accent on the sovereignty of God. We have bought into the lie that we are the captains of our salvation, the masters of our fate. And we need once again to place ourselves under the mighty hand of God. This kind of holy surrender and holy obedience is a necessary part of the formation of our souls.

Another thing: Calvin's work on prayer is a corrective to our egocentric ways. For him prayer is not so much a transactional matter by which we get things out of God. Rather it is first and foremost a transformational matter in which we learn to adjust ourselves to the divine will. Calvin writes,

> Now, let this be the first rule of right prayer, that we abandon all thought of our own glory, that we cast off all notion of our own worth, that we put away all our self-assurance, in our abjection and our humility giving glory to the Lord, so as to be admonished by the prophetic teaching: "We do not pour forth our prayers unto thee on the ground of our righteousness but on the ground of thy great mercies."[34]

This forming of the heart and mind in a Christward direction is a major burden in prayer. Commenting on the Lord's Prayer, Calvin writes, "When, for example, we pray that 'his name be hallowed' we should, so to speak, eagerly hunger and thirst after that sanctification."[35] Once, however, we are oriented body, mind, heart and soul toward Christ and his righteousness, we are to come boldly with our requests knowing that we have "a promise to assure us we will receive whatever we ask."[36] This then is that interactive life of prayer with God whereby we are constantly receiving into ourselves the divine loves and joys and aspirations as we learn to ask in faith for what we need. This is how we develop a life "zealous for piety."

Allow me to mention one final observation. It was John Calvin who brought the threefold office of Christ as prophet, priest and king into dogmatic theology. This holds the most profound implications for our spiritual formation. The threefold office of Christ is a way of speaking about Christ's continuing action among his people. He is alive. He is here. He is active. He is our prophet to teach us. He is our priest to forgive us. He is our king to rule us.

The threefold office of Christ is the divinely revealed solution to the threefold disease of sin: ignorance, guilt and corruption. Christ by prophetic light overcomes our ignorance and the darkness of error. Christ by priestly merit takes away our guilt and reconciles us to God. Christ by kingly power removes our bondage to sin and death. The prophet enlightens the mind by the spirit of illumination; the priest heals the heart and soul by the spirit of compassion; the king subdues our rebellious affections by the spirit of sanctification.

The threefold office of Christ reminds us that in the person of Jesus is summed up the whole of the biblical narrative. Calvin is here offering a compelling way to make sense of a large block of diverse biblical data. It captures in one phrase the offices of ancient Israel and underscores Jesus as the fulfillment of messianic hope.

And for us today? Well, it shouts loud and clear that Jesus Christ is fully sufficient. In his roles as priest and king, Christ is the one who is both king and priest forever after the order of Melchizedek. As prophet Christ fulfills the messianic longing for the coming of the prophet like Moses: "The LORD your God will raise up for you a prophet like me [Moses] from among your own people; you shall heed such a prophet. . . . I [the LORD] will put my words in the mouth of the prophet, who shall speak to them everything that I command" (Deut 18:15, 18). Jesus is the fulfillment of the prophet like Moses who will teach his people himself. He is our ever-present, ever-living teacher. We are to listen to him.

Heavenly Father, we hate to admit it, but emotionally we take a step back when we hear the word piety, not to mention the idea of being "zealous for piety." Everything in the culture and (dare we admit it?) everything within us draws back from the idea.

It sounds bland and uninteresting and slightly sanctimonious. Everywhere we're told today to seek intelligence and cleverness and shrewdness. Not piety.

Yet, what is piety but all goodness and grace and devotion? In our best moments it is what our hearts long for. O Lord, incline our hearts toward bona fide, sterling piety. May we even be zealous to seek it out. In the holy name of the triune reality—Father, Son and Holy Spirit. Amen.

INTIMACY WITH JESUS CHRIST

Therefore be imitators of God, as beloved children,
and live in love, as Christ loved us.

EPHESIANS 5:1-2

Tired and lonely Francesco Bernardone climbed Mount La Verna to flee the crowds and draw close to God. He had come here before when the press of his responsibilities had grown too much and his sense of God's presence had grown too small. Now he was back. Exhausted. Dispirited. Old. After spending much of his adult life pursuing a perfect expression of the life of Christ, his tired body was breaking down. The years of disciplined neglect had taken their toll.

And then it happened. In the midst of a forty-day retreat, the fiery presence of the living Christ overwhelmed him. Coming in the form of the six-winged seraph from Isaiah 6 and hanging on the cross, Christ presented himself directly. Francesco was never the same. His body changed physically. The stigmata marks left on his hands, feet and side were identical to those of Jesus. He seldom spoke of the experience, but those who were present witnessed to his transfigured state. These eyewitnesses would later recount this experience and tell how the external marks confirmed what they had known for a long time: that Francis was in word, thought and spirit a perfect imitation of Jesus Christ.

Francesco Bernardone is known today as St. Francis of Assisi (1181–1226). His experience on Mount La Verna in 1223 is the famous story of the visitation by Christ. This dramatic miracle would shape Franciscan spirituality for the next three hundred years and would ignite universal interest in the imitation of Christ as the ultimate destiny of every Christian. This is the central issue of Christian spirituality: learning to become like Jesus.

De Imitatione Christi

From the time of Christ, Jesus' followers have sought ways to imitate him. The New Testament is filled with examples of how experiences from Jesus' life became the model for early Christians. And Paul emphasizes at the outset of the church how our life of prayer and our efforts to imitate Christ are part of a larger goal to become like him.[1] The apostle John places a unique focus on Jesus as the enlightener of all life. Through both his Gospel and his epistles we see how our efforts to imitate Christ raise us to new levels of awareness and understanding. John helps us see how Christ connects us organically with God. As we seek to imitate Christ, we are literally joined to God through him.

Across the long expanse of Christian history and culture, the effort to imitate Christ has played a primary role in the cultivation of the highest ideals and understandings of the Christian life.[2] Beginning in the fourth century, the *virgines sacrae* were consecrated to perpetual virginity as an expression of the imitation of Christ. Syriac Christians followed suit, initially understanding discipleship as a literal imitation of the poor, homeless, celibate Jesus. In Ireland, the Celtic Christians practiced a form of voluntary exile and deprivation known as "the green martyrdom," traveling as itinerant ministers in faith and obedience just as Jesus had done. These are just a few of the examples that illustrate the way culturally conditioned efforts to imitate Christ have guided the church through the centuries.

At the rise of the thirteenth century, the church began to look again to Jesus. After the highly speculative love-mysticism of earlier centuries, medieval Christians renewed their focus on the person and work of Christ. Europe was beginning a significant cultural transformation, and the earliest vestiges of what would become the modern economy were under way. Major shifts were destabilizing society, and during this time the church looked to the figure of Jesus and a life of imitating him as a stabilizing force for all Christians.[3]

During earlier centuries, the cloistered monk toiling in prayer had been the noblest expression of the Christian life. As the world changed, however, the image of the ideal Christian changed as well. In time this new approach became known as the *devotio moderna*, the new way, and it defined the goal of the Christian life as learning to live as Christ had lived. No longer were Christians called to a life of solitary prayer. Now they were to be in the world, preaching, praying and facing the same challenges Jesus had. Over the next four centuries this new understanding would gain ascendancy. By replacing the ideal of the cloistered life with the growing belief that we were to express in word, thought and spirit the very life and teachings of Jesus, this new approach recovered the essence of the New Testament message.

Francis of Assisi

The World as Our Cloister

Almighty, eternal, just, and merciful God,
grant us . . . to be inwardly cleansed, interiorly enlightened and inflamed
by the fire of the Holy Spirit . . . able to follow in the footprints
of your beloved Son, our Lord Jesus Christ.

A PRAYER OF ST. FRANCIS

LIKE SO MANY BEFORE HIM, FRANCIS OF ASSISI (1181-1226) had to break free of his fascination with himself before God could use him in a meaningful way. Biographers tell us that until he was twenty-four, he wasted his life in a pampered, self-indulgent lifestyle shielded from the harsh realities of everyday life. His father was a rich textile merchant and the family wealth prevented Francis from facing the truth of his condition.[4]

But then he changed. Around 1205, Francis underwent a dramatic spiritual experience that forever changed him.[5] After a brief imprisonment and a long illness he realized his life was meaningless. This recognition propelled him to find a new anchor for his existence and Jesus became the key. His conviction: to live for God alone by imitating Christ alone.

Renouncing his wealth and even his family, he set out on a new path believing the only way he would find meaning was through a life fully devoted to God. While reading Scripture and listening to a sermon, three separate passages instantly captivated him: "Go, sell your possessions, and give the money to the poor" (Mt 19:21), "Take nothing for your journey" (Lk 9:3) and "If any want to become my followers, let them deny themselves" (Mt 16:24). Taking these passages to heart, Francis embarked on one of the most arduous and sustained imitations of Christ in all of history.

Francis's Approach

These three passages form the foundation of Franciscan spirituality. With them in hand and fully aware of his changed condition, there was no turning back for Francis. Every day became a relentless pursuit of perfection in Christ. As days became years, the passion only intensified. This passion in turn became the unrelenting magnet for the entire movement as followers flocked from across Europe to this new way of life. Between 1205 and the Fourth Lateran Council in 1215, scholars document that several thousand people from all walks of life flocked to the "evangelical" life as expressed by Francis.[6]

By "evangelical," Francis meant a recovery of the life, teachings and spirit of Jesus as contained in and communicated by the four Gospels. Francis firmly believed that the Gospels call believers to express in their own lives a complete and perfect embodiment of the life and spirit of Jesus. His new emphasis conveyed a purity that attracted people. There was nothing sophisticated or hidden in it; the goals and purposes of the Christian life were articulated clearly and simply in concrete terms.

As this movement spread across Europe, Francis's stature in the eyes of the church increased as well. His combination of sincere humility and transcendent love captivated a society reeling from massive turmoil and disruption. As Bonaventure writes, "Francis longed to be transformed by the fire of ecstatic love. . . . Like a glowing coal he seemed totally absorbed in this flame of divine love."[7] Bonaventure goes on to note, "[Francis] was drawn to Christ with such a fervent love and the beloved returned such intimate love to him that God's servant always seemed to feel the presence of his savior before his eyes."[8]

These recollections and many like them are vivid indications of the passion with which Francis pursued intimacy with Jesus Christ. Known as one of the earliest vernacular theologians, Francis's simple speech patterns and self-deprecating manner cloaked a highly sophisticated understanding of how we grow in our love and knowledge of God. What is so striking is his unflinching interest in the actual events of the life of Christ. He was not looking for the deeper meaning beyond the event, but believed our experience of the event itself would initiate in our life the very same spiritual response experienced and expressed by Christ.

Francis's Teaching

The central theme for Francis was imitation of Jesus. Our attempts to imitate Christ connect us with the expression of God in the world. We must be obedient to God in everything, which means following the life and spirit of Jesus always. This imitation not only identifies us with Jesus but allows us to experience the realities of his life directly. When we enter the wilderness to be tried and tempted, we encounter the same spiritual realities Jesus faced. When we journey to a foreign place, we experience the same ambivalent response Jesus did. When we seek to find God and discover instead long, dry periods of spiritual wasteland, we understand Christ's sense of abandonment during his darkest hours. These experiences and others allow us to see the parallels between our own existence and that of Christ. Drawing on a long-held medieval interpretation, Francis believed the temporal experiences of life express the incarnational realities of Jesus. And these realities ultimately mediate our perfect communion with God.

Francis also emphasized being fully open to the ministry and inspiration of the Holy Spirit. The ability to imitate Christ is a direct result of the Holy Spirit's power in our life. Beyond our experiences of God and our rational reflections on them, Francis believed first and foremost in pure, unmediated revelation by the Holy Spirit. Thus God can be known only to the extent the Holy Spirit makes him known to us.[9] In all things Francis taught the transparent, inconspicuous and unassuming ways of the Holy Spirit.

By living with openness to the inspiration of the Holy Spirit, we discern the third key reality: God's presence in all creation. When we live with a sacramental view of life, we see how every aspect of the created order bears witness to God and in the process we learn how to look for God in every aspect of our life. In fact, all of creation leads us to love God, honor God's church, love our neighbor and regard every created thing as a part of our deeper life with God.

As the one institution given by God to bear witness to God's created order, the church is to be honored and respected. Its teaching is to be followed. It is a key way God is made present to the world, so it is critical that we participate fully in its life and remain true to its teaching.[10] Just as

Christ was originally made present through the virgin, so he is now made present through the visible church.

It is in this context that the fifth key theme comes to the fore as we recognize Francis's unique and intense focus on the Eucharist. Francis viewed the Eucharist as the way in which Christ enters us in order that we might become like him. We make Christ present to the world by ingesting his life and mission through the sacraments and expressing them through acts of love and service.

Francis taught that the Christian community is our context for finding our companionship in Christ. We need spiritual friends for the journey. We need companions who can encourage and sustain us in our life with God. We need Spirit-led, trusted brothers and sisters who can challenge and convict us. Our companionship is determined not by blood lines or race or even nationality. It is determined by our common bond in Christ. It is through spiritual friendship that we understand our spiritual relationship to God.[11]

The seventh key theme is expressing this companionship through gospel living. From his conversion, Francis strived to lead an intense Christian life. His desire to identify totally and fully with Christ even led him to make careless attempts at martyrdom, traveling on three separate occasions to hostile lands in hopes of meeting his demise for the cause of Christ.[12]

Finally, gospel living is manifested in the control we exert and the power we display through the expression of the virtues. True love of our enemy is manifested when we are not upset when an injury is done to us. Patience is displayed not when things are going well, but when they are going poorly. Purity of heart is born of peace of mind and compassion of spirit. Graciousness toward others is achieved when we protect ourselves against envy and wrongdoing by never talking poorly of another.[13] Chastity protects us from utter corruption. Ultimately, Francis emphasizes that we should do nothing but follow the will of the Lord.

The Need for More

Eventually, however, problems with this approach developed. The generation that followed Francis was not sure what to do with his literal interpretations of the life of Christ. Some wanted to continue in the very same path Francis had taken when he started and led the Franciscan order. In reality, however, there was no practical way for this to happen and the order eventually succumbed to the pressure to become an official part of the church. Fortunately, this change received an able defense through the brilliant work of St. Bonaventure. Without his convincing polemics, it is unlikely the Franciscan movement would ever have endured.

REFLECTING AND RESPONDING

I stood with my friend Dallas Willard in Santa Croce, the famous Franciscan church in Florence, Italy. Only a short walk away was the magnificent Duomo cathedral, the de facto center of Florence. The two churches are a contrast in extremes. Both are magnificent but in different ways. The cathedral is simply overwhelming with its ornate bronze doors, which Michelangelo said were "fit to be the gates of Paradise," bands of elegant green, red and white marble across its entire facade, all marble floors and gilded dome—the largest in the world until Michelangelo outdid it with his design of St. Peter's Basilica in Rome. Santa Croce is marvelous in its own right, but in a straightforward, simple way with giant wooden beams.

I was puzzling over the mass of tombstones in Santa Croce. The walls are lined with tombs and the floor is paved with some 276 tombstones. Some of the most famous names in Italian history are inscribed there—Michelangelo, Galileo, Dante, Machiavelli, Rossini and more. I wasn't surprised at the tombs—they are commonplace in medieval churches. What surprised me was that so many prominent figures were buried here and not at the Duomo, which by all accounts is far more impressive and important in the scheme of things. "Why?" I asked. "Why would all these renowned people choose to be buried here and not at the cathedral?"

"Well," Dallas replied with his characteristic wisdom, "it was because of the extraordinary holiness of Francis and the Franciscan friars that came here. Their power resided in their holiness. Even a hundred years later that holiness still filled the place. It drew people by the thousands and they wanted to be near such uncommon holiness, even in death." Standing there in Santa Croce, I felt it too. I had been in innumerable European churches, large and small, but here in Santa Croce it was as if the very air was still scented by the quiet, peace-filled holiness of those Friars Minor.

And it is this holiness that has continued to draw millions to the "little brother of Assisi" over the almost eight centuries since. It is what draws me, this holiness of life. It is so attractive. It is so winsome. It is so compelling. It is a holiness that is revealed in passionate devotion, in radical simplicity, in joyful humility.

In Francis of Assisi we see passionate devotion. A story is told of the Lord Bernard of Assisi, one of the richest and wisest noblemen in the city. He had watched Francis for two years and was deeply impressed by how he could endure all the ridicule and abuse with such patience and serenity. Hoping to learn the heart of his spirituality, he determined "to put St. Francis' holiness to a test." He invited Francis to supper and to stay the night. He had a bed prepared in his own room, in which a lamp was always kept burning. Francis, wanting to "conceal the divine graces which he had," climbed into the bed and pretended to fall asleep. Lord Bernard, it seems, was better at this game and "he pretended to be sleeping soundly, and he began to snore loudly."

Francis, believing that Bernard was fast asleep, arose and knelt by the window and began praying with "intense fervor and devotion," saying, "My God and my all!" All through the night he continued this way with "intense fervor and devotion," sobbing out the words with "many tears" and saying only, "My God and my all! My God and my all!" Lord Bernard, watching the whole scene from his bed, was "touched by the Holy Spirit in the depths of his heart." When morning came Bernard declared, "Brother Francis, I have definitively resolved in my heart to leave the world and to follow you in whatever you order me to do."[14] Passionate devotion.

In Francis of Assisi we see radical simplicity. Illness and a military disappointment were among the influences that led the sensitive Francis through a lengthy series of intense struggles of the spirit, climaxing in 1206 when his enraged father brought him before the bishop to disinherit him. Francis stripped himself naked and walked away, determined to follow the Lord's bidding into apostolic poverty.

This espousal of "Lady Poverty" led to numerous ventures. Once Francis and Brother Masseo went begging for bread in a small village. Returning with a few dried crusts, they searched until they found a spring for drinking and a flat rock for a table. As they ate their meager lunch, Francis exclaimed several times, "Oh Brother Masseo, we do not deserve such a great treasure as this!" Finally Brother Masseo protested that such poverty could hardly be called a treasure. They had no cloth, no knife, no dish, no bowl, no house, no table. Elated, Francis replied, "That is what I consider a great treasure—where nothing has been prepared by human labor. But everything here has been supplied by Divine Providence, as is evidenced in the baked bread, fine stone table, and the clear spring." Joyfully they finished their meal and then journeyed on toward France "rejoicing and praising the Lord in song."[15] Radical simplicity.

In Francis of Assisi we see joyful humility. Francis called his humble band "God's jugglers," whose task was to "revive the hearts of men and lead them into spiritual joy."[16] Paul Sabatier wrote of Francis, "Perfectly happy, he felt himself more and more impelled to bring others to share his happiness and to proclaim in the four corners of the world how he had attained it."[17] And away he went, traversing much of Italy, preaching to the sultan in Egypt and engaging in ministry among Muslim peoples. His "Friars Minor" (little friars or little brothers) fanned out over Europe and beyond.

They not only preached, but also sang. Exuberant and joyful, they were often caught up in ecstasy as they worshiped. With the soul of a poet, Francis would improvise their hymns. Best known is his "Canticle of the Sun," with its celebration of Brother Sun and Sister Moon, Brother Wind and Sister Water. Francis and his Friars Minor knew the joy of the Lord. They were stamped by simple love and joyous trust. They led a cheerful, happy revolt against the spirit of materialism and double-mindedness. Joyful humility.

When Francis was absorbed in prayer at the deserted church of San Damiano in Assisi he heard a command of the crucified Lord. "Francis," the voice told him, "go and repair my house, which, as you see, is falling completely into ruin." In response Francis uttered the following prayer as he knelt beneath the crucifix of San Damiano:

Most high,
glorious God,
enlighten the darkness of my heart
and give me, Lord,
a correct faith,
a certain hope,
a perfect charity,
sense and knowledge,
so that I may carry out Your holy and true command.[18]

St. Bonaventure

The Fullness of Life in Christ

Since imagination aids understanding, I have arranged in the form of an
imaginary tree the few items which I have collected . . .
and have ordered . . . them in such a way that the first or lower branches
depict the Savior's origin and life are described;
in the middle, his passion; and in the top, his glorification. . . .
How wholesome it is, always to meditate on Christ.

THE TREE OF LIFE

MANY OF TODAY'S FOLLOWERS OF CHRIST hesitate to embrace Francis of
Assisi because there is too little nuance in his treatment of the Christian
life. At times he seems so literally minded that he is of little earthly good.
Even so, his popularity and that of the Franciscans exploded throughout
Europe. What Francis distilled in life became even more revered after his
death: humility as the gateway to the spiritual life, the call to be a fully
devoted follower of Jesus Christ and the commitment to lead an exem-
plary Christian life. Tugged along by the zeal to emulate his life and legacy, the Friars Minor gave rise to a whole new wave of "holy literature."
In the midst of the upsurge of interest in Francis's life and ministry, the
young Bonaventure (1217-1274) felt compelled to follow his leader's example and then to preserve this example in writing.[19]

History bears scant reference to Bonaventure's early years. He was born
in 1217 in Borgnoregio, a small Italian village near the Mediterranean
Sea. Sprinkled among the few insights that do exist is a dramatic story that
explains his debt to St. Francis. While still a young boy, Bonaventure
became deathly ill. His future was in doubt and his illness worsened. In
desperation his mother cried out in the name of St. Francis. Shortly there-

after, the boy's fever broke and his health began to improve. Believing that the saint had played a direct role in his healing, Bonaventure felt forever indebted to Francis.[20] His vast intellect and broad experience (monk, professor, colleague of Thomas Aquinas at the University of Paris, and minister general of the Franciscans) compelled Bonaventure to find a grand unified theory of the spiritual life.

Of all the personalities of the thirteenth century, few stand as ready and able as Bonaventure to interpret the church to the world and the world to the church. His ideas are challenging and complex. He is prolific in his output but frequently opaque in his meaning. His original writings, which fill more than thirteen volumes, range from devotional literature to speculative philosophies to systematic theology to biblical interpretation and even include theories of education. Bonaventure provides us with a comprehensive philosophy of life. Unfortunately, much of his writing is simply too obscure—even some of his writings on Christ remain remote and inaccessible. What he does provide, however, is one of the most striking and attractive portraits of the spiritual life developed during the thirteenth century.

Although Bonaventure's writings cover such a wide range, the topics that concern us come from the period of his life when he devoted his abilities to helping us understand the nature and destiny of our life with God.[21] His nickname, the "Seraph Doctor," betrays history's view of his indebtedness to Francis. The title comes from the central image he uses to convey the nature of the spiritual life: the account of St. Francis seeing the fiery Seraph on Mount La Verna. Bonaventure uses the account to provide an allegorical interpretation of the spiritual life. It is this allegorical interpretation that becomes his central contribution to articulating the nature of our life with God.

Sources of Spiritual Knowledge

Bonaventure identifies six sources of spiritual knowledge, each of which acts in unique ways to guide us on our spiritual journey.

The literal and allegorical understanding of Scripture. In the thirteenth century, the Bible was read with the goal of receiving its depth and complexity over time. We often speak of the "allegorical" interpretation of Scripture, but this phrase diminishes the dynamic interplay between God's interpretive Spirit, our spirit and God's inspiring Spirit that gave rise to the original text. Eventually, this method became standardized and known as *lectio divina,* the oldest and most widespread method for reading and understanding both the literal and allegorical senses of Scripture.

Lectio divina, which means "divine readings" or "reading divine things," originated with the greatest minds in the history of the early and medieval church. They were often sophisticated people with powerful intellects. Many contributed to the development of doctrinal teachings of the church, using the Scriptures as their primary source. Over time this prayerful reading of Scripture became normative, and for many centuries faithful Christians never second-guessed the reliability of the text. Receiving its message as the will of God, devout believers found help and guidance for their life with God from their reading and prayer.[22]

The enduring writings of the great saints of the church. Since each generation must bear faithful witness to our life with God, this witness in turn nourishes every new believer. For Bonaventure, tradition does not stifle Scripture but incorporates it, along with its various uses and interpretations in the life, practices, experiences and teachings of the church through the ages.

The contemporary writings of the great spiritual masters. In this respect Bonaventure uses the work of St. Francis and others to show how his contemporaries live and think about their life with God. This allows him to use these writings to amplify and build his own understanding of God and demonstrates how this understanding grows over time through interaction with other great Christians.

The integrative writings of experts in the human disciplines. This reflects the right use of reason. He shows that Christianity is based on faith, but this does not mean that we oppose or reject reason. Our minds are a gift from God that allow us to understand Scripture, construct doctrine, make sense of our life and offer a meaningful contribution through our work.

"The book of nature." Bonaventure shows how learning to read the book of nature enables us to perceive the active presence of God in the world. All of the church for most of its history has believed that God created the heavens and the earth. In more recent times there has arisen a dispute over how old or young the earth actually is, but always there is a recognition that because God created it, the world is good and worthy of our respect.

   The mature wisdom to read "the book of experience." Bonaventure's most dramatic use of spiritual experience[23] is the way he appropriates St. Francis's experience of the fiery Seraph to illustrate the process and goal of the spiritual life. Ultimately, he believes everyone has a real and personal experience with God so that we have confidence in our faith in him.

Stages of Spiritual Growth

Next come the seven stages of our spiritual growth. As we work through each stage, the discoveries made at one level must be appropriated into the next until the highest level when we experience perfect union with God. The six sources of spiritual knowledge help us understand how the seven stages of spiritual growth are intertwined. Each stage must be dealt with in its proper order, and our ability to understand the role of each stage in our life with God is necessary for our complete transformation. We must see our senses transformed at stage one, for example, gaining a sense of our spiritual senses beyond our natural senses if we are to see our imagination transformed in stage two. The first six stages show Bonaventure's massive integrative mind at its finest. Stages one and two reflect the influence of St. Francis. Stages three and four reflect the influence of Augustine. Finally, stages five and six reflect the influence of Dionysius (we'll look at him in chapter 7). Let's consider each stage briefly.

   Stage one consists of the senses. Through seeing, hearing, touching, tasting and smelling we gain information that leads to human knowledge.[24] The senses are the gateway to intelligence. The sense world always mediates the intelligible world. For Bonaventure, although all thoughts do not arise from experience, all thoughts depend on experience.

   The second stage is the imagination. This is not a casual or frivolous activity but a special way in which we understand our sense experience and what it can teach us about God. Although this is a distinct stage, it cannot be considered independent of the others. Because the temporal always mediates the eternal, the work of the imagination organizes our sensory knowledge in such a way that we understand our life with God and express our devotion to him.

The third stage is the intelligence. Augustine emphasizes that we bear the image of God through our capacity to reason. Likewise, Bonaventure highlights that our intellectual capacities are formed by reflecting on temporal realities, eternal realities and unchanging truths.[25] We use our intelligence to understand terms, delineate propositions and investigate inferences. Bonaventure amplifies this understanding with an illustration. "How could the intellect," he begins, "know that a particular being is defective and incomplete if it had no knowledge of the Being which is free from all defect?"[26] In other words, because we have an idea of perfection implanted in us, by nature we are able to understand imperfection.

In this stage, our intellect is able to put sensory knowledge and reasonable thoughts into proper alignment. As a result, the transformed mind that is aware of God's reality is able to see the form of the Trinity in every aspect of knowledge.[27] Bonaventure's culminating illustration in this section demonstrates how the three powers of human reason (memory, understanding and will) lead us to enjoy eternity, understand truth and embrace God.

Stage four is the understanding, the intersection of our natural powers with our supernatural destiny. Christ is the linchpin that transforms every aspect of our earthly existence in order to assist us in our journey to God. "No matter how enlightened one may be by the light of natural and acquired knowledge," Bonaventure asserts, "he cannot enter into himself to delight in the Lord unless Christ is the mediator."[28]

This stage is critical because at this level we transition from the right use of our natural senses to the recovery of our spiritual senses. "When by faith the soul believes in Christ, it recovers its spiritual hearing, seeing, smelling, tasting and touching."[29] When our spiritual hearing and seeing are restored, we are able to receive and understand the words of Christ and view the splendor of his illumination. When our spiritual smelling is restored, we recover our ability to understand Scripture properly. When we recover our spiritual sense of taste and touch, we experience the love and life that originate in God.

Stages three and four form the two middle wings of the Seraph and lift us above the earthly plane to the final plateau on our way to union with God. At this point, Bonaventure pauses to emphasize that God is outside us in the physical world as demonstrated in stages one and two, within us through the rational world as demonstrated in stages three and four, and beyond us in the spiritual world as he will now demonstrate in stages five and six.

Stage five (the intelligence) begins our entrance into the "holy of holies" as we see the essential attributes of God.[30] Stage six (the conscience) prepares us for stage seven (union with God) by guiding us to understand the interrelationship of the Father, Son and Spirit in the Trinity.[31] Together, God's essential attributes and interrelated nature are made known to us through Christ our teacher, who alone mediates these truths to every one of us who is faithful. These truths are not discoverable by human reason alone. On our own and apart from God we can recognize our need for God, but we cannot recognize his nature or internal relationship. It is here that Bonaventure makes his beautiful statement that "evangelical perfection" is the process by which we come to imitate Christ perfectly in word, thought, deed and spirit.

Everything Leads Through Christ

Bonaventure states that no one can understand the nature of God and the destiny of the Christian life without Jesus Christ. We can all work our way through stages one, two and three. But at the pivotal juncture in stage four, unless Jesus is our mediator there is no way to develop a proper understanding of God or arrive at the ultimate destiny of the Christian life.

Like creation itself, stage seven brings us to a state of complete alignment of every thought and desire through union with God. This is to experience *apatheia,* the state of existence where all our longings are satisfied exactly as God intended and we are able to live free of disordered thoughts and emotions. This is to experience shalom, a state of complete peace.

Bonaventure completes our ascent by returning to Francis and the spellbinding encounter he experienced on Mount La Verna. For Bonaventure, Francis is the example of evangelical perfection, of the person who imitates Christ so completely that he becomes like him. The ultimate goal of the Christian life is to experience the mystical Christ and in this way recognize that our life with God both includes and transcends our earthly thoughts and experiences.[32]

REFLECTING AND RESPONDING

Did you notice that Bonaventure actually believed in such a thing as spiritual knowledge? Not just feelings or speculations, but actual knowledge. For the most part we today can hardly comprehend the idea of a body of knowledge about the spiritual life. I mean real knowledge. Knowledge in character formation that we can test and verify. We have much to learn in this area and Bonaventure can help us. We are only now recovering some of Bonaventure's insights into the sources of spiritual knowledge. I want to highlight three of these that are of special interest today.

The first is the value of approaching Scripture by means of *lectio divina.* The recovery of this approach has come in reaction to the detached, mechanical, higher critical view of Scripture we have had for some time now. With *lectio divina* we are gaining a new appreciation for the character formation purposes of Scripture.

What is involved in *lectio divina?* It involves listening to the text of Scripture—really listening, listening yielded and still. It involves submitting to the text of Scripture, allowing its message to flow into us rather than attempting to master it. It involves reflecting on the text of Scripture, permitting ourselves to become fully engaged—both mind and heart—by the drama of the passage. It involves praying the text of Scripture, letting the biblical reality of life with God to give rise to our heart-cry of gratitude, confession, complaint or petition. It involves applying the text of Scripture, seeing how God's Holy Word provides a personal word for our life circumstances. It involves obeying the text of Scripture, turning, always turning, from our wicked way and into the way everlasting (Ps 139:23-24). As we do this the river of God's life will flow through the Bible and into the thirsty wasteland of our soul.

Second, we are gaining a new appreciation for the "book" of nature today. To be sure, nature has experienced the effects of the Fall with its decay and corruption. As the wise apostle Paul puts it so graphically, "The

whole creation has been groaning in labor pains" waiting for the day
when it will be "set free from its bondage to decay and will obtain the
freedom of the glory of the children of God" (Rom 8:21-22). Yet even in
its present decay, the book of nature teaches us much. We see beauty and
symmetry and glory there, for nature is always doing the will of the Father. The trees stretching skyward, the birds singing and swooping
through the air, the little creatures that scurry about the earth, all are doing the will of the Father. Most days when I am writing I will take an
hour or two to hike in a nearby canyon just so I can see some of the will
of the Father. In his poem "God's Grandeur" Gerard Manley Hopkins
tells it straight: "The world is charged with the grandeur of God." In the
silence of this canyon I experience something of that grandeur.

Finally, we come to the "book" of experience. Learning to "read" our
experience and the experience of others is so valuable. In this we are following the ancient dictum "know thyself" . . . with a caveat. As we seek
to understand our inner motivations, scruples and desires, we also look for
the footprints of God in our experiences. We most certainly ask, "What
does this experience teach me about myself?" In addition, we also ask,
"What does this experience teach me about God?" "Can I discern the
good hand of God in all things?" "How does God reveal himself through
my experiences?" "In what ways is God hidden to me?" "And why?"

All this asking and discerning is best done in community. Frankly, we
humans are capable of infinite self-deception. Thus it helps when we have
trusted friends who are wise in the ways of the Spirit and can help us track
the footprints of God in our experiences. This is, of course, the work of
spiritual direction, but it need not be a formal arrangement. Where there is
a loving, nurturing community, we can open our lives to one another and
help each other discern where God has been at work in our experiences.

I hope it does not take away from the importance of the man and the
greatness of his teaching if I beg to differ with Bonaventure on one important matter. And it is not just Bonaventure; this same issue comes up
with many others in this book, for it was a fairly common belief of the
time, especially in desert monasticism. I am referring to what the ancients
called *apatheia,* this ability to live completely free of all emotion or desire.
I hate to be blunt about it, but human beings simply cannot live without

desire. Without desire we will not eat or drink or sleep. The Christian message is not the elimination of desire but the transformation of desire. The overcoming of destructive desire and developing the inward reality of right desire is what we are after and what we can experience as our life is soaked in Jesus and his way.

A Prayer of St. Bonaventure

"Pierce, O most sweet Lord Jesus, my inmost soul with the most joyous and healthful wound of Thy love, and with true, calm and most holy apostolic charity, that my soul may ever languish and melt with entire love and longing for Thee, may yearn for Thee and for thy courts, may long to be dissolved and to be with Thee.

"Grant that my soul may hunger after Thee, the Bread of Angels, the refreshment of holy souls, our daily and supersubstantial bread, having all sweetness and savor and every delightful taste.

"May my heart ever hunger after and feed upon Thee, Whom the angels desire to look upon, and may my inmost soul be filled with the sweetness of Thy savor; may it ever thirst for Thee, the fountain of life, the fountain of wisdom and knowledge, the fountain of eternal light, the torrent of pleasure, the fullness of the house of God; may it ever compass Thee, seek Thee, find Thee, run to Thee, come up to Thee, meditate on Thee, speak of Thee, and do all for the praise and glory of Thy name, with humility and discretion, with love and delight, with ease and affection, with perseverance to the end; and be Thou alone ever my hope, my entire confidence, my riches, my delight, my pleasure, my joy, my rest and tranquility, my peace, my sweetness, my food, my refreshment, my refuge, my help, my wisdom, my portion, my possession, my treasure; in whom may my mind and my heart be ever fixed and firm and rooted immovably. Amen."[33]

Thomas à Kempis

Imitating Christ

The words of Christ remind us that we must imitate
his life and his ways if we are to be truly enlightened and set free
from the darkness of our own hearts.

THE IMITATION OF CHRIST

IT IS PERHAPS THE SIMPLICITY OF THE WRITINGS of Thomas à Kempis (1379-1471) that draw us in. His reflections match our own life experience: "When I had journeyed half of my life's way, I found myself in a dark wood for I had lost the path."[34] Every one of us has wandered off the path. Sometimes we have wandered accidentally, sometimes intentionally, but always because we lacked a clear sense of where we needed to go and the cost of not arriving at our destination.

The Imitation of Christ was written in the fifteenth century to help us find our way back onto the path. It was an instant success and came to represent a watershed of fifteenth-century Christian spirituality. By the end of the century it had been translated into multiple languages and spread around the known world. It would be one of two primary texts that guided Ignatius of Loyola back to his life with God. Once it was translated into English, it became and has been a perennial bestseller, along with *The Pilgrim's Progress* and the Bible.

It is believed that à Kempis wrote the *Imitation* while caught up in a great renewal movement sweeping Europe. The simplicity of its message and the accessibility of its ideas make it especially attractive, but it also reveals the turmoil sweeping the continent at the time. How does one become like Christ while facing political and social unrest on a grand scale?

As Europe endured the aftermath of the great schism of the fourteenth century, it was also seeking relief from the bubonic plague that ravished Europe for one hundred years, killing a third of the population initially and then recurring every three to ten years. Furthermore, the continent had to address the growing decay that was undermining the organized church. All that à Kempis believed should happen through God's power at work in the world had collapsed. The schisms that began long before his birth continued deep into his own century. In a desperate attempt to find a deeper life with God, à Kempis entered a monastery in order to engage in patterns of life and instruction that would strengthen himself and the church.

The Priorities of Faith

The *Imitation* itself is straightforward: it provides timeless instruction in spiritual direction for those who will in turn give spiritual direction as well. Every one of us who seeks to balance our love for God with our work in the world could be guided by this classic. Its very strategy seeks to answer the question that haunts every honest seeker: how can we change for the better? Because the book was originally written as journal entries, it does not follow any organizational pattern, but it does cluster around eight central priorities.

First, when we cultivate humility we destroy self-centeredness and enter the pathway to God. Then, humility allows us to develop a clear conscience based on the active cultivation of virtue. Next, we discover inner peace. As a result, everything in our life begins to flow out of a spontaneous response to the pure love of God. Then we are prepared to encounter the cross and discover the full impact of Christ. This helps us see that God wants to lead us into the life-changing experience of eternal life. As a result, we strive to become true imitators of Christ. Finally, we become ruled not by nature but by grace.

As we consider each priority in detail, we recognize that the first step to spiritual transformation is to destroy our self-centeredness. The ability to move beyond our ego in order to discover God begins by cultivating a spirit of humility. Humility is based on perceiving reality accurately, including the truth that life does not revolve around our needs and desires. Thomas à Kempis recognizes that all of us believe our natural desire for happiness will cause us to find happiness. But this is simply not the case. The very nature of the spiritual life runs counter to our natural desires. We do not discover happiness naturally. In fact, our self-centeredness is so powerful that we fail to see that we cannot engineer our own happiness but only prepare for it.

The second priority builds on the first and insists on the need to cultivate virtue. Throughout the early part of his book, à Kempis repeatedly reminds us how easy it is to fall prey to temptation. Our vulnerability to temptation is a result of a life that is not fully integrated. We are not stable, we are not patient and we are not kind. Our feelings are easily thrown off by our day-to-day affairs. The cultivation of virtue, on the other hand, gives us an ordered consistency that stabilizes us.

The third priority is to discover inner peace, or *eirene*, a Greek word that is similar in meaning to the Hebrew *shalom*. It means much more than the absence of conflict but signifies our discovery of complete well-being. Today there are so many fashionable attempts to discover well-being that we forget the central teaching of our faith: complete well-being can only be accomplished through our relationship with Jesus Christ.

The fourth priority is to live every day as a spontaneous response to the pure love of God. This is understood as *agapé* love, the love that is free of egocentric desire. The best expression of this love is the fruit of the Spirit. To be able to exhibit the fruit of the Spirit authentically is to be an integrated person full of love and free of evil.

The fifth priority is to encounter the cross in order to understand Christ. Eventually, all of us must die to self and the world in order to enter the fullness of our life in God. No matter where we start, our life with God must pass through the cross. In a day filled with all sorts of spiritual options, it is hard to recognize the enduring testimony of this uniquely Christian approach. The idea of the cross and the sense of sacrifice it entails call us to a path different from every other.

The sixth priority is to experience eternal life, or *zoë*. This Greek term comes from the New Testament and is different from *bios*, which means only physical existence. The prevailing mood of our society draws all our energy and attention toward *bios*, not *zoë*. Every place we turn emphasizes our biological existence without paying attention to our eternal end. Yet *zoë* is the experience of eternal life that originates in God alone even while we live. It is a glimpse of the meaning of this life as a foretaste of the life to come.

The seventh priority is to imitate Christ. Although this is à Kempis's entire theme, when he defines it more specifically, he states that to imitate Christ is to embody in our own life the same spirit with which Jesus lived when he was on earth. He elaborates by showing how Jesus is the way (the path to God), the truth (the ultimate source and foundation of life that makes truth possible) and the life (*zoë*—the eternal, uncreated life that originates in God alone).

The eighth priority is to be ruled not by nature but by grace. And here we encounter one of the most interesting features of à Kempis's entire book: his discussion of the difference between those ruled by nature and those ruled by grace.

The Contrast of Nature and Grace

The difference between nature and grace covers several pages but is easily compressed into thirty key contrasts. These ideas played a significant role in how Ignatius would eventually structure his thirty-day retreat. Here is a brief summation of the contrasts, with the caveat that these differences are discernible only by those who are spiritually enlightened.[35]

- Nature is crafty and seductive, while grace walks in simplicity.

- Nature is self-centered, while grace does everything purely for God.

- Nature is unwilling to be under a yoke of obedience, while grace moves beyond self-centeredness to minister for God.

- Nature works for its own benefit, while grace does not consider how to prosper for its own ends.

- Nature willingly accepts honor and respect, while grace attributes all honor and glory to God.

- Nature is afraid of shame and contempt, while grace is happy to suffer reproach for the name of Jesus.

- Nature is lazy, while grace joyfully looks for something to do.

- Nature seeks the unique and different, while grace delights in simple, humble and even shabby things.

- Nature keeps an eye on fashion, rejoices in material gain and is depressed at loss, while grace attends to eternal things and does not cling to passing ones.

- Nature is greedy and likes to take, while grace is kind, sharing and content with little.

- Nature focuses on the body, the vanities of life and the worries of self-preoccupation, while grace turns its back on anything that stands in the way of God.

- Nature gladly accepts any comfort that gratifies the senses, while grace seeks comfort in God alone.

- Nature is motivated by selfish gain, while grace seeks no reward other than God.

- Nature revels in friends and relatives, while grace loves everyone and focuses on the wise and virtuous rather than the powerful and rich.

- Nature is quick to complain of want and trouble, while grace bears poverty resolutely.

- Nature turns all things to itself and pushes itself into the spotlight, while grace refers all things to God.

- Nature longs to know secrets and to have the inside story, while grace pursues what is useful for the soul.

- Nature is quick to complain, while grace endures all things resolutely.

- Nature wishes to be seen in public, while grace seeks to avoid vain displays.

- Nature longs to be steeped in sensual experience, while grace exercises restraint of the senses.

- Nature wants to be noticed by others, while grace wants to be noticed by God.

- Nature is ruled by sin, while grace is ruled by grace.

- Nature represents vice, while grace represents virtue.

- Nature attempts to judge between good and evil, while grace teaches us the eternal law of God.

- Nature does not act on what it knows to be good, while grace flees sin and evil.

- Nature relies on natural gifts, while grace relies on the gift of God's mercy.

- Nature succumbs to vice, while grace radiates virtue.

- Nature flees the truth, while grace submits to truth.

- Nature runs on its own energy, while grace relies on energy from God.

- Nature ignores its failures and refuses to learn from them, while grace humbly embraces shortcomings and learns from them.

One of the ways I have found this list helpful is to use it as an interactive guide as I write in my journal. I have focused on one contrast a day for six thirty-day periods and recorded the results in my journal. The effect is staggering. It is natural to see and experience life only as it affects me. To break out of our egocentric posture is nearly impossible, but when we do, we are learning to live not by nature but by grace.

The ultimate priority of the spiritual life is to enjoy the fullness of life by coming to completion in Christ. This completion is possible only through active involvement in the Christian community. À Kempis places a strong emphasis on the role of the sacraments in our life with God. None of us ever knows God in isolation. Rather, our life with God is a series of individual and corporate experiences that guide us over time.

Throughout his text, à Kempis repeatedly asks what attitudes are desirable and what disciplines are necessary if we are to imitate Christ fully. It is only when the totality of who we are expresses the totality of who Jesus is in us that we imitate him. Few of us attain this level of identity with Christ, but the possibility of complete fulfillment in this way provides the most attractive vision of life possible. Although à Kempis articulated this approach it was left to Ignatius to systematize how it could be attained.

REFLECTING AND RESPONDING

For half a millennium, *The Imitation of Christ* has been the unchallenged devotional masterpiece for Christians everywhere. We have been immensely enriched by this simple book, which distills the insights of a dynamic Christian community in the fifteenth century known as the Brethren of the Common Life. The *Imitation* is one of the finest expressions of the spiritual movement known as *devotio moderna* (modern devotion), which swept through the European continent from the fourteenth to the sixteenth centuries. It stressed an inner life of devotion and cautioned against an outer life of excessive busyness and preoccupation.

The *Imitation* has a way of drawing me back to the things I value the most: simple love for Jesus, prayerful devotion, ongoing character formation into the image of Christ and more. A single insight from the *Imitation* can transport me onto an inner venture of discovery and spiritual growth: "No one speaks securely except the person who willingly keeps silent. No one leads securely except the person who freely serves."[36] Or it settles me into thoughtful meditation and introspection: "What good is it to live long when we improve so little?"[37] Or it rouses me to strive all the more toward deep character formation: "Fight bravely, for habit overcomes habit."[38]

Over the years, I have profited immensely from the *Imitation*. But, frankly, I have always thought of it as a collection of rather random, independent sayings. Hence, what Gayle Beebe has done in ordering the *Imitation* into general themes is quite unique. And it works. The ordering is not forced and is right on the mark. It opens the *Imitation* up in a whole new way. For this we can be grateful.

It would be worthwhile to slowly read the *Imitation* with these eight themes in mind and see where we would place each section. This would give us an entirely new way to approach à Kempis's teaching. We could consider his insights into humility, for example, by reading at one setting the dozen or so sections that consider that theme.

Further, it is helpful for us to see how one theme drives us into the next. This does not come so much from à Kempis himself, but it certainly is a quality that shines in Gayle Beebe's ordering of à Kempis. A spirit of humility, for example, is essential before we can even consider the cultivation of virtue, and humility, once acquired, of necessity drives us into the cultivation of virtue. Or consider how inner peace as a settled reality of life is needed before we can live every day as a spontaneous response to the pure love of God, and how both of these are essential for us to endure the sufferings which come with taking up our cross daily.

The summation Gayle Beebe has developed to characterize the theme of being "ruled by grace rather than nature" is brilliant. I have not seen as clear and accurate a summary of à Kempis on this topic anywhere. Gayle's idea of using these thirty statements one at a time as a daily examen of conscience is excellent—though five or six days may be all some of us can take at one time!

I do hope you will consider making *The Imitation of Christ* one of those few books you will return to and draw strength from for a lifetime.

A Prayer of Thomas à Kempis

"*Grant me most sweet and loving Jesus, to rest in you above every other creature, above all health and beauty, above all glory and honor, above all power and dignity, above all knowledge and precise thought, above all wealth and talent, above all joy and exultation, above all fame and praise, above all sweetness and consolation, above all hope and promise, above all merit and desire, above all gifts and favors you give and shower upon me, above all happiness and joy that the mind can understand and feel, and finally, above all angels and archangels, above all the hosts of heaven, above all things visible and invisible, and above all that is not you, my God. Amen.*"[39]

Ignatius of Loyola

Guided by the Mysteries of Christ

The following are some rules for perceiving and understanding the different movements that are produced in the soul—the good that should be accepted; the bad that should be rejected. . . . This takes place in those who earnestly strive to purify themselves from their sins and who advance from good to better in the service of God our Lord.

THE SPIRITUAL EXERCISES

ENTERING THE MIX AT THE END OF THE fifteenth century and growing into full maturity in the sixteenth, Ignatius of Loyola (1491-1556) represents one of the greatest conversion and growth stories in Christian history. His transforming experience occurred in 1521, when he was wounded in battle and suffered severe injuries to both legs. His own autobiography records that until this time he had been fully given to the vanities of the world and especially to acts of heroism in war.[40] But the brutal wounds in 1521 meant a subsequent rehabilitation requiring months of rest. From this experience of suffering came a remarkable reflection on his life with God. These reflections triggered a moral and spiritual transformation that changed his life and forever changed the world.

While recovering in his native Spain, Ignatius was given a variety of books, including *The Life of Christ* by Ludolph of Saxony, *Golden Legends* by Jacobus de Voragine, a book on the life of St. Francis and a copy of Thomas à Kempis's *The Imitation of Christ*. These books stimulated a spiritual awakening that inspired Ignatius to think long and hard about the ultimate destiny of his own life and that of every human being. He wondered to himself, Why not become like St. Francis and imitate Christ? While traveling on a pilgrimage through Manresa, a small town near the

Benedictine monastery of Montserrat, Ignatius experienced a deep conviction that our true destiny as individuals is to return to God in order to find the peace and contentment we so desperately seek.

This insight completely changed Ignatius. He came to see that our life with God could fundamentally reshape us. He also recognized that we could be given to spiritual excesses that would distort us. Out of these observations and experiences Ignatius gathered ten men in 1534 and formed the Society of Jesus (the Jesuits) in order to send disciples throughout the world to provide an educated "middle way" to God. His best work, *The Spiritual Exercises*, outlines the disciplines we must undergo if we are to become like Christ and accomplish his vision for our life in the world.

In his writings, Ignatius reflects on the tremendous difference between what Christ expects of him and how he actually responds in his effort to imitate Christ. Troubled by this gulf, he begins to review the life and teachings of Jesus as recorded in the Gospels. During one of his extended meditations on Jesus, Ignatius recognizes how his moods shift and his thoughts change. Intrigued, he begins to examine how best to understand these discrete experiences in the larger scheme of life with God. It is in the midst of these reflections that Ignatius realizes that our experiences of God must have reasonable explanations. In other words, we need to know what they mean if they are to have enduring power in shaping the destiny of our life.

The Goal of *The Spiritual Exercises*

This conviction resulted in a body of writings and correspondence that fills twelve volumes.[41] *The Spiritual Exercises* forms the centerpiece of this work, and its enduring influence has been the remarkable impact individuals undergo when they work their way through the thirty-day Ignatian retreat, a series of disciplined practices meant to form our character into the very expression of the character of Christ. Of the writing of this landmark work, Ignatius recalls, "*The Spiritual Exercises* are all the best that I have been able to think out, experience and understand in this life, both for helping somebody to make the most of themselves as well as being a profit to others."[42]

The Spiritual Exercises comes from Ignatius's own experience of learning to understand life with God. This understanding is guided by his desire to find the middle way between the excess of religious enthusiasm and the sterility of philosophical reflection. The exercises require a disciplined imagination and a specific pattern of guided reflection and are to be completed in thirty days. None of the weeks is perfunctory. Each requires discernment so that we know we have learned what the specific "experience" is meant to teach us before we move on. As we attend to the person and work of Jesus Christ, God's work unfolds in our life dramatically. The *Exercises* captured a psychological truth long before it was scientifically proven: namely, that it takes roughly thirty days to change virtually any behavior-based habit.[43]

It is important to note that Ignatius never intended for these exercises to replace regular participation in the church or to jettison our understanding and appreciation of orthodox theology. Additionally, Ignatius emphasizes that the evidence for our movement into a deeper reflection on the mysteries of Christ is manifested by our movement outward into a deeper life of service.

Week one: Moral reform. Ignatius begins week one by laying out the process of moral reform. The purpose of moral reform is to channel our desires and harness our passions in a way that allows us to attend to the mysteries of the life of Christ. Since we are created to praise God, we need to understand how this can occur.[44]

In this context Ignatius explains the difference between venial and mortal sins. Venial sins pertain to one's thought life. Mortal sins are the sins we commit with our body and are more pernicious because they are based on deadly thoughts giving rise to sinful actions. Three stages of reflection guide us in understanding the way God breaks the grip of this sin in order to redirect our life to him.

First, we must reflect on our sin, acknowledging its severity and power to disrupt our life with God. Second, we must recognize how the sin of Adam and Eve is the pattern for all of us as devious thoughts lead to wayward actions. Finally, we must reflect on the sins of others, not to judge or despise them but to recognize how human sin can ruin God's destiny for our life.

Week two: Our life with God. After outlining spiritual and moral "purgation," Ignatius opens week two by focusing on the role of the imagination in "illuminating" our life with God. Throughout the history of the church, the imagination has played a key role in directing or diverting us from life with God. Imagination is the power we have to generate possible explanations for why we experience life the way we do. The imagination creates understanding. It clarifies meaning. It permits our conceptions and our perceptions to connect with one another. Without imagination, we would never be able to know, understand or even conceptualize our experience of the world. Imagination, then, operates to synthesize the specific experiences of our life into a meaningful whole.[45]

Ignatius sees the imagination as creating contact with the living reality of Jesus Christ. This dramatic recovery of the life of Christ is meant to lead us into a full identification with the Savior. Beginning with the nativity, Ignatius identifies key events from the life of Christ and helps us to identify with these experiences. After reflecting on Christ's birth, we continue by contemplating his presentation in the temple, the parallels between his life with the life of Moses, his flight to Egypt, his obedience to his parents, his baptism, the Sermon on the Mount, the calling of his disciples, his public ministry and his humiliation as he was preparing for his passion.

In each case, these reflections are meant to produce in us a capacity for unbroken contemplation of God. In concluding the disciplines of week two, Ignatius introduces the idea of three classes of people: those who are free of worldly attachments but only at the end of life; those who are free of attachments spiritually, but still own them; and those who are fully devoted followers of Jesus Christ, living and responding to life exactly as he did.

Through this ascending scale, Ignatius outlines the way he envisions our spiritual growth occurring: we grow to the extent that we are free from our attachments to this world. Positive engagement is not only possible but quite necessary. We cannot be like Christ unless we are free from the physical possessions of this life while enjoying the spiritual vitality of identifying with his life.

Week three: Identifying with Christ. Week three is devoted to imaginative reflection on the passion of Jesus. Like week two, week three uses real stories from the Gospels to draw us into full identity and union with the life and sufferings of Jesus. But for Ignatius, the goal of the spiritual life is not only "union" with Christ but also full devotion to his life and ministry. In this way he differs dramatically from Dionysius and others who emphasize that the goal of life is perfect union with God and complete contentment and rest in him. For Ignatius, contemplation is not an end in itself but a means of preparation for expressing as best we can the active love of God in the world.[46]

Week four: Full identity with Christ and service to the world. Week four completes the exercises and opens with Christ's appearance to Mary. Here, Ignatius takes us through a wonderfully imaginative tour of the tomb and Christ's conversation with her. The point of week four is to celebrate our full identity with Christ and to re-engage by celebrating our role and responsibilities within the created order. In this final week, Ignatius insists that no meaningful life with God can occur apart from our active life in the world.[47]

These four weeks complete the threefold way. Week one guides us through "purgation." Week two brings "illumination." Weeks three and four bring us into "union" with God for greater service in the world. In this way we are able to see and know the ways of God and his will for our life. This is to be converted into a living embodiment of Jesus Christ as a result of our imitation of him.

Throughout his writings, Ignatius emphasizes two seven-step approaches that are integral to the right use of the exercises. One is for evaluating all truth claims in which we use our mind to discern the truth of God. The other is for understanding how we can make a greater contribution to the common good in which we see the motives that lead us to display a heart for the world.

Seven Steps to Truth

The seven steps for evaluating all truth claims include:

- Always test the claim in light of the example of Christ.
- Consult other Scriptures.

- Look for confirming examples from the desert fathers.

- Consult the leading Christians of our own day.

- Pray.

- Study.

- Balance prayer and study with action and contemplation in order to know God and express his will in the world.[48]

Seven Contributions to the Common Good

The seven steps for determining what is true are followed by seven steps for making a greater contribution to the common good.

- Always place our hope in God.

- Lead an upright life.

- Live a life of humility, modesty and charity.

- Be likable.

- Always maintain a middle position between opposing forces.

- Exhibit strong moral authority by showing respect, being thoughtful in speaking and exercising discretion in giving advice.

- Win friendship with those in high positions so that we can be more effective in achieving our God-given goals and ambitions.[49]

Ultimately, Ignatius lays the groundwork for those who seek a deeper life with God while pursuing a broader impact on society. Despite being a contemporary of Luther and Calvin and actively resisting the Protestant Reformation, he provided many of the very same tools for Catholics that Luther and Calvin provided for Protestants. Both sides demonstrate a desire for a closer walk with God by engaging in a life of prayer and active service. Ignatius's highly structured retreat method (including meditation, contemplation, application of the senses and examination of conscience) reflects his belief that we can have a direct experience of God that not only changes us but also helps us contribute something worthy to society.

Although all four of the individuals we have considered in this chapter lived during the premodern era (before the seventeenth century and the scientific method), their insights span into our postmodern era because of their unique understanding of our life with God. Eventually, the Western church would settle into the patterns of separation we know today as Roman Catholic, Protestant and Anglican. In the sixteenth century, however, it was unclear what would happen politically, and eventually these fissures led to the Thirty Years' War.

Today we face a new opportunity. For the most part Christians no longer feel threatened by resources coming from other expressions of Christianity. As a result, all four of these individuals are experiencing a renaissance today that likely will provide guidance deep into the twenty-first century.

REFLECTING AND RESPONDING

The four-part structure of the Ignatian spiritual retreat is quite ingenious. The first week centers on our need—indeed our sin—in the light of God's overcoming love. The second week centers on the life of Christ, the third week on the death of Christ and the fourth week on the resurrection of Christ.

Whatever details of *The Spiritual Exercises* you may disagree with, I want to commend this four-part rhythm to you. Oh, how we need a deeper musing on our perennial knack for disobedience and God's unbounded habit of mercy. Oh, how we need a richer contemplation on that Life that is life indeed and that shows us the way so we may follow in his steps. Oh, how we need a fuller meditation on that death that sets us free. And, oh, how we need a more profound experience of that resurrection that empowers us to obey Christ in all things.

I hope you noticed how highly Christocentric this structure is. This is no accident. Ignatius wanted to anchor the Christian life in the life, death and resurrection of Jesus, especially as it is expressed in the four Gospels of Matthew, Mark, Luke and John. This was done in order to give a solid foundation for the spiritual life. In addition it provided guardrails for the excesses of both the religious mystical experiences that abounded at the time and the philosophical speculations of the day. This is the central "middle way" to which Gayle Beebe refers. Center your efforts on the

Jesus revealed in the Gospels and everything else will find its proper place. This is the Ignatian vision.

Ignatius believed church reform was to be based on individual reform. Hence his *Spiritual Exercises* are intently personal. The individual does not just read this book but enters into a retreat experience designed to reform the inner spiritual space. I know people who in the third week of an Ignatian retreat have entered genuine death to self only to emerge in week four into personal existential resurrection. Their heart is changed. Their affections are changed. Their values are changed. All for the better.

Now, a word about the dynamic use of the sanctified imagination that is so central to Ignatius and the retreat experience he designed. In placing such a strong emphasis on the imagination, Ignatius was helping ordinary people enter into the life of Jesus in a vivid, emotive, affective way. To "see" Jesus standing by the sea of Galilee, to "hear" the waves splashing against the side of the boat, to "touch" the hem of his garment, to "smell" the sea air, to "taste" the bread and the wine—all are dramatic visual aids that draw us into the story until the story becomes genuinely autobiographic of us. We stand before Jesus as he asks us, "Who do you say that I am?" With the woman at the well we ask, "Where do I get this living water?" We, with Nicodemus, puzzle over spiritual realities, asking, "How can these things be?" We tremble at the issues of life and death, exclaiming, "I believe, help my unbelief!" We humbly sit with the other disciples allowing Jesus to wash our feet. And we join Thomas in confessing, "My Lord and my God!" This is how the imagination can be sanctified and used for the purposes of God.

I wonder if you found it as interesting as I did that Ignatius laid out seven approaches for making a greater contribution to the common good. This is, of course, a natural outflow of his conviction that the evidence of the effectiveness of the thirty-day retreat is a movement outward into a deeper life of service to others. I especially like his fourth point: be likeable. How simple and how very important. Grumpy, sarcastic, opinionated people make life difficult for everyone around them. Conversely, when the goodness of God flows from us naturally and easily, it brings life to all. In so doing we contribute to the common good. May it be so for us all.

Dear Lord, we too want to imitate Jesus as was true for Francis and Bonaventure and Thomas and Ignatius. But imitation is a tricky thing. It easily becomes so superficial, so outward. It is easy to see this in the "disciples" of our contemporary celebrity figures. They mimic their idols in the silliest ways. It would be comical if it weren't so tragic.

But then, we quickly fall into the same trap. We so want to be like Jesus and so desperately try to follow the way of Jesus that, more often than not, we end up in some silly, superficial mimicry that has nothing to do with righteousness and peace and joy in the Holy Spirit.

What we long for, Lord, is a richer, deeper, fuller imitation of the heart of Jesus. Give us, we pray, the compassion of Jesus. Grant us today an increase of the spirit of mercy and joy and peace. Most of all, may our lives become more and more characterized by divine, agapé *love.*

Translating these graces into our world of laundry and computers and deadlines is the real key. For that we will need your boundless wisdom. Lord, help us always to draw from the deep well of your wisdom. Amen.

THE RIGHT ORDERING OF OUR EXPERIENCES OF GOD

I will go on to visions and revelations of the Lord.
I know a person in Christ who fourteen years ago was caught up
to the third heaven—whether in the body or out of the body I do not know;
God knows. And I know that such a person . . . was caught up into Paradise.

2 CORINTHIANS 12:1–4

It happened one day quite unexpectedly. For five long years he had struggled to make sense of his faith. Every time he felt settled, a new challenge arose that threatened to undo him. The further he went in life the more it troubled him. Is Christianity really true, he wondered? Could it hold up in the marketplace of ideas? Did it have the intellectual credibility he needed to continue believing in God? And what should he make of suffering? How could he believe in a loving God when evil and suffering ravished the world?

These questions haunted him. As the questions intensified, his despair grew. Would there ever be answers, or would he live the remainder of his days with only the questions?

And then it happened. Of all places, he was in school. Far removed from the grind of everyday life he had come to graduate school in hopes of finding God. While sitting in class one day listening to a lecture on Pascal's three orders, the barriers to deeper belief suddenly collapsed.

He had been troubled by his inability to find God and make sufficient sense of a universe under God's care. But he was also a person of faith who lived with an open and willing heart. The barriers created by the modern mentality and its confidence in human reason had hindered the natural flow of the Spirit of God. Yet with learning and especially an understanding of Pascal's treatment of the relationship of the heart, mind and emotions, he experienced a life-giving surge.

He was overcome with a sense of the goodness and graciousness of God. Recognizing the different levels of reality helped him make sense of his own spiritual journey. Even the problem of evil and suffering, although never fully resolved, made sense to him when placed in the broader perspective of God's ultimate plans for our life. A perceptual shift occurred as a profound and new understanding of the Christian life unfolded.

Years later he experienced a second brief encounter with God. During his early days in pastoral ministry he suffered a severe leg injury that required surgery and a long rehabilitation. His leg was placed into a large, long, heavy cast that greatly reduced his mobility. His spirits slumped and his confidence in the goodness of life disappeared. Early one Sunday morning, however, as he was preparing to lead worship, he was suddenly and unexpectedly overcome with a profound sense of the presence and love of God. The experience lasted only a few moments, but it fundamentally confirmed the reality of God's love and produced a renewed confidence in God's presence in his life.

These two experiences taken from the life of a close friend are like countless similar stories reported in the Bible and throughout Christian history. They are included here not because they are so unusual but because they are so commonplace. They illustrate the way both individual and corporate experiences of God help bolster our confidence in the truth and goodness of the Christian life. However impressive teachings about God's love may be, if divine grace were not ever experienced, these teachings would remain a mere abstraction.

But religious experiences are not of themselves the highest authority in the Christian faith. A simple way to recognize this is to compare our religious experiences with the views we see as we climb a mountain. As we climb higher and higher, we get different views. We cannot say that any one of the views we experience is the definitive view, no matter how much more beautiful and overwhelming it may be compared with the others.

Likewise, we need a reasonable theological account of the Christian faith to provide a basis for the validity of our experiences and to form a framework we can use to understand their significance. This lets us measure the legitimacy of religious experiences when others make similar claims. As Paul put it so succinctly in 1 Corinthians 12:3 when facing the turmoil caused by people who claimed authority because of their experiences, "No one speaking by the spirit of God ever says, 'Let Jesus be cursed!'" Nor are various experiences enough to sustain our spiritual life. We need a reasonable foundation for these experiences to help us understand their real meaning.

Very early in the church's life, it was generally accepted that our knowledge of God had two main sources: the Bible and the natural order. These are referred to in the literature of the time as the "two books of God." Scripture is more important, as it reveals God's purposes and intentions far more clearly than nature, but nature is seen to support and confirm what the Bible reveals.

In addition, a major way we describe the goal of the Christian life is to see God "face to face." Nothing created is necessary as a medium to know him, neither Scripture nor nature, since we can come before God directly. The phrase "face to face" is partly an allusion to Moses, who met God on the holy mountain, and also to Paul's statement that we now see God only dimly, as in a mirror.

All of us are promised an ultimate intimacy with God, while a few of us seem to enjoy this reality here and now. It seems that God gives this life to a few people in order to encourage the rest of us and let us know what awaits each of us in the life to come. These ecstatic or mystical experiences are a gift to encourage the church. They are not given so that an individual can elevate him or herself over any other Christian who has not had this specific experience. They are meant to lead us all to knowledge of God through Jesus Christ.

Although few of us have had overpowering mystical experiences, many if not all Christians have had some degree of spiritual experience. This reality was given renewed emphasis in the twelfth century, especially through the influence of Bernard of Clairvaux. The variety of types of spiritual experience is vast, but at its core it is focused on Jesus Christ. Through the Holy Spirit we receive both a sense of his presence and the many graces he promised us, such as love, joy, peace, patience, kindness, generosity, faithfulness, gentleness and self-control (Gal 5:22). In general, the role of spiritual experiences is to confirm the teaching of Scripture through the effects of God's Spirit on us and to enable us in time to enjoy God's habitual presence.

Defining Mystical Experience

To experience God is to have a mystical experience of him. The word *mystical* is derived from the Greek verb *muein*, which means "to remain silent; to shutter the senses, to quiet down, to come to rest." Originally it pertained specifically to the Greek mystery religions and included the acquisition of special knowledge leading to religious insight. Writing at the turn of the twentieth century, W. R. Inge offered twenty-six different definitions of this term.[1] Others offered additional explanations, but the most prominent simply states that mystical experience is "the type of [spiritual experience] which puts the emphasis on immediate awareness and experience of God, on direct and intimate knowledge of Him."[2]

Consider these two examples from Scripture. In 1 Samuel 3, Eli and Samuel are in the private quarters of the temple, almost asleep, when Samuel hears a voice he believes to be Eli's. Three times he hears the voice, and three times he believes it is Eli calling to him. From the text it is apparent that Samuel has not yet acquired the capacity to hear and understand the voice of God. After the third experience, however, Eli realizes that the voice is coming from God, even though he has never heard God's voice himself. Eli instructs Samuel how to respond the next time God speaks. Eventually, it happens a fourth time and Samuel responds appropriately because he now enjoys both the experience and the right understanding of the nature of this experience. What is unique in this story is not how Samuel's experience is alike or different from other mystical experiences, but the way he has to learn to look for God. In the process his perceptions of God are changed.

A second illustration, taken from the life of the apostle Paul, amplifies this point. In Acts 9, Paul has a mystical encounter with God that fundamentally changes the destiny of his life. Traveling to Damascus to further his campaign against the first Christians, Paul is blinded by a light and hears a voice telling him to change his ways and come to a new understanding of God. Eventually Paul's sight is restored, and his perception of God is changed forever.

Both experiences teach us that our mystical experiences help complete our perception of God. Our experiences of God confirm the validity of our life with him. They also help us conceptualize the vast varieties of experiences that exist among Christians and our multiple understandings of God. As we consider the following four writers we will see just how varied and complex the Christian life truly is.

Julian of Norwich

Enfolded in the Goodness of God

As the body is clad in clothes, and the flesh in the skin,
and the bones in the flesh, and the heart in the whole, so are we clothed,
body and soul, in the goodness of God and enfolded in it.

SHOWINGS

JULIAN OF NORWICH (1342-1416) WAS BORN shortly before the black plague ravished England, eventually killing nearly half of its population. Historians tell us of the enormous instability that accompanied the "Black Death," while Julian speaks of a greater longing to know and love God. She was an anchoress, a woman who lived in a one-room apartment attached to a church. In the late Middle Ages Norwich was a commercial hub and vibrant cultural center. An anchoress in such a setting spent her days praying, reflecting on God and providing spiritual guidance for those who sought her counsel.

Julian is the first woman openly identified as such to write a spiritual classic in English. Other women had no doubt written devotional literature before she did, but always anonymously or under an assumed name. Julian is especially provocative because she combines a wide range of theological knowledge with deep spiritual insight. Her words are especially riveting when we consider how she helps us make sense of our experiences of God. Earlier in the same century, a profound renaissance of interest in the role of religious experiences had swept the church. One after the other, a number of original works appeared to help us know how to interpret our experiences of God.

Beginning in the twelfth century, a shift was under way that focused increasing attention on the earthly existence of Jesus. As life with God migrated beyond the cloistered community of monks, the "new devotion" became more Christocentric and more affective than many earlier expressions of Christianity. The emphasis was on the emotional side of life with God, and many women who were inclined this way began to write about their experiences. But most women were not allowed to be educated or write, so many of their earliest works were ascribed to the men who helped produce these manuscripts and place them into circulation.

Julian's Experiences of God

In the midst of this renaissance but without any knowledge of it, Julian wrote a book based on her sixteen religious experiences that began on May 8, 1372. The work would turn out to be a classic. "Of these sixteen revelations," she recounts, "the first began early in the morning, about the hour of four, and it lasted, revealing them in a determined order, most lovely and calm, each following the other, until it was three o'clock in the afternoon or later."[3] She recorded these experiences first in a short version and then, after years of reflection, in a longer text, both of which survive today.

These texts reveal a brilliant and able mind grappling with the reality of God. Each "showing" takes Julian into a deeper understanding of God and of the truth that can be known through our experiences of him. As we read her visions it is important to remember that we are not evaluating the reliability of her claims. We are simply seeking to understand how she understood these experiences and how they stimulated a deeper life with God.

JULIAN'S SIXTEEN SHOWINGS

1. Julian sees blood trickling from the crown of thorns on the crucifix and has experiences of the Trinity and of the blessed virgin.
2. Julian sees the face on the crucifix change color.
3. Julian sees God in an instant and understands that he is in all things.
4. Julian sees blood flowing from the wounds on Christ's body and then vanishing.
5. God shows that Christ's Passion defeats the devil.
6. God thanks Julian for her suffering and shows her the bliss of heaven.
7. God gives Julian alternating experiences of joy and sorrow.
8. Julian sees Christ's body drying as he suffers bodily death, and shares in the pain caused to all creatures. Her reason suggests to her that she should look

up to heaven, but she chooses instead the dying Jesus as her heaven.

9. Jesus affirms his pleasure in suffering for Julian's sake, and shows her three heavens in his humanity.
10. Jesus shows Julian his heart within his wounded side.
11. Jesus allows Julian to see the blessed virgin.
12. God reveals himself in glory.
13. God affirms that, despite sin and suffering, all shall be well.
14. God tells Julian that prayers are inspired by him and please him.
15. God promises Julian that he will be her reward for suffering.
16. God shows Julian Jesus in her soul and grants her certainty that her showings come from Jesus, thus confirming his existence and truth to her.[4]

Julian explains each vision by following a set pattern. First, she shows how the vision helps her understand why she is to be contrite. Then the vision helps her understand to whom she is to show compassion. Finally, the vision helps her express a particular aspect of earnest longing for God. This pattern reflects an internal state, external awareness and eternal longing. The first showing ushers us into the presence of God and demonstrates the role of Christ and the importance of Mary. These three personalities play a key role in every aspect of Julian's understanding. Using the "spiritual imagination," a faculty she first identified, she synthesizes bodily sight, the words formed in response to our bodily sight, and spiritual perception.

This is one of the most innovative processes ever contributed to help us understand our spiritual life, particularly when it comes to knowing the role of spiritual experiences in our life with God. What Julian shows us is how we must move from physical experience to conceptual understanding to spiritual insight. To a certain extent it is a reality we experience every day, but Julian adds a unique twist. Here is a basic example to illustrate this point.

When we drive a car, we see a red light, a yellow light and a green light. Our sensory experience reports this data. This sensory data in and of itself is not enough to motivate behavior. Likewise, through our conceptual understanding, we have ideas of stopping, slowing down and accelerating. But, again, this conceptual understanding is not enough to motivate our actions. It is only when we combine sensory data and conceptual understanding that we realize a red light means stop, a yellow light means slow down and a green light means accelerate. This third step, in which perceptions and conceptions are combined through interpretation, is what Julian means when she speaks of spiritual insight. Thus, every divine showing she describes includes sensory experiences, conceptual understandings and spiritual insight.[5]

Interpreting Julian's Visions

The first showing, the image of blood trickling down from the crown of thorns, returns us to the scene of Christ's Passion and the principal players involved in that drama: the Holy Trinity, Christ himself and Mary. She tells us what these images mean to her, but she cannot make them mean the same thing to us. She can only accent their reality and then leave it up to our own longing for God to reconcile these perceptions and conceptions in a way that reaches the same spiritual insight.

Her second showing involves seeing Christ's face on the cross. Covered in dry blood and with anguish etching the contours of his face, Christ hangs before her in the shadowy darkness.[6] Although she longs to see Christ more distinctly and clearly, Julian realizes through spiritual insight that God allows us to see only enough to continue for that moment in our life with him. We do not need to see more than he desires to reveal to us at any given time.

Her third showing is seeing God in everything.[7] This showing opens up some of the earliest and most innovative theological speculation in the English-speaking world. Julian begins to ponder the wonder of God, the reality of sin and the future of humanity. She minimizes the enduring alienation from God that befalls the sinner. She realizes that God alone rules the world and everything in it. Additionally, all that happens occurs under God's divine care.

The fourth showing is Christ's blood running everywhere. Julian understands this scene to signify that Christ's blood is for the whole world. As much as we need water to survive physically, it is even more important that we avail ourselves of Christ's blood in order to thrive spiritually.[8]

The fifth showing teaches us that God uses the Passion of Christ to overcome the devil.[9] Not by any sense experience, but strictly by words formed in her mind Julian realizes this is the way to overcome the "fiend," or Satan. As she recounts this insight she sees how Christ defeats the wicked ways of Satan and wants us to use his example to guide us in our own response.

The sixth showing helps us understand the importance of trials and suffering and the bliss we will enjoy in heaven.[10] First, Julian recognizes that the Lord God experiences gratitude himself. Second, she sees that all of us who are in heaven find joy in recognizing the gratitude God feels when all suffering is finished. Finally, this bliss remains as eternally new and fresh as it did the first day we experienced it.

The seventh showing is key to experiencing the assurance of salvation we all desire. Here is how Julian renders it: "And our Lord's next showing was a supreme spiritual pleasure in my soul. I was filled with eternal certainty. This feeling was so joyful to me and so full of goodness that I felt completely peaceful and at rest."[11]

Julian goes on to realize that the very purpose of these experiences is to convince us of our salvation. Again, here is how she expresses it in her own words: "I understand that it is necessary for everybody to have such experiences. God wishes us to know that he safely protects us and that we should pass beyond experiences of suffering and pain in order to remain in eternal joy, which is God almighty, who loves and protects us."[12]

The eighth showing focuses on Christ on the cross in the midst of his Passion and approaching death. In addition to all the pains he suffers with which we are to identify, Julian also identifies with Christ's suffering as she tells us of her own mother keeping vigil by her bedside as she nears death. This association with Christ's suffering is reminiscent of the medieval belief that our sufferings should approximate Christ's sufferings if our glory is to approximate his.[13]

The ninth showing is to realize how happy Christ is when we understand and appreciate his suffering and Passion. It is as if our gratitude and recognition is the only joy God needs in order to feel good about his ultimate sacrifice. This is an unusual thought. We often think of salvation only as a remission of sins to appease an angry God. What Julian is saying, however, is that we bring joy to God when we love and serve him simply because our love and joy demonstrate our understanding and appreciation for all God has done for us.[14]

The tenth showing reveals the joy of Christ in suffering for our sake. When we are unable to think abstractly about God, Julian prompts us to think concretely about Jesus. It is in recognizing the purpose of the wounds in his side that we realize the joy Christ experiences in making the ultimate sacrifice.[15]

The eleventh showing causes Julian to elevate Mary. Believing Christ prefers Mary to all earthly creatures, Julian calls us to venerate her as well. In this veneration we recognize the initial joy she experienced at the conception of Christ, the enormous grief she felt in his crucifixion and her eternal joy to be with him forever. She is the perfect example of how we are to anticipate and experience Christ.[16]

The twelfth showing teaches us that every soul that longs for Christ and finds him must pass through Mary. She is the perfect example of the path we are to follow. During this showing, Julian realizes that although there are many earthly teachers provided by the church, there is only one ultimate teacher, Jesus Christ.[17]

The thirteenth showing involves the redemption of sin and suffering. Here Julian comes to understand that no matter how little or big our sin and suffering are, God will redeem them for good. God's goal is to help us embrace all of life, not just our particular interests or positive experiences. She introduces the concept of a lower animal nature that is vulnerable to sin and a higher godly nature that can think only of God. By taking comfort in God, we are able to see that despite sin and suffering, all will be well.[18]

The fourteenth showing answers the question, Why pray? Often when we think of God's providence, we wonder what good it will do to pray. If God wants to do something, he will do it whether or not we ask him to. What Julian realizes, however, is that prayer is not so much about getting God to hear our requests as helping us to change our perceptions. Prayer makes us pliable. Prayer restores elasticity to our soul. Prayer is God's way of reorienting us to his will and helping us develop the spiritual insight to embrace it. Prayer is also the way we join with God in the fulfillment of his purposes for the world.[19]

The fifteenth showing teaches us how to develop patience and endure suffering. Julian is clearly at the height of her own physical suffering when she realizes that patient endurance has helped her understand how God comes to us in suffering. In this way, suffering is not a barrier to our belief in God but a passageway.[20]

After the fifteenth showing, Julian begins to recover from her illness. She realizes she is going to live. After recovering her sense of life she enjoys rest, and her confidence and peace of mind return.

The sixteenth showing, which comes a day later, teaches us to have confidence in our salvation. This final, confirming vision helps Julian believe in the reality and validity of all she has experienced. She writes, "In all eternity Jesus will never leave the position which he takes in our soul; for sitting in us is his most familiar home. This was a ravishing and restful sight, for the sight of this sitting gave me certainty that he dwells there eternally."[21]

The Culminating Effect

The culminating effect of the sixteen showings is to help us learn how to resist the devil in order to draw close to God. Through the process of these sixteen experiences, Julian undergoes a spiritual and perceptual reorientation that helps her see God and understand what is real. She concludes her comments on the showings by confronting other human responses that keep us from God. Ultimately, Julian's hope is that we will hate sin, love God and do his will.[22]

Because of her remarkable insight and her sensitivity to the movements of God's Spirit, Julian elevates vernacular theology to a new level. With its focus on the legitimacy of spiritual experience, vernacular theology does not dismiss formal and doctrinal theology but shifts its emphasis to show how reason and theology must serve God's greater purposes in order to bring us into a deeper understanding of him. Although her writings include long, interactive considerations of several major Christian doctrines (creation, human nature, the role of reason, the incarnation, the passion, sin, the church, eschatology and so on), her greater concern is to help us experience God and understand our experiences of him.

One final note will help us put Julian's experiences in context. There is little doubt that individual readers either really like her or really don't. There seems to be little middle ground in how people respond to her. Part of this can be attributed to the unique emphasis of fourteenth-century English spirituality and its recovery of interest in the validity of religious experience. Another and perhaps greater factor may be her graphic descriptions of her own encounters with God.

The Motivating Insight

When I first read about Julian's experiences, I must admit I had mixed emotions. At one level, they riveted my attention and made me think long and glorious thoughts about God. At another level, they seemed so unusual. No matter how we respond, though, these accounts help us realize that God is revealed to us over time and through a variety of circumstances and experiences. Julian's revelations illustrate that God breaks in on our life in distinct and powerful ways. And these encounters rarely if ever happen early or instantaneously in our spiritual life but are a result of a long and arduous process of drawing near to God. The process of spiritual formation has as its goal a deep and abiding life with God. Julian's experiences remind us of this goal and encourage us along the way.

In fact, all four of the individuals examined in this chapter reflect a pattern prominent in the history of the church: each of their individual experiences of God was the result of years and years of meditation, prayer, study and effort. The value of spiritual experiences generally, and visions and revelations specifically, is to confirm the presence of God in long expanses of a life joined with him. This is not a works/righteousness approach, but a reflection of our understanding that God expects each one of us to make a tangible response to him through how we live and express our life.

Nevertheless, Julian's approach to God is unprecedented and distinct. From physical perception to reasonable conception to spiritual interpretation, Julian demonstrates how we come to a full knowledge of God and enjoy eternal contemplation and rest with him.

REFLECTING AND RESPONDING

I first encountered Julian when I was teaching a college course on the devotional classics. We had studied Augustine and Bernard of Clairvaux, Thomas à Kempis, Martin Luther, John Calvin, John Wesley and more. For one particular session I assigned Julian's *Showings*, thinking it was appropriate for us to read this first book written by a woman in English. When we gathered the next week, however, I found my students in an uproar. We had discussed many great writings with intelligence, reason, even good humor. But this was different. No one sat back in proper academic detachment. Everyone was speaking, debating, even shouting. Some loved the book, others hated it, but all were passionately engaged.

As I tried to referee the discussion, I searched for a reason for this turn of events. How could a book whose only concern is the love of God cause such intense controversy? As I listened to my students I soon realized that the heart of the problem centered on her passionate love language. Now, these students were quite familiar with such language—movies, books, television and the Internet abound with it. What they were unfamiliar with was using this kind of language in Christian devotion. Julian writes, "For truly our lover desires the soul to adhere to him with all its power, and us always to adhere to his goodness."[23] She did not approach the crucifixion with endless theories of the atonement. Oh, no. She drew near to see "the body bleeding copiously . . . the fair skin . . . deeply broken into the tender flesh through the vicious blows delivered all over the lovely body. The hot blood ran out so plentifully that neither skin nor wounds could be seen, but everything seemed to be blood."[24] In speaking of the Trinity Julian made no attempt to parse the mystery. Rather, she declared, simply and profoundly, "The Trinity is our everlasting lover."[25]

We, my students and I, were learning a valuable lesson that day. Contemporary culture had conditioned us to think of passionate love exclusively in erotic and sexual terms. Julian's dramatic language was freeing us to look at God's love for us and our response of love with new eyes. That day we began allowing for a deeper range of emotion in our relationship with the divine Center. Tenderness, intimacy, passion, yearning—all these and more became legitimate ways of responding to divine love. It was a *kairos* moment, that day in the classroom.

The mystical revelations in Julian's book *Showings* revolve around the passion of Christ, and perhaps the key take-home value for me is that they remind me to approach the cross of Christ with all my heart. I might find the various theories of the atonement a useful intellectual exercise: ransom theory, substitutionary theory, moral influence theory and others. But Julian reminds me to come to the experience of Christ on the cross with passion, with affection, with empathy, with soul. Am I able to feel the nail holes in hands and feet, touch the rough-hewn cross, mourn the dying of the king of heaven?

This is all deeply emotive language, and the experience of full-hearted emotion does not come easily to many of us. So how do we begin? Where do we begin? Well, we begin with a broken and contrite heart. We begin with inward godly sorrow. Abba Anthony observed, "Whoever wishes to advance in building up virtue will do so through weeping and tears."[26]

I once received a special grace of the soft rain of tears. I had been meditating on the ancient teaching of the church on "compunction"—heart sorrow. As I did this, God graciously helped me enter into a holy mourning on behalf of the sins of the people of God and a deep tear-filled thanksgiving at his patience, love and mercy toward us. This heart weeping lasted only a few days. I wished for more. Julian is our teacher in this more emotive side of worship and adoration.

I am especially glad for the fourteenth revelation to Julian about prayer. The observation in this chapter that Julian's approach to prayer "restores elasticity to our soul" is so descriptive of her experience. I love her prayer, "Lord, you know what I want if it be your will that I have it, and if it be not your will, good Lord, do not be displeased, for I want nothing which you do not want."[27] I long for more of this spirit in my own experience of prayer.

Julian, of course, could pray in this way because she had an abiding confidence in the goodness of God. God, she knew, was after her to do her good always. She could trust God's will utterly, for the will of God would be the very best for her. Always. This was her confidence.

At one point she writes, "This revelation was given to my understanding to teach our souls wisely to adhere to the goodness of God. . . . For the highest form of prayer is to the goodness of God. . . . For truly our lover desires the soul to adhere to him with all its power, and us always to adhere to his goodness."[28] Julian reveals a spirit and a confidence in the goodness of God that I long to imitate.

I find Julian to be at her best when she is sharing insights into prayer. She is a rich gold mine in which we can dig and explore to our heart's content. In times of dryness and barrenness Julian tells us that God is speaking over us, saying, "Pray wholeheartedly though you may feel nothing, though you may see nothing, yes, though you think that you could not, for in dryness and in barrenness, in sickness and in weakness, then is your prayer most pleasing to me, though you think it almost tasteless to you. And so is all your living prayer in my sight."[29]

Perhaps Julian's most famous line about prayer comes at a time when she despaired whether God ever heard her prayers. It was then that she heard the Lord saying to her, "I am the ground of your beseeching. First, it is my will that you should have it, and then I make you to wish it, and then I make you to beseech it. If you beseech it, how could it be that you would not have what you beseech?"[30] From this perspective prayer is like a reflex action to God's prior initiation on the heart. The experience of the years could cause Julian to announce confidently, "Prayer unites the soul to God."[31]

Some of the showings I find problematic. The eleventh showing, with its veneration of Mary, and her fifteenth showing, which idealizes suffering, seem to reflect more medieval underpinnings than is warranted by Scripture. These, however, are small objections to a work that calls us to a passionate, head-over-heels love affair with the great God of the universe.

Perhaps it would be good to close with the most well-known of Julian's words, words that speak to the ultimate restoration of all things: "But all shall be well, and all shall be well, and all manner of thing shall be well."[32]

Our Savior and our Friend, Julian had the most wonderful transcendent mystical experiences. Our experience seems rather petty by comparison. The focus of our attention seems to be the mundane stuff of life. We worry about stretching our finances through to the end of the month, and how to help our children do well in math and reading. We mow lawns and wash the clothes. Yet, we are learning to do these things with you, Lord. We thank you for caring about all our petty daily cares.

Perhaps a time will come when the idea of transcendent mystical experiences will be higher on our priority list. We look forward to that time. In the meantime we will do our best to be faithful in the common ventures of life. Amen.

George Fox

Learning to Follow the Light of Christ Within

Then I heard a voice which said,
"There is one, even Christ Jesus, who can speak to thy condition,"
and when I heard it my heart did leap for joy.

THE JOURNAL

GEORGE FOX (1624-1691) WAS BORN in the small village of Fenny Drayton in Leicestershire, England. He belonged to a heroic age of great kings, great poets and great unrest. He died in 1691, three years after the English Revolution formally and finally defeated the crown.[33] He was raised in the Church of England, but the religious and political ferment overrunning England forever marked him. For five years he pursued answers to his religious questions and found no one capable of helping him. Only when he had a dramatic experience of Christ was his religious thirst satisfied. Eventually he left the Church of England, and for the next forty years he underwent some of the most severe persecution anyone in the church has ever endured. Before he died, though, he saw many laws enacted to protect the Religious Society of Friends (Quakers) and bring religious liberty to the English-speaking world.

All great movements begin long before their time. Around 529, the Academy in Athens where Plato and Aristotle had studied and taught closed its doors, and in the same year the first Benedictine monastery opened, signifying a shift that came to dominate the Christian world. This shift had a marked influence not only on the religious life of England but eventually on the understanding of George Fox. Several individuals played a role in this transition, including Augustine, Bernard of Clairvaux, Bonaventure, Francis of Assisi, Jacob Boehme and Julian of Norwich, but the influence of Augustine and Francis is especially noteworthy.

The thinking of these two saints helped Christianity understand its reliance on Neoplatonism while also moving beyond it. Over time the emphasis of Christian mysticism shifted from its Neoplatonic context in the Greek world back to the biblical tradition of the Hebrew prophets and ultimately Jesus himself.[34]

The Inward Christ

In his own time Augustine made a strong case for following the inward Christ as Lord and Teacher. This inward guide was the foundation of knowledge and supplied our mind with what we needed in order to understand the spiritual life. "Jesus alone," Augustine writes, "teaches me anything who sets before my eyes, or one of my other bodily senses, or my mind, the things which I desire to know."[35] Eventually, Fox modified Augustine to emphasize Christ as the light within. Still, this inner light was tied directly to the biblical Jesus.

The teachings of the Franciscans, Fox's second primary influence, focused on the unique qualities of Jesus. Four components were especially important to Fox: the Franciscan emphasis on itinerant ministry, a willingness to suffer at the hands of the authorities for a greater cause in the tradition of martyrdom, a belief that the true church is made up only of those whose life exemplifies the life and teachings of Jesus, and a recognition that union with God is possible only through the person and work of Jesus Christ. The inner light might govern our understanding, but the reality to which it speaks is governed by our experiences of the historical Jesus. As a result, Fox advocates seven basic, progressive steps to understanding our experiences of God.

SEVEN ELEMENTS IN OUR LIFE WITH GOD

1. Every true Christian has direct, immediate experiences of Jesus.
2. These experiences are best understood by relating them to evidences from Scripture.
3. These experiences not only confirm current leadings but also provide new insights as we move through life.
4. Scripture teaches us how to relate our experiences of the historical Jesus with the leadings of the inward Christ.

5. By identifying with Jesus we enter into his sufferings and understand our own experiences of suffering in relation to him.

6. The community of faith is more important than religious traditions.

7. All of these insights and experiences lead us into the pure love of God.

Experiencing God. Throughout his life, George Fox emphasized the importance of experiencing the living presence of God. This emphasis was born of his own experience. Here is how he came to the full wealth of conviction in his own life: "And when all my hopes in them and in all men were gone, so that I had nothing outwardly to help me, nor could tell what to do, then oh then, I heard a voice which said, 'There is one, even Christ Jesus, that can speak to thy condition,' and when I heard it my heart did leap for joy."[36]

This experience cemented Fox's belief that each of us needs to have a real and vital experience of God through Jesus Christ. Fox believed this knowledge comes directly and immediately. We do not need anything other than a desire for God to find him—mediated knowledge is not necessary or even desirable since Christ alone is sufficient.

Understanding our experiences. The need to reconcile our experiences with Scripture can be found in Fox's own writing. When we read his *Journal* we are immediately struck by how much he quotes the Bible. In fact, many of his contemporaries marveled out loud that if the Bible were ever destroyed, Fox could recite three-fourths of it from memory. In the first one hundred pages of his *Journal* alone, there are at least 148 direct references or allusions to Scripture.[37] Fox consistently uses the Bible to gain insight into the realities of life and to show the relevance of the spiritual life to these realities. In every instance, our experiences of Jesus unlock the hidden mysteries of God and of our life. Fox expresses it this way: "Jesus is the opener of the door by his heavenly key, and it is through Christ that the entrance is given."[38]

The challenge for Fox is to move us beyond the objective text of Scripture to embrace the Spirit of God, which is love. For Fox, this meant that the spirit of Scripture, which is God's love, must be exalted over the text of Scripture.[39] Inevitably, this position heightened the conflict between himself and the religious authorities.

Always growing. Fox's third element, how these experiences not only confirm current leadings but also provide new insights as we move through life, is taken from the life of the apostle Paul. As early as 1647, Fox writes that following the light of Christ brings new insights into our life with God. These insights are acquired as we learn to love God, and this love for God brings us into a deeper union with him. These perceptual shifts do not occur easily or often, but when they do we gain insight and a deeper life with God.

Borrowing from the life and witness of Paul, Fox demonstrates how the outward law of his Jewish heritage prevents Paul from realizing the inward reality of Jesus Christ. It is only on the road to Damascus, when Paul's entire life and perspective are changed, that we see the reality and power of the inward Christ. This perceptual reordering is a result of a direct experience of Jesus Christ. It is critical for Paul and critical for Fox and the early Friends as well.

The importance of Jesus. This is probably the most significant contribution Fox makes to our life with God. Following the example of Augustine, Fox identifies Christ as the inward Teacher who alone brings insight. In developing this understanding of Christ, Fox uses two phrases interchangeably. One is the "light of Christ within," while the other is "Christ as inward Teacher." Both embody the Augustinian ideal and stand apart from either Locke's understanding of the "light of reason"[40] or Descartes's understanding of the "light of nature."[41]

As early as 1648, Fox begins to comingle references to the Holy Spirit with the divine light of Christ evident in all things. His intent is to direct us to the "Light within," which is Christ, who can teach us all things.[42] Fox amplifies his position by stating, "I was sent to bring people off from all the vain religions of the world in order to turn them to the inward light by which all might know their salvation."[43] These teachings further alienated Fox from the religious authorities. Criticizing the ministry of the professional clergy for being hollow and vain, Fox encouraged the people to turn to "your true teacher, Jesus Christ, and not these hirelings such as teach for fleece and prey upon the people."[44]

The role of suffering. The fifth element for Fox is to enter into the sufferings of Jesus and understand our own experiences of suffering in relation to him. For much of Fox's life the Quaker movement was officially banned. Much like Christianity in its first four centuries, waves of persecution against Quakers ebbed and flowed according to the attitudes of different rulers. Not until 1689, with the passage of the Act of Toleration, were Quakers able to gain legal status in English society.

This persecution subjected Fox to some of the most brutal religious oppression of his time. When we suffer at the hands of nature or other human beings, we can sometimes doubt the goodness of God. Fox, however, never allowed this to happen. Though he experienced repeated stonings, beatings, general misfortune and torture, Fox always saw it as an opportunity to experience Christ apart from the limits of conventional religion.

The true church. Fox was perceived as a huge threat to the religious and political order of his day. Essentially, his positions initiated religious innovations long before their time. He also sabotaged several religious rituals and traditions that he believed stifled the spirit. As an alternative, Fox advocates a whole new community of faith based on a common love of Christ. True Christians, in Fox's mind, are those who live with a perfect expression of the life and teachings of Jesus. Thus, Fox emphasizes that the true church is not the building down the street but "living stones, those who are part of God's spiritual household of which Christ is the head."[45]

The pure love of God. The final element is the realization that all of these experiences and insights lead us to a pure love of God. Fox believes that our experience of God's love must propel us into public service. We are not to retreat from society as monks in earlier times had done. Our experience of love propels us into the world in order to accomplish God's work. Every social engagement, therefore, is an expression of our Christian beliefs.

Pacifism, according to Fox, is not a nice social position but an expression of the active love of God capable of bringing peace to the world.[46] Prison reform is not the latest crusading notion of a social activist but the active love of God restoring human dignity to all of God's creatures. Honesty in business is not the accidental product of social upbringing but the outworking of God's love to live with integrity.[47]

In each case, Fox sees the endless love of God as the satisfaction of all our needs as humans and the ultimate pattern for our life. Thus, to love our neighbor is to love ourself and to hate our neighbor is to hate ourself. Ultimately, Fox's emphasis on our experiences of God is central to understanding our life with God. Such experiences usher in spiritual confirmation and provide the assurance that produces peace and personal rest.

REFLECTING AND RESPONDING

George Fox is an absolute marvel. Self-taught, he had the most astonishing insights (he called them "openings") into the heart of the gospel message. Using the seven elements discussed in this chapter, I want to comment on a few of these insights.

The first and the fourth elements go hand in hand: that we can have direct, immediate experiences of Jesus and that Scripture teaches us how to relate our experiences of the historical Jesus with the leadings of the inward Christ. Now, these notions may sound tame to modern ears, but they caused a firestorm in Fox's day. And when we understand the full import of the teaching we can see why it was so revolutionary in his day—and in any day.

In its shortest form, Fox's gospel message was, "Jesus Christ is alive and here to teach his people himself." Jesus is the fulfillment of the great eschatological prophet—"the Prophet like Moses"—who will teach his people, here and now (Deut 18:15-19; Acts 3:22; 7:37). Fox often spoke of taking people off of human beings and leading them to Christ, their present Teacher. He writes, "I was commanded . . . to bring people off all their own way to Christ the new and living Way, and from their churches which men had made and gathered, to the church in God . . . which Christ is the Head of . . . and off from all the world's worships."[48]

This utter confidence in Jesus as the inward Teacher and leader of the Christian community was deeply threatening to the religious authorities. We can see why. If Christ has come to each of his people himself, all human authoritarian rule and control is effectively undermined.

But, of course, that is precisely Fox's point. His contention is that the living Christ can be trusted to lead, discipline and guide his people. At one point he exclaims, "Christ Jesus, who was dead and is alive again, and lives forevermore, a prophet, counselor, priest, bishop and shepherd, a circumciser and baptizer, a living rock and foundation for evermore, the beginning and ending, the first and last, the Amen."[49] This was Fox's way of expressing Jesus' multiple functions among his people. Jesus forgives us, teaches us, guides us, comforts us, oversees us, rules us and so much more. During a huge gathering at Firbank Fell, Fox taught the people that they can truly "know Christ to be their Teacher to instruct them, their Counselor to direct them, their Shepherd to feed them, their Bishop to oversee them, and their Prophet to open divine mysteries."[50]

This kind of highly functional Christology insists that Christ alone is in charge of his church. Even more to the point, human beings are not in charge. And no human being can control the outcome. Well, you can quickly see how this teaching could lead to the creation of a loose association of freewheeling religious individualists. Fox was well aware of this potential danger and set in place a double guardrail to guide those who had accepted Christ away from this outcome.

This brings us to elements two and six from this chapter. Element two says that we always need to reconcile our experiences with the testimony of Scripture. Scripture is central, not as an outwardly imposed authority but as an inward testimony to the life we have with God.

Element six stresses that all our experiences of Christ are tested and confirmed within the living community of faith. While it is certainly true that Fox undermined the vested interests of the religious authorities, at the same time he highly elevated the place of the Christian community. Fox called this community life "gospel order." For him the church is "raised up" by the power of God without the aid of any religious apparatus or human paraphernalia whatever. To use a contemporary term, Fox was developing a unique form of "religionless Christianity."

The true church then is found wherever people gather together in the name of Christ and experience his living presence in their midst. Christ has the power to rule and govern his people and give them an orderly corporate existence under his sovereign leadership.

Christ gathers his disciples together and they live under his authority: learning together, obeying together, suffering together. Gathered by Christ as a living community we do not scatter in times of persecution. Rather we are prepared to die for one another and our Master, Jesus.

Christ is our prophet to teach us, our priest to forgive us, our king to rule us, our friend to come alongside us. His life becomes our life. And by means of his transforming power we wage the peaceable war of the Lamb against evil in all its manifestations: personal, social, institutional.

One final comment. Element number three affirms that our experiences with the inward Christ provide us with new insights as we move through life. This is a frank recognition that Christ, our ever-living Teacher, continues to teach his people. And so, new understandings emerge. For example, early Friends were on the forefront of literally every social movement of their day. Witness their vigorous attack on slavery, their efforts in mental health and prison reform, and more. Why was this so? What caused them to do this? They were not more intelligent or better able to see the currents of history. No. Their profound experiences of Christ as a living, inward Teacher gave them confidence that when they gathered together, openly acknowledging Jesus as the leader of their worship—"the Presence in the midst," as they put it—they received the guidance for which they waited.

O Living Christ, teach us what we need to learn. We will do our best to live in a listening mode. Amen.

John Wesley

The Role of Our Religious Experiences in Knowing God

In the evening I went very unwillingly to a society in Aldersgate Street. . . .
About a quarter before nine . . . I felt my heart strangely warmed.

JOURNAL

THE TALE OF THE CONVERSION OF JOHN WESLEY (1703-1791) is one of the most dramatic in the history of the church. History reports that Wesley pursued God with all his might, yet he could never find assurance for his soul. On his trip home from America, Wesley writes, "I came to save the souls of Indians, but who should save my soul?"[51] After countless hours and endless days, his rigorous discipline and his search for lasting assurance paid off when he encountered the living Christ at a meeting of Moravians in the south of London. This meeting forever transformed him.

For many years, Wesley had been dogged by doubt. But this experience in south London was so profound that it completely changed his outlook and reoriented his thinking. He became convinced that the only sure way to heaven was to experience the confirmation of God's love in our heart.

Because of his great experience, Wesley realized that "experience" did not contradict Scripture but served to organize, illuminate and apply the truth of it to our life. Up until now he had been a faithful adherent of three-point Anglicanism, accepting the primary authority of Scripture with the secondary authorities of reason and tradition. Now, experience offered a fourth path to knowing God.

Understanding Our Experiences

To help graft this fourth source of religious authority onto a mainstream system, Wesley borrowed liberally from John Locke, the great seventeenth-century British empiricist philosopher. Locke believed that all knowledge arises from experience or reflection on experience. Wesley appropriated this understanding into his spiritual application and defined our relationship with God as ultimately resting on "the felt experience of the Holy Spirit in our lives as believers."

This emphasis on religious experience opened a whole new dimension of theological understanding. Wesley states that heart religion is confirmed by direct, immediate, inward experiences of God. Just as we know physical reality because of our natural senses, we know spiritual reality by our supernatural senses. He defines this type of religious experience as helping determine the "true, scriptural, experimental religion."

By using the term "experimental," Wesley is saying something crucial. He means, first, that our life with God is built on the vitality of our experiences of God. Second, it is based on experiment and the way in which our experience aligns with those recorded throughout the history of the church. Finally, it is an experience of God that can be known by test and experiment in a way similar to the new scientific approaches that were sweeping England.[52]

As Wesley settled into these new understandings, his preaching and writing took on greater power and clarity. In one of his best-known passages, Wesley defines the whole purpose of Christianity as helping us "find the way to heaven." "I have accordingly set down in the following sermons," he writes, "what I find in the Bible concerning the way to heaven, with a view to distinguish this way of God from all those which are the inventions of men."[53] Wesley continues by noting, "I have endeavored to describe the true, the scriptural experimental religion so as to omit nothing which is a real part thereof, and to add nothing thereto which is not." By true religion Wesley meant our knowledge of our spiritual relationship with God.

On his famous trip to the colony of Georgia in 1736, Wesley was overwhelmed by the courage and faith of his fellow passengers, the Moravians. As waves crashed across the top of the ship and their demise seemed imminent, Wesley could hear the Moravians singing and praising God. He realized in that moment that although he had head knowledge of God, he had no real living faith. Eventually they arrived safely in Savannah harbor, but the disquiet in Wesley's soul would take two years to calm.

Over time Wesley refined his position further. Eventually he came to anchor his thoughts to the idea of the truth of Scripture confirmed in our hearts by the inward testimony of the Holy Spirit. This truth was ably seen by the manifestation of God's love in our life. The ability to express the fruit of the Spirit is evidence that God's love is fully active in our life in the world.

The Wesleyan Quadrilateral

The inclusion of experience as a fourth source of religious authority took real courage and helped open the way for Wesley's innovation in religious knowledge. As an Anglican he had asserted the primacy of Scripture and the corroborating witness of tradition and reason. But his own journey to God convinced him that right thoughts about God were not enough. We need to experience the reality of God in our heart to know the assurance of salvation for our life.

Yet Wesley was concerned about the excesses of religious experience that were echoing back and forth across the Atlantic. He had witnessed some of these excesses himself. As he sorted out their validity, he began to articulate what we know today as "the Wesleyan quadrilateral."[54]

Wesley believes all knowledge of God originates with Scripture, but all knowledge of God is not contained in Scripture. Although Scripture is the source of our primary knowledge of God, we have the secondary sources of tradition, reason and experience. In 1756, Wesley published his only formal systematic piece, *The Doctrine of Original Sin, according to Scripture, Reason, and Experience*. This monograph is his only foray into a systematic study of Christian doctrine. It teaches us a great deal about Wesley's approach to our life with God.

Wesley begins by observing the facts of Scripture that identify the nature of original sin. Then he shifts to a litany of examples from world history, citing both the known history of the English-speaking peoples as well as great works of Western civilization by Cicero, Seneca, Ovid and so on. He then notes examples from recent events and finally concludes by examining personal experience.

Wesley's innovative approach to religious experience is a tremendous help for understanding our life with God. Here is how he establishes the legitimacy of experience as one of the four sources of religious knowledge and places it in dynamic interplay with the other three.

Beginning with Scripture. First, Wesley begins the quadrilateral with Scripture. To understand Scripture properly, it is important that we learn to read it at three levels: literally, in context and in conversation with itself. By literally, Wesley means we have to understand the stories of Scripture. By understanding the stories of Scripture we gain an appreciation for the various personalities who make up the grand sweep of God's interaction with humanity. Here we witness both the great triumphs and the devastating tragedies and come to appreciate God's sovereign hand at work in every age.

In order to gain mastery of the scope and sequence of Scripture we move beyond literal reading to reading Scripture in context. At this second level we gain an appreciation for the nuances of Scripture, for the purposes behind various forms of writing and for the roles different authors play in our life with God. When we read Scripture in context we learn the significance of historical saga, epic narrative and psalms of lament. We feel the pathos of the major and minor prophets. We are electrified by the advent of our Savior and captivated by our call to a gospel life. We are riveted by the explosive growth of the early church while feeling both encouraged and chastened by Paul's writings to the first Christians. Here we see the messy reality of human life as it encounters the gospel. And just like these first Christians, we are drawn into the grandeur of our own life with God.

As our knowledge of Scripture expands, so our knowledge and experience of God expand as well. We may come to recognize that Scripture appears to contradict itself. Deuteronomy 21, for example, instructs a father to take a mouthy son outside the camp and stone him to death, while Ephesians 6 cautions parents not to provoke their children to wrath. This recognition opens up our third and highest level of reading Scripture: reading Scripture in conversation with itself.

Consciously or unconsciously, we interpret Scripture in ways that make sense to us within the framework of our knowledge of God and our lived experience. We recognize the higher teachings of the Gospels and Epistles and devise our own process of biblical interpretation, even if we lack formal training. No reasonable person, for example, reads Deuteronomy 21 and believes we should still take rebellious children to the edge of the city limits and kill them. No reasonable person believes that Jesus' instructions in Matthew 5 to pluck out our eye in order to avoid lusting after a woman is something we should literally do. Common sense and the Holy Spirit help us interpret Scripture so that our interpretation leads to the best life possible, not one filled with people who have harmed themselves or others because of a distorted understanding of our life with God.

Tradition. Living the best life possible requires the able help that comes from the legacy of the great saints of the church, our rich theological traditions, our own thinking capacities and the experiences that come when we live in the fullness of our life with God. The great saints of the church fortify the relevance of tradition as they articulate their understanding of Jesus' person and work throughout history. It is their engagement with the historic faith that provides a relevant and guiding witness in each age.

Reason. Wesley's inclusion of reason demonstrates the need for our theological reflections to make sense. As humans, our God-like capacity to reason allows the construction of doctrines and theologies that place our individual experiences of God in a broader framework of meaning and understanding. Throughout the history of the church, reason has played a central and primary role in our theological understanding. Pascal notes, "If we submit everything to reason, our religion will be left with nothing mysterious or supernatural. If we offend the principles of reason our religion will be absurd and ridiculous."[55] Wesley amplifies this understanding by noting, "Reason constitutes a precious gift of God. It is the candle of the Lord, which he hath fixed in our soul for excellent purposes."[56]

The role of religious experience. Although treated last in the quadrilateral, Wesley believes our experiences of God are critical in confirming the teachings of Scripture. In fact, only by faith do we understand Scripture properly, since our understanding of Scripture is guided by our life of prayer.

Religious experience is more than just an incident of thought and feeling. It is an inward knowing that validates the truth of Scripture. It combines our natural sensations, perceptions and observations and then reorders them so we can perceive our reality accurately and recognize the presence of God. When we move beyond our natural senses, we come to a whole new level of knowledge and understanding. This knowledge is derived from a personal, experiential encounter with God that Wesley considers "objective inward knowing," a phrase he borrowed from Robert Barclay, the famous Quaker apologist.[57]

God is hidden. That is, God is not discernible through our natural senses. But the testimony of the Holy Spirit with our spirit makes a unique inward impression whereby "the spirit of God directly witnesses to [our] spirit," thus confirming our relationship with God.[58] This is how we experience the assurance of salvation. This brings the joy, peace and contentment we long for and seek.

Growing in Christ: Societies, Classes, Bands

One of Wesley's most unique contributions to spiritual formation was an innovation that helped new followers of Christ grow in their faith. Because of his vast travels, Wesley quickly realized many were coming to faith in Christ without any knowledge of how to grow in this new life. As a result, Wesley formed his movement into three differently-sized groups for varying levels of spiritual growth and support.

"Societies" were essentially congregational churches. "Classes" were mixed groups where no more than fifty individuals would gather for instruction and prayer. "Bands" were single-sex groups of no more than ten individuals who met every week to discuss direct and probing questions in order to bring about character formation and Christlikeness.

In order to join a band, you had to answer a set of very specific questions. After being granted entrance, weekly you were asked questions as part of the group's effort to achieve a depth of commitment that led to a deeper life with God. First, the questions for joining the band:

- Have you the forgiveness of sins?
- Have you peace with God through our Lord Jesus Christ?
- Have you the witness of God's Spirit with your spirit that you are a child of God?
- Is the love of God shed abroad in your heart?

- Has no sin, inward or outward, dominion over you?

- Do you desire to be told of your faults and that plain and simple?

- Do you desire to be told of all your faults?

- Do you desire that every one of us should tell you, from time to time, whatsoever is in his heart concerning you?

- Consider! Do you desire we should tell you whatsoever we think, whatsoever we fear, whatsoever we hear concerning you?

- Do you desire that, in doing this, we should come as close as possible, that we should cut to the quick, and search your heart to the bottom?

- Is it your desire and design to be, on this and all other occasions, entirely open, so as to speak everything that is in your heart without exception, without disguise and without reserve?

Once a person joined a band, another set of questions would be asked each time the group met. These questions were quite provocative, and anyone willing to answer them regularly and honestly could not help but grow spiritually. Here they are in outline form:

- What known sins have you committed since our last meeting?

- What temptations have you met with?

- How were you delivered?

- What have you thought, said, or done, of which you doubt whether it be sin or not?

- Have you nothing you desire to keep secret?

This organizational structure has helped millions of Christians worldwide come to saving and sustaining faith in God. Its commitment to the pursuit of holiness has led to an understanding of the process of becoming more like Christ. As Christianity expands around the world (by 2050, it is estimated that there will be three billion Christians worldwide, eighty percent of these outside of Europe and North America), the interesting thing is that many of these new Christian groups reflect Wesley's worldwide reach, including the explosion of charismatic and Pentecostal congregations that have their original roots in Wesley and Methodism.

REFLECTING AND RESPONDING

John Wesley impresses me on so many fronts. His passion. His love for Christ. His organizational skills. His bold field-preaching. And more. Here, I want to reflect with you on two insights into the spiritual life from this astonishing man.

The first is what we have come to call the "Wesleyan quadrilateral" of Scripture, tradition, reason and experience. This synthesis was Wesley's way of breaking the horns of the perennial dilemma of religious authority. We do not need to study Christian history or be among Christian fellowships for long before we see how groups and even whole denominations end up gravitating toward one of these sources of authority to the exclusion of the others. And the battles people have fought over these matters are enough to create rivers of blood and an ocean of tears.

In contrast, Wesley wisely brought these four sources of authority together as a kind of delicate balancing act: asserting the primacy of Scripture with the corroborating witness of tradition, reason, and experience. His sophisticated understanding of the role of Scripture, his ability with tradition to draw on the great legacy of the saints and the rich theological history of the people of God, his careful use of reason as "the candle of the Lord" and his understanding of experience as "objective, inward knowing" provide us with the four pillars necessary to give us a solid structure of Christian life and faith. Having studied with care the ways these issues have played themselves out through history, I am convinced that Wesley has given us the best articulation of the necessary combination of sources for religious authority that is to be found anywhere.

The second insight is the unique way Wesley was able to bring the growing number of converts into fellowships of loving, nurturing accountability. This was the "method" in Methodism. By establishing the societies for fellowship and nurture, the class meetings for instruction and training, and the bands for mutual, loving confession, Wesley gave a structure for growth to ordinary Christians that is comparable to what Benedict and his rule did for the monastic world.

This "method" was Wesley's unique way of fleshing out the theological notion of *ecclesiola in ecclesia*, "the little church within the church." This structure, of course, can easily fall into legalism, but when it is done well it provides an exceptional means for growing people up in "the nurture and admonition of the Lord." The searching questions Wesley used to decide if a person should gain entrance into the bands are by themselves enough to build backbone in any Christian. And the weekly questions thereafter can search us to the depths.

Wesley established this structure everywhere he went. Well, almost everywhere. In the county of Pembrokeshire in the northwest of Wales, he failed to organize the people into societies, class meetings and bands. Twenty years later he reflects on this failure in his *Journal:* "I was more convinced than ever that the preaching like an apostle, without the joining together those that are awakened and training them up in the ways of God, is only begetting children for the murderer. How much preaching has there been for these twenty years all over Pembrokeshire! But no regular societies, no discipline, no order, or connection. And the consequence is that nine in ten of those once awakened are now faster asleep than ever."[59] Hence, this failure underscored to Wesley the vital importance of his organizing structure of societies, classes and bands.

So, these two insights into our life with God: a solid foundation for spiritual authority and a practical strategy for growth.

For me, my study of Wesley and his vast influence all came together on one memorable day when I journeyed alone to the John Wesley house in London. I had been traveling and speaking hither and yon. Drained from all the ministry activity, I decided to take a day by myself at the Wesley house.

Of course I knew well the story of the man who had declared, "The world is my parish." On an earlier trip I had traced Wesley's steps at Lincoln College in Oxford, where he had been a fellow and where the "holy club" had often gathered. I'd even been to sites of his ill-fated missionary sojourn in Savannah, Georgia. But I had never been to the Wesley house. The Wesley chapel and the home next door had both been built around 1778. In the latter years of his ministry Wesley used this home for his London base during the winter months and then traveled the length and breadth of Britain on horseback the rest of the year. It was in this home in the upstairs bedroom that Wesley died on March 2, 1791, just before ten o'clock a.m. He was eighty-seven years of age, having traveled and preached far and wide for over sixty years.

How is it possible that a place that sees multitudes of tourists regularly could be totally vacant on the day of my visit? Maybe the cold, gray weather played a part. Perhaps divine Providence. I do not know, though I am inclined to favor the latter explanation, for what happened to me on that day was deep and lasting. I had taken the London Underground to the Old Street Station and then walked the short distance to the chapel and house. Once there the only person I saw was the curator of the museum, who kindly unlocked the doors and gave me freedom to spend all the time I wanted, alone and undisturbed.

I began in the chapel. It was the first Methodist church built specifically for the celebration of Holy Communion and, of course, for preaching services. In time it became known as the "mother church of world Methodism." I found it exactly as Wesley himself described it: "perfectly neat but not fine." Beautiful in a straightforward sort of way with its Georgian architecture, excellent woodwork and stately stained glass. Beautiful but not overly ornate. I liked it immensely.

The five or six steps ascending the pulpit were roped off. But there I was in the chapel completely alone. I couldn't resist. Gently stepping over the rope I ascended the pulpit where Wesley and many other luminaries of the early Wesleyan movement had preached. I stood there soaking in the goodness of the moment. The earnest sermons of two hundred years, still embedded into the woodwork of the pews, seemed to call out to me. The time was strengthening and humbling.

Leaving the chapel I walked across the street to Bunhill Fields, the famous burial place for Nonconformists and Dissenters. I had been told that the front of Wesley's chapel looked directly out onto the grave site of Susanna Wesley, mother of John and Charles—even more, the mother of Methodism. I found it easily. Other famous Dissenters were buried there as well: William Blake, Daniel Defoe, John Bunyan, Isaac Watts and more. With much ado I even found the grave marker for George Fox just outside of Bunhill Fields. The Dissenter's Dissenter, I guess!

Finally, I made my way to the Wesley house. It is an excellent example of a small Georgian house, all brick with three stories, as I remember. But, of course, I had not come for a lesson in eighteenth-century architecture. No, I was seeking out the spiritual core of this remarkable man's life. Hence I gravitated to the second floor, which contains Wesley's study, his bedroom and a small prayer room. I studied the study with keen interest. In the desk I was able to find the secret drawer where Wesley would keep the monies for the poor collected from the latest class meeting.

The bedroom too was of interest. The bed where Wesley died especially drew my attention. As he lay dying, his friends gathered around him, Wesley grasped their hands and said repeatedly, "Farewell, farewell." At the end, summoning all his remaining strength he cried out, "The best of all is, God is with us." He then lifted his arms and raised his voice again, repeating the words, "The best of all is, God is with us." With that, one of the great witnesses for Christ passed from this life into greater Life.

At last I slipped into the small prayer room, which extends off the bedroom. Here, early every morning, Wesley would come to study his Bible and seek God's empowerment for preaching the everlasting gospel of Jesus Christ throughout the world. Over time this little room has come to be known as "the power house of Methodism." In my mind's eye I recall only a small table with an open Bible and a kneeling bench. The bench looked out through a window, and from that vantage point I could see Wesley's grave behind the chapel. Whether the kneeling bench was the original that Wesley used or a replica I do not know. My guess would be a replica, but it was of no consequence to me. I knelt, completely alone with the God who hears in secret. For the longest time I did not try to make any prayer with my mouth or my mind. I remained still. Listening. Ruminating on the great events of that dynamic movement of the Spirit over two hundred years ago. Time was suspended for me at that kneeling bench in that little prayer room in the Wesley house in London. Finally, I spoke words. A longing hope of my heart, I guess. A prayer, too. "Do it again, Lord," I cried. "Do it again!"

O Christ, Son of the living God, so much of our life feels a lot like Wesley's ill-fated journey to Georgia. We start out filled with such hope and enthusiasm. But we fail to count the cost. Or we don't have a realistic vision of what is needed. Or we make fatal blunders along the way. And we end up with our hopes dashed and our mission in ruins.

Jesus, can you make something out of our failure? Will you? The Bible stories make it clear that you are the God who majors in restoration. Could this be true for us? You gave Wesley another run at life—and what a journey it was! His story gives us hope that you just might do something of value with us. O come, Lord Jesus. Give us a renewed vision of what you can do . . . what you will do . . . with the tangled mess of our lives. It is in your name that we dare to make this prayer. Amen.

Friedrich Schleiermacher

Making Sense of Our Experiences of God

What is religion? Religion's essence is neither thinking nor acting;
but intuition and feeling. Religion is the sensibility and
taste for the immediate experience of the infinite.
This feeling must accompany everyone who really has religion.

ON RELIGION

IT MAY SURPRISE YOU TO FIND FRIEDRICH SCHLEIERMACHER included here, known as he is as the "Father of Modern Theology." But, many aspects of his thought started out right even if they eventually veered off course. Unfortunately, over the years, the criticism of Schleiermacher has mounted to the point that some of his most powerful and reliable insights have been completely forgotten. So, now we offer an opportunity for you to see into the complexity of this remarkable intellect, recognizing as we do that amidst the ocean of valid criticisms there still exists streams of living water that can refresh and nourish us.

As the nineteenth century opened, the cross currents confronting Christianity began to exact a huge toll on organized religion. Religious participation in many industrialized countries plummeted. The missionary expansion of Christianity throughout the world did little to stem the tide as more and more European churches declined. As these new developments gained momentum, former bastions of ardent belief collapsed. One of the most telling examples was in nineteenth-century Prussia, where the legendary theologian Friedrich Schleiermacher was born, lived and worked.

Friedrich Schleiermacher (1768-1834) was born during a period of intense turmoil. His father was a civil servant and many of his uncles and grandfathers were pastors. Early in his life his father moved the family to

Herrnhut, where they quickly fell under the spell of Count Zinzendorf and the Moravians. This time forever marked young Schleiermacher, who spent the rest of his life working out the implications of a religious faith based on vital experiences of God.

In early adulthood, while studying theology, he read translated editions of Robert Barclay and John Wesley. Both men articulated a confidence in religious experience that impressed Schleiermacher. Although he was never a Quaker or a Methodist, elements of each man's thought influenced Schleiermacher long after he reached his mature thinking.

At the turn of the nineteenth century, Schleiermacher's Prussia was experiencing the general religious demise sweeping Europe. The most educated members of society had stopped participating in organized religion. More and more writers across all disciplines were condemning what they saw as the stifling effects of Christianity. Fewer and fewer intellectuals were pursuing a life with God. As a result, a general malaise settled over the educated members of many Christianized societies, robbing them of the opportunity for a life with God.

In the midst of this collapse, Schleiermacher wanted to recapture the vital necessity of our life with God. As a result, he wrote one of the most significant theologies of religious experience ever penned. Of all his works, his first treatise, *On Religion*, and his last and most significant work, *The Christian Faith*, do the best job of articulating his understanding of our experiences of God.

Beginning in 1799, with the writing of *On Religion*, Schleiermacher began to articulate a defense for religious experience that remains relevant today—relevant today because it captures the vital core of every legitimate experience of God. He was invited to do so by the cultured despisers of his day, the elite intellectuals who believed a life with God was irrelevant since they had outgrown their need for him.[60] In quick order he compiled his thoughts into five distinct speeches, each capable of communicating the vitality of Christian experience he believed and cherished.

The Universal Experience

The first two speeches are introductory by nature and set the groundwork for his main thoughts. Speech Three begins with Schleiermacher outlining the way individual religious experience is available to every believer.[61]

Schleiermacher's goal is to show that our inward religious experiences and the way we express these religious experiences directly reflect our understanding of the spiritual life. That is to say, where we fellowship as Christians fundamentally shapes how we understand our personal experiences of God and whether we even believe they are possible. Our participation in what Schleiermacher calls the "outer forms of religious expression" guide and form our understanding of the spiritual life. In other words, it is no accident that Pentecostals report a much higher incident of religious experience than Presbyterians.

By contrast, the inner form is the context for our immediate experience of God. This intuition lays the foundation for the formation of the self, and continual attention to it drives us toward the completion of our nature. Schleiermacher believes every one of us is born with an innate capacity for God. This is the God-shaped vacuum of Augustine and Pascal. But our capacity for God does not mean we will experience him or even understand this experience properly when it occurs. We need guidance.

How Communities of Faith Form

In Speech Four, Schleiermacher addresses the role of the religious community in helping us understand our experiences of God. Schleiermacher makes a wonderful defense of the importance of the true church. A true church, he says, is one that believes and teaches the vitality of religious experience and helps each of us to understand our personal experiences of God. In his day, critics lampooned the church as the cause of all society's problems. Schleiermacher, on the other hand, insisted that we recognize that a church is always comprised of the individuals who are in it. Thus, it is unwarranted to blame the church when it is always the people within the church who are the problem.

First, it is human nature to gather in groups. Humans are social beings and are drawn naturally to one another. It is also the nature of religion to draw people into groups. Therefore, the existence of religious communities is not innately evil or even bad, but normal and natural. Thus, rather than condemning the church, we should think together about why religious communities exist at all and how we can make the best use of them.

Then, Schleiermacher shows the way specific communities of faith help us understand our experiences of God. Through speaking, hearing and worshiping together, we are able to share our experiences of God and gain further insight by having others share theirs. This process guides us in understanding our spiritual experiences and demonstrates that the true church is based on mutual exchange, not repressive hierarchies. In this emphasis, Schleiermacher advocates a community where true religion is the mutual exchange between equals who have experienced God.[62]

Why Communities of Faith Matter

In Speech Five, Schleiermacher deals even more specifically with the role of the community of faith.[63] Here Schleiermacher outlines how various spiritual experiences take on particular forms. No single individual or religious group possesses the experience of God fully. From within the context of various Christian communities, we are able to interpret these experiences of God accurately. Since religious experiences are experiences of an infinite God, and since communities of faith are finite in nature, every experience of God must take on finite form if we are to understand its relevance in our life with God.

Ultimately, Schleiermacher argues for Christianity's supremacy above all other religions because it provides the best explanation for understanding the role of our experiences of God. In every case, we are vulnerable to human interpretations that can distort our understanding. Although some have argued that participation in any religious community corrupts our experiences of God, Schleiermacher never subscribed to this belief. By contrast, he believed and advocated that the Christian life is known and understood only through the work of Christ and the mediating role of the church.

Toward the end of his life, Schleiermacher provided a penetrating interpretation and theology of our experiences of God in his work *The Christian Faith*. This work is rich and complex and represents an inversion of Calvin's *Institutes of the Christian Religion*. Calvin, as you remember, begins with God: "Knowledge of God and knowledge of man is inextricably linked; one cannot be had without the other. But out of deference to God we will begin with God."[64]

Schleiermacher, by contrast, wants to focus on how humans know, and he begins with how we interpret and understand our experiences of God within the context of our community of faith. He develops an elaborate system of interpretation and demonstrates the role of every aspect of our Christian life in helping us understand our experiences of God. "Piety" is the avenue to understanding these experiences, and the perfect experience of piety is mediated through our feeling of absolute dependence on God.

This inverted starting point raises important questions, but it is more accurate to view Schleiermacher as constructing the most compelling theology of spiritual experience in the modern era. All of this would influence the European elites to whom he was writing. At least it did so for a time, then their interest in God would fade quickly as they wandered off to pursue other interests.

REFLECTING AND RESPONDING

So many hats can be placed on Friedrich Schleiermacher: father of modern Protestant theology, distinguished professor at the University of Berlin, respected author, popular preacher and, perhaps preeminently, apologist for our experiences of God. In his lectures at the University of Berlin he engaged almost every branch of theology and philosophy: ethics (both Christian and other), history of philosophy, church history, psychology, logic, metaphysics, politics, New Testament studies, dogmatic and practical theology, pedagogy, aesthetics and more. Schleiermacher was the first world-class theologian to confront head-on the Enlightenment's critique of Christianity. The subtitle of his book *On Religion* makes clear his intended audience: *Speeches to Its Cultural Despisers*. In answering the critics of Christianity, Schleiermacher rooted Christian faith in a highly sophisticated understanding of our experiences of God. In his early writings he spoke of a "feeling" or "intuition" of the universe—what he called "the sense and taste for the infinite." Later he spoke of "the feeling of absolute dependence." Throughout, Schleiermacher was showing European intellectuals that religious experience was a valid means of human knowledge.

William James, a century later, sought to do much the same thing for American intellectuals in his *Varieties of Religious Experience.*

Schleiermacher inverted the way in which we "know." Calvin, for example, began with knowledge of God and moved from there to understand human nature. Schleiermacher instead begins with human nature, especially our experiences of God, and seeks to move from there to a robust theology of God. It is to Schleiermacher's credit that he took the skepticism of his day seriously, engaging the critics of Christianity on their own turf, and sought to give a careful rationale for the Christian faith by appealing to religious experience as a valid means of moral knowledge.

What he sought to do for skeptics in *On Religion* he attempted to do for believers in *The Christian Faith.* Many have viewed this systematic effort to be one of the true classics of Christian theology. In this sense he should be considered the classical representative of the modern effort to reconcile science and philosophy with religion and theology. He sought to accommodate Christian faith to modernity.

Over the years many have questioned Schleiermacher's orthodoxy on key points, even dubbing him the "father of modern liberalism." Perhaps so. However, when I consider his twenty-five-year ministry at Trinity Church, Berlin, his poignant sermons, his fervent prayers and the thousands who lined the city streets upon his death, I cannot escape the vitality of his experience of Christ. And his desire that we experience this life as well.

The contrast between Schleiermacher and John Wesley is quite instructive. While both stressed the importance of experience, Wesley did so within the context of the primacy of Scripture. Schleiermacher, on the other hand, begins anthropologically, with how we as humans make sense of our experiences of God. Perhaps he could not have done otherwise, for those to whom he was speaking did not welcome or accept either Scripture or Christian tradition as authoritative sources of human knowledge.

Still, I cannot help but wonder if by beginning with religious experience Schleiermacher inadvertently undermined the confidence of a whole generation searching for a meaningful life with God. Karl Barth, in the twentieth century, along with many others, felt that Schleiermacher had taken theology down the road of human potentiality at the expense of

God's reality, majesty and grace. Barth's critique is compelling. Even so, Barth retained a wistful appreciation for Schleiermacher, even speculating that "all might not be lost" with Schleiermacher if there can emerge a theology "predominantly and decisively of the Holy Spirit."[65]

The Pentecostal explosion in our day might be a partial fulfillment of this hope. It is certainly experiential to the core and deeply dependent on the work of the Holy Spirit. The additional element needed now, and an element that we are beginning to see in various places, is a sufficiently rigorous theology that can match the passion of Holy Spirit experience.

Gracious God, how do we engage our world faithfully and at the same time on terms others will find persuasive? Schleiermacher was dealing with Enlightenment ideas and the emergence of modernity. We're faced with postmodernity. Experience is certainly important to our postmodern friends. But their idea of experience all feels so slippery and individualized. What are the anchors, the moorings for the ship of faith?

You want us to think this one through on our own, don't you! Okay, we will do our level best. But please, Lord, come alongside us and guide us in our thinking. Amen.

PATH SIX

ACTION AND CONTEMPLATION

Jesus . . . came to a village where a woman named Martha
opened her home to him. She had a sister called Mary, who sat at the Lord's
feet listening to what he said. But Martha was distracted by all the
preparations that had to be made. She came to him and asked,
"Lord, don't you care that my sister has left me to do all the work by myself?
Tell her to help me!" "Martha, Martha," the Lord answered . . .
"Mary has chosen what is better."

LUKE 10:38-42 (NIV)

If you want to visit, you'll have to see me in my garden." My first deep exposure to Benedictine spirituality occurred during graduate school. I had read about Benedict, browsed his *Rule* and knew his place in the development of monasticism. But I had never studied him seriously. Then, during my doctoral studies on phenomenology and Thomas Aquinas, I met Father Winance, a Benedictine monk from Belgium living at the monastery in Vallermo on the high desert of California. He taught on Tuesdays but held office hours on Fridays. In his garden. To discuss any readings you first had to attend Mass, eat a common meal and pray. Then you were ushered outside to his garden for conversation.

It was during these conversations that the range and influence of Benedict began to make sense to me. His commitment to an active life lived contemplatively captivated me. The authors from whom he borrowed (*The Rule of the Master* and Cassian specifically) and the authors who borrowed from him (Gregory the Great) cultivated a stream of spirituality that guided monasticism for a thousand years and can still guide us today. As Father Winance emphasized, to understand Benedict and to understand the active and contemplative life, you have to begin with Cassian.

John Cassian

Balancing the Active and Contemplative Life

First there is practical, that is active knowledge,
which is perfected in correcting moral actions, and purging vices;
and second the theoretical knowledge, which consists in the contemplation
of divine things and the grasp of the most sacred meanings of Scripture.

CONFERENCES

JOHN CASSIAN (360–435) IS CREDITED with focusing monastic attention on the need to balance the active life and the contemplative life. He was born in the region of Europe now known as Romania. In early adulthood he traveled to the Holy Land where he joined a monastery near Jerusalem, migrated to Egypt and fell under the spell of Evagrius of Ponticus (see Path Two). Shortly after Evagrius's death in 399, Cassian left Egypt and returned to Constantinople. He accepted a post under John Chrysostom, eventually migrated to southern Gaul and introduced desert monasticism to Western Europe. Eventually Benedict fell under his spell, and the *Rule of St. Benedict* distills many of Cassian's thoughts as well as those found in *The Rule of the Master,* including how to order the monastic life and what qualities we should look for in our leaders. The exact time of Cassian's death is unclear, but after 432 we never hear from him again, and scholars have estimated that he died somewhere around 435.

Even though Cassian always exalted the life of the monk over the life of the lay person, he displays a grasp of the tensions that exist between the two approaches and shows unusual grace while striking a balance between the two. Cassian's *Conferences* was written in the context of spiritual direction, in which a mature director guides young understudies in their spiritual journey. The entire book is based on a series of exchanges that teach discretion and provide guidance on the big issues of our life with God.

One of his most provocative thoughts is captured in a well-known passage from the *Conferences* in which he states, "First there is practical, that is active knowledge, which is perfected in correcting moral actions, and purging vices; and second, the theoretical knowledge, which consists in the contemplation of divine things and the grasp of the most sacred meanings of Scripture."[1]

Finding the Balance

This famous quote defines the nature of the spiritual path: this life is never simply action or contemplation but a discovery of the balance that exists between the two. Since the beginning of time, followers of Christ have struggled to find this balance. Although the influence of Evagrius on his thinking is undeniable, Cassian develops more thoroughly the way in which our active life opens us up to contemplative prayer and the way in which contemplative prayer becomes an integrating center for our thoughts, reflections and actions.

This understanding recognizes that the balanced spiritual life is a "going out" and a "coming in," an initiation of active living and a contemplative rest in God alone. We are commanded to love God with our heart, mind, soul and strength and our neighbor as ourselves. This requires a life of prayer but also engagement with the world. As Gregory the Great would so aptly put it, the active life and the contemplative life are not opposed to each other but are two sides of the same coin.[2]

As straightforward as this dynamic seems, the church has not always welcomed or embraced this way of thinking. In 430, the greatest intellect in the Western church passed into his eternal rest. With Augustine's death an era ended just as a new and disastrous season was beginning; over the next one hundred years the Roman Empire descended into the waste heap of world civilizations. And shortly after Augustine's death, John Cassian's untimely demise took the other great spiritual intellect of the time.

Initially friends, Augustine and Cassian ended life as adversaries and theological enemies. The great strain came as a result of Cassian's unrelenting emphasis on the Christian's responsibility to become like Christ. Today, the tales of these ancient tensions are hard to fathom. Resting as they do on the important but nonessential doctrines of election and free will, Augustine and Cassian refused to find common ground. For Augustine, God alone initiates and saves. For Cassian, our life with God carries a deeper nuance. Yes, of course, the initiative always begins with God, but that initiative always requires a human response. After all, the Bible reveals God's initiation in all things but also identifies how we are to respond in love to his activity.

Jesus summarizes the whole law and the prophets with the command to love God and love our neighbor (Mt 22:37-39). It is easy to recognize how an emphasis on loving God becomes deeper and richer when we learn how to love God by loving our neighbor. But if God initiates and all responsibility lies with him, what is our obligation to respond? And if we place even a little of the responsibility on ourselves, are we allowing a works/righteousness emphasis to distort our understanding of grace and the Christian faith? Augustine thought so, but Cassian believed not.

For Cassian, the ultimate goal of the Christian life is a direct, one-to-one encounter with God. "Every art and every discipline has a particular objective, that is to say a target and an end peculiarly its own."[3] Cassian defines this objective and end as follows: "To gaze with utterly purified eyes on the divinity is possible, but only to those who rise above lowly and earthly works and thoughts and who retreat with Him into the high mountain of solitude."[4]

How do we achieve this objective? Cassian is specific and direct: "Every kind of knowledge has an appropriate sequence, a logical order."[5] So in order to achieve our ultimate goal we must follow this appropriate sequence. First, we must master two levels to the active life. We begin by knowing the nature of our sin and the means of finding a cure for our afflictions. Then we discern the order of the virtues and have our spirit shaped by their perfection. Finally, after we have mastered the active life, we are able to cultivate the contemplative life. But we must also recognize that without the active life in proper order, it is impossible to enter into, let alone sustain, the contemplative life. Contemplation rises above action, making us aware of divine things and sacred meanings.[6] The table below provides an overview of Cassian's thought.

On the lowest plane and the first rung of the active life, we work to eradicate vice. This is where we confront the eight deadly thoughts of

Table 6.1. Ordering the Active and Contemplative Life

Levels of Reality	Types of Knowledge	Faculties of Discernment	Activities of the Soul	Books of the Bible	Three Renunciations	Desires of the Soul	Theological Virtues	Goal of Life
Highest	Theoretical, contemplative knowledge	Charity	Love of God and love of neighbor	Song of Solomon	Mind transcends all earthly concerns	Perfection	Love	See God face to face
Middle	Action leading to virtue	Reason	Love of virtue	Ecclesiastes	Vanity of all creation	Longing for heaven	Hope	Master virtue
Lowest	Action eradicating vice	Desire	Hatred of vice	Proverbs	Despise the riches of the world	Fear of hell	Faith	Destroy vice

Evagrius (gluttony, lust and avarice affect the lowest level; anger, sadness and discouragement affect the middle level; and vainglory and pride affect the highest level).[7] We are ruled on this level by desire—the desire to respond to God's initiative with a faithful response. We work to hate vice, and the book of the Bible that guides us in our deliberations is Proverbs, with its deep understanding of human wisdom. When we are in a state of mind that recognizes the right response, we renounce the riches of the world. This is the first and formative step in being able to ascend to the next level. The motive in our spirit is a fear of hell and our initial response to God is one of faith. The kind of life that results is one that destroys vice.

The middle level on the active plane leads to the full cultivation of virtue. The faculty that guides us is reason as we recognize the right way to use all aspects of our life. Reason in turn leads to the development of discernment, and our soul's most important activity is the cultivation of virtue. We are guided in this phase by the book of Ecclesiastes and its recognition of the vanity of everything under the sun. We renounce the transitory nature of all creation and indeed its complete vanity, and our soul's desire is a longing for heaven. The theological virtue that matters most is hope, and the goal of life is to fully live out the eight godly virtues.

Finally, the highest level is typified by contemplative, theoretical knowledge. The faculty of discernment that matters most is charity. The soul's most important activity is to love God with all our heart, soul, mind and strength, and our neighbor as our self. Song of Solomon properly understood guides us on this plane, and we renounce our mind's attachment to the earth so that we can be joined to God in contemplative union. All of this is guided by the desire of the soul to achieve perfection, defined as a state of uninterrupted meditation on God alone. Our primary theological virtue here is love, and the kind of life that results is one in which we see God face to face in fulfillment of the biblical promise.

This entire scheme reflects Cassian's conceptualization of the spiritual life.[8]

The Role of Discernment

Discernment is the linchpin for Cassian's system. He refers to discernment as the mother of all the virtues.[9] As he does throughout the *Conferences*,

Cassian articulates his ideas by entering into conversation. All truth comes to light through dialogue. In this case, the dialogue is with Abbot Moses.

We learn through this conversation about the nature of true discernment, how the early fathers of the church defined it, what happened when it was done poorly and how we can find its goodness and value for our own walk with God. Discernment is the virtue that keeps us from the snares of the devil and on the path to God. It is the lamp of the body, the guide of life and the source of sound judgment. It teaches us how to make wise decisions in human affairs and also about God. We will not ascend to the highest levels of our life with God without the proper exercise of discernment. To illustrate this reality Cassian chooses several negative examples.

First, he uses the horrific tale of a monk named Hero. Hero disregards the teachings of the holy community. Despite the ardor of his discipline and the soundness of his life, he goes against the council of the elders and in a delusional state jumps into a deep well believing God will protect him. As the monks draw his broken body from the depths of the deep empty well, they ponder the demise of their once legendary monk.

Cassian follows this graphic story with more germane ones: two brothers, one who is able to discern and one who is not, and the differences that mark their lives. A third man, deluded by Satan, offers to sacrifice his own son. At the last moment he is turned away by the timely intervention of several brothers. As the mother, guardian and guide of all the virtues, discernment is the only virtue that will help us do the right thing at the right time for the right reason in the right way. But discernment requires spiritual maturity, and the key to spiritual maturity is the cultivation of a spiritual disposition that is rare.

"True discernment," Abbot Moses says, "is obtained only when one is really humble." In every case, humility allows us to cultivate a spiritual disposition pleasing to God. Humility allows us to listen and receive from the collective wisdom of those who have gone before us and have themselves lived with a spirit of discernment. We do not listen to every person who is older, but only to Spirit-led, trusted friends who have walked with God.

Cassian's emphasis at this point is a fascinating one. He helps us see that

God rarely if ever addresses us directly. Instead, he works through indirection. Indirection requires that we learn how to look for God. He uses the beautiful example of Samuel and Eli to illustrate his point. God could have come to Samuel directly, but instead he wanted Samuel to learn how to look for God. The result was that Samuel relied on Eli to help him understand God's initiation and our appropriate response.

Another of Cassian's conferences focuses on turning away from the world and ascending higher in our life with God. This is a remarkable principle, showing that we cannot engineer our own salvation and growth in grace, but we can work to limit the influence of Satan and the deadly thoughts that threaten to undo us.

Throughout the *Conferences*, the role of spiritual experiences is paramount. Again and again Cassian emphasizes that we cannot teach or understand what we have not experienced.[10] We must grow spiritually if we are to teach faithfully.

The Role of Prayer

Prayer is the other primary vehicle for learning about God.[11] Like his teacher Evagrius, Cassian emphasizes that it is impossible to enjoy uninterrupted communication with God if we are distracted. But what distracts us? Not just one temptation but five elements lead us astray: the concerns of the body, worldly thoughts that invade our mind, anger, lack of true humility and memories that rise up at the most inopportune times.

Our ability to pray develops as our life progresses. In a unique and honest examination, Cassian describes how prayer differs according to the purity of our soul. He concludes this conference by providing a definition of the four dominant types of prayer and then an extended treatment of the Lord's Prayer that outlines exactly how we should pray and what our expectations regarding prayer should be.

The four types of prayer are supplication, petition, intercession and thanksgiving. Essentially, supplication and petition are the lowest level, intercession is the middle level and thanksgiving is the highest level, where we rise above earthly concerns and see the world and our life as God does.[12] The Lord's Prayer follows a seven-step pattern that demonstrates the ascent of our soul to God.

The Seven-Step Pattern of the Lord's Prayer

- recognition of God

- recognition that we exist in God's kingdom

- knowing that God's will governs all

- knowing God provides for our every need

- learning to forgive as God forgives

- overcoming temptation

- recognizing that God's kingdom, power and righteousness deliver us from evil[13]

Prayer plays an important role in shaping our soul.[14] As noted earlier, the ultimate goal of the Christian life is to see God face to face. This can occur only if our soul arrives at a state of perfection exemplified by uninterrupted attention on God alone. But Cassian's highest form of prayer requires an arduous ascent. The steps to praying well and arriving at our ultimate summit begin modestly. He compares the process to the way a child learns to read: First we learn the individual letters. Then we see their place in the alphabet. Next we learn the rules of grammar. Then we learn to read. Finally, we show complete mastery by learning to write. This is also the grammar of faith and divine ascent.

The key, of course, is purity of heart. Our growth in God requires self-denial and self-discipline. It also requires that we follow the path God has laid for us. Writing empathetically, Cassian notes, "Let every personality try to pursue the chosen path faithfully and there is a chance of perfection."[15] The path of perfection ends in the perfect love of God.

Ultimately, Cassian is concerned to eradicate the eight deadly thoughts, cultivate the eight godly virtues and find equilibrium between action and contemplation. Humility and charity should always be present if we are to stay on track. Likewise, we need to use our mind discerningly to sort out the options we must pursue, both for our body and for our spirit.

Acquiring Spiritual Knowledge

The last section of Cassian's work focuses on different aspects of spiritual knowledge and how we complete our ascent to God. Of critical importance is his conference on spiritual knowledge. Here we see Cassian's view of Scripture and also come to understand the theological framework he uses to make sense of our life with God. Cassian believes that a logical sequence of knowledge can always be found[16] and leads through the lowest level of the active life where we eradicate vice, through the middle or second level of the active life where we cultivate virtue, to the highest level of theoretical or contemplative knowledge where we understand God.

All knowledge derived from Scripture progresses through the appropriate order of the fourfold sense of Scripture.[17] *History* is simply a knowledge of what went before us and an understanding of the importance of these events. *Allegory* is discerning from the events of history the deeper meanings they carry that convey the purposes of God. *Anagogy* reveals the mysteries of heaven, and *tropology* leads us to apply scriptural teaching to our own life and derive a principle and guide for holy living.[18]

Knowledge of Scripture leads us into a deeper life with God. For Cassian, spiritual knowledge is impossible without Scripture, the community of faith, the guidance of devout believers who have gone before us and a disposition of humility. Ultimately, Cassian launches a theological approach that takes seriously the various levels of meaning of Scripture, the importance of tradition, the right use of reason and a respect and belief in the value of spiritual experience. This would take on greater amplification in the centuries ahead, but Cassian was among the first to coordinate these various theological sources as he worked to help us understand life with God.

REFLECTING AND RESPONDING

John Cassian is, I think, among the most modern of the ancient writers. Why? Because his insights into the spiritual life begin with the world of action—and the world of action is right where the majority of us live the major part of our lives. Of course he doesn't leave us there, but this is where he starts.

Cassian's beginning point is fundamental, basic. It is only in the rough and tumble of real life experience that we can truly understand vice and

virtue. And truly know the difference between the two. When we watch
vice in action we see how very real it is. And how genuinely destructive.

A few years back a group of philosophers gathered at a resort in Aspen,
Colorado, for a conference on the problem of evil. As they delivered their
learned papers, it quickly became clear that they were having difficulty
deciding whether there really was such a thing as evil. I wonder if they
might have had more success in their deliberations if the venue for their
event had been in the heart of Los Angeles or Hong Kong or any major
city in the world, really. I don't know . . . I am just wondering.

Vice. Evil. Sin. Whatever we want to call it, it is bad—really bad. It
destroys human beings and wreaks havoc on all manner of real-life situations. It is death-giving. Conversely, virtue is good—genuinely good.
And when we see these two realities played out in the gut-wrenching
situations of home and work, we understand by experience that to eschew
vice and pursue virtue is the path of life.

So Cassian begins right where we are in the world of action, but the
story does not end there. He moves us from the world of action into
the world of contemplation. The amazing thing in this, especially given
the world from which he comes, is that in moving us into contemplation,
he does not leave action behind. No, instead Cassian places us right in the
center of a delicate teeter-totter balance between the two.

We need both, says Cassian, both action and contemplation. And why
is this? Well, Jesus' summation of all the law and the prophets requires it.
Love God and love our neighbor. We cannot fully love God without contemplation; we cannot fully love our neighbor without action. And so we
live in a balance between the two. So simple . . . yet so profound.

This balance of action and contemplation is essential for us today. We
moderns have gone completely off the charts on the active side of things.
Doing, doing, doing. Our lives are defined by doing. Indeed, our doing
can do us in. So it is vital that we listen to Cassian here. Without asking
us to leave our doing behind, Cassian invites us into another world, a
world of stillness and contemplation. Here we discover the discernment to
live rightly, in balance.

Now, it is at the point of discernment that Cassian intrigues me the most.
You remember that he calls discernment "the mother of all virtues." Over

the years the most frequent and consistent prayer of my life has been for an increase of the spirit of discernment. What measure of it I have entered into has always left me longing for more. Perhaps you have similar longings. Is it possible that the ancient words of John Cassian could be the most contemporary of words to speak to the haunting yearnings of our heart?

Perhaps it would be helpful to consider how we might begin to bring Cassian's insights into our everyday experience. I would suggest we begin right where we are. In the jobs we have. In the families we are in. In the ordinary tasks of laundry, work assignments and family responsibilities. We, of course, do not leave these tasks behind; instead we engage in them contemplatively. That is to say, we undertake our daily routine in a listening, attentive spirit. Whispered prayers of guidance and discernment accompany our everyday tasks. "Teach me, Lord, how to work prayerfully." "Show me new, creative options in this family situation." "Open to me new doors of loving, caring and blessing." "Help me to see vice for the slop it truly is, and show me the goodness of rightness." And more.

Beyond this, it might profit us to set aside a day with the single objective of evaluating our life situation. A quiet day of perhaps six or seven hours. In this time above all else we are asking for an increase of discernment. "What am I doing that could be left undone?" "Are there ways for me to be with my children that are more life-giving?" "My job, Lord; help me approach it with a vision and a hope that is from you." "What do I do in my work that is life-giving and what is death-giving?" You get the idea.

Balance and discernment. These are things we most certainly will be working toward for many years to come. We could have no better teacher than Cassian.

DISCIPLE: *Dearest Lord Jesus, if discernment truly is "the mother of all virtues," then I want to be seeking hard after it. But where do I begin? How do I begin?*

JESUS: *My precious child, it is important for you to begin right where you are. Begin with your children and your neighbors and those you work with every day. Listen . . . really listen to what they say. Look . . . really look into their eyes. Discernment begins with loving attention. In time loving attention will grow into heart compassion.*

DISCIPLE: *Yes, Lord, I see the value of loving attention and of heart compassion . . . though I'm not sure I truly understand heart compassion. Still, I don't see how these things lead to discernment.*

JESUS: *First things first, my eager child. The first thing is not discernment but love. So, first learn to be with those around you without demanding anything or getting anything from them. Simply be with them. Enjoy their company, not for what they can give you but for who they are. Take interest in the things they find interesting. Each person in your circle of nearness is of infinite worth. Discover, my child, the great worth in each person. Move past the human superficialities of style and social custom which tend to hide the soul. Stay with them until you can see the soul. Once you see the soul, really see the soul, you will stand back in wonder at the treasure in your midst. This will draw you into heart compassion. In time these things will enable you to see the spirit in a person, and once you see the spirit animating the person the process of discernment will begin. But you don't want to run ahead of yourself. Begin with love.*

DISCIPLE: *And so I will. Thank you. Amen.*

Benedict of Nursia

Learning to Live by a Rule

Listen carefully, my son, to the master's instruction,
. . . and faithfully put it into practice. . . . [E]very time you begin a good work
you must pray to him most earnestly to bring it to perfection. . . .
In this way everything must be arranged so that the strong have something
to yearn for and the weak nothing to run from.

THE RULE OF ST. BENEDICT

BETWEEN THE CLOSE OF CASSIAN'S LIFE and the opening of the Crusades, some of the most significant social and cultural shifts occurred. On virtually every major front dissent and turmoil raged across the Holy Roman Empire. With the social fabric of the ancient world unraveling, the theological assumptions of the first five centuries began to crumble as well. As these transitions gathered momentum, key thinkers emerged to help develop thoughts and practices that would guide the new communities of faith. Chief among these architects was Benedict of Nursia (480-547).

Benedict was born in Nursia, about seventy miles north of Rome. He was sent to Rome as a young man but was repulsed by the corruption he discovered there. Falling under the influence of Cassian and Egyptian monasticism, Benedict incorporated many desert practices into the monasteries he helped to create in southern Europe. His monasteries were carefully planned and known for their distinct practices, including the choice of a specific number of monks: twelve monks formed a community and a thirteenth served as the monastery leader, or abbot. The abbot was selected on the basis of exhibiting the qualities of Jesus. These monasteries grew in number and stature and when Benedict died, he left behind numerous communities and one complete rule.[19]

Benedict's *Rule*

In his time, Benedict's *Rule* was considered the most unique contribution to monastic literature. By 700, thirty additional rules had been written, all patterned off Benedict's. Today, scholars consider *The Rule of St. Benedict* to be based on the slightly older *Rule of the Master*. Benedict's *Rule* includes the general framework of this earlier work as well and presents the first seven chapters almost verbatim.

In Rule 1 Benedict's interest is to elevate the "cenobite," or community-based monk, as the highest ideal, a theme echoed thirty years later by Gregory the Great. Benedict demonstrates that life in community forms the best context for undergoing growth and change. "Anchorites," monks who live by themselves, are good, but ultimately anchoritic spirituality prevents us from facing the complexity of human relationships and moving forward in our life with God. As a result, Benedict identifies key resources that help guide our progress.

Discovering Eternal Life

Benedict begins by identifying the ultimate goal of the spiritual life to be eternal life. How then do we order our life to accomplish this great goal? Benedict outlines the path: prayer, work, study and rest, all undertaken in the context of stability, humility and community. The importance of community is the way it forms the foundation and stability we need in order to make progress in our life with God. When we awaken to our life with God, our spiritual senses come back to life. But this awakening must follow a process guided by the sources of the spiritual life. The process develops in several key ways.

Scripture. God's Word is the touchstone for all elements of understanding and supersedes every other source of religious insight. Benedict helps us understand how to read Scripture for wisdom and understanding. Discretion is cultivated through learning to read Scripture using the ancient practice of *lectio divina,* a method that shows us how to understand the external environment around us, intuit our own inner thoughts and feelings and develop an integrated understanding of our life with God.

The writings of the saints and spiritual masters. Benedict is particularly attentive to Cassian's *Conferences* and requires it as regular reading at every monastery. His point is to show how Cassian assimilates the wisdom of the saints and how we are to do the same in our own spiritual life.

Our spiritual life. Benedict believes we can learn a great deal by paying attention to our deeper motives, our spontaneous thoughts and our emotional reactions. By examining these personal dynamics, we become attentive to the deeper movements of God. This is where we learn to imitate Christ.

Active engagement with others through community. The tensions of our interpersonal life play themselves out in our life with God. In fact, Benedict believes community is the highest expression of the spiritual life because of its innate tendency to force us to grow and change. Being in relationship helps us learn how to view life sacramentally, to see the sacred tapestry of God woven together by every fiber of life.

The Rule. By studying *The Rule*, by hearing it read aloud and engaging with its contents, we develop a reflexive response to its purpose. It is not meant to stifle the human spirit but to free it. When I read the *Rule of St. Benedict* for the first time, its profound summary combined with its sheer simplicity moved me. As we expose ourselves to it over time, its very contents become a source of God's living wisdom guiding us daily through our life with him.

In *The Rule,* Benedict calls us to understand and apply the instruments of good works. The seventy-two instruments deal with developing a perfect love of God and a balanced love of neighbor. They conclude by addressing how we express the life and spirit of Jesus in word, thought and deed.[20] The point of Benedict's list of good works is not to give us a catalogue of virtue and vice but to remind us of the elements of our character that must be formed after Christ if we are to become like him. Every single instrument reminds us of a specific element of our life with God.

Cultivating Humility

Benedict also leads us through the twelve degrees of humility that usher us into the presence of God. First, we must cultivate humility by always keeping the fear of God before us and express this attitude in a spirit of obedience. Obedience is crucial if we are to learn to follow God. It forces us to subjugate our ego to divine love and service.

The second degree of humility is to follow the Lord's will and not our own. The greatest challenge to our life with God is our predisposition to be egocentric, to insist that life be seen and lived only from our perspective. The objective is to break out of our egocentrism and see the world and our life as God sees it.

The third degree of humility is that we develop an ability to take input from others. Specifically, we are to learn obedience by submitting to a superior. One of the most significant indicators of success in life is the ability to accept the authority of others. An inability or refusal to do this is one of the greatest stumbling blocks to a successful life.

The fourth degree of humility is to accept the superior's instruction in learning perseverance. Persevering in our life circumstances develops constancy of character. It is rare for life to go exactly our way.

The fifth degree of humility is full disclosure to the abbot, the ancient image of the spirit-led, trusted friend. The abbot is the spiritual director for the monks in the monastery and is also their boss. To fully disclose to the abbot teaches us how to take responsibility for our attitudes and actions in ways that hold us accountable. It is impossible to face this reality if we share only bits and pieces of the story.

The sixth degree of humility is to learn contentment in all things and consider everyone greater than ourselves. To be content in every circumstance means to accept willingly whatever life presents. However, this can also sometimes have the unintended consequence of hindering us from correcting bad circumstances. Discretion helps us determine when to correct unbearable circumstances and when to be content with things as they are.

The seventh degree of humility is always to put ourselves lower then everyone else. In a sense, this teaching supports the belief that if we abase ourselves, others will lift us up. This practice works best if we are in a situation where others help us see our role in the greater purposes of the community.

The eighth degree of humility is for a monk to do only what is permitted by the common rule of the monastery or what is permitted by the senior monks. The lines of seniority are clear. No one advances beyond his rightful place.

The ninth degree of humility is to speak only when spoken to. The discipline is meant to help us realize that our value lies in the community and not in ourselves. The hope is for our words to be thoughtful and true, resting on reflection and delivered in proper sequence and order.

The tenth degree of humility is to avoid laughter. *The Rule* interprets Scripture so literally with this instruction that it seems to overstate the case, almost suggesting a suppression of joy. However, Benedict is more concerned that we not get caught up in frivolous activity. Laughter expressing a spirit of contentment comes from a deep relationship with God. Laughter that springs from ridicule destroys community.

The eleventh degree of humility teaches a monk to speak gently, using reasonable words and humane tones. This instruction emphasizes the way human speech can lift up or tear down. Speech is the single most significant vehicle for communicating our noblest ideals or our most destructive motivations.

The twelfth degree of humility is to always demonstrate a posture of humility, whether before others or before God. As we ascend each degree of humility, our spirit is refined until humility comes as an instinctive and immediate response. Together, these twelve steps usher us into a state of mind that allows us to express the highest ideals of the community and the deepest possible understanding of the spirit of Christ.

The Essential Qualities of Our Leaders

All of these attributes are good, but what makes this sort of growth and development possible? Leadership. The leadership of the community fundamentally shapes what values are articulated and embraced in the community. How, then, should we choose the abbot, the leader of the community of faith? In one of the most compelling entries in the entire *Rule*, Benedict provides brilliant insight into the nature and responsibility of leadership. Elsewhere throughout the work he lists qualities and characteristics that are the litmus test for selection of an abbot, and they should also be the litmus test for every leadership position, whether of an abbot or the head of a major corporation or even the leader of a local nonprofit. Here they are in outline form.

- The abbot holds the place of Christ in the monastery and should show forth his goodness and holiness by his deeds rather than his words, being an example of integrity.[21]

- The abbot should call together the council of the monks and weigh their input while making his decision.[22]

- The abbot gives an account of his behavior to God.

- The abbot is learned in divine law.

- The abbot is sober and chaste.

- The abbot prefers mercy to justice.

- The abbot hates sin but loves the brothers.

- Even in his corrections, the abbot exercises prudence.

- The abbot keeps his own frailty and shortcomings ever before himself.

- The abbot cuts off vices in each brother as he determines, distributing guidance to each as they have specific need.

- The abbot works to be loved rather than feared.

- The abbot is not violent, anxious, obstinate, jealous or prone to suspicion.

- In all matters, the abbot is prudent and considerate.

- The abbot is discreet and moderate so that the strong may have something to strive after and the weak nothing at which to take alarm.

- The abbot observes *The Rule* in all things so that he may reap his eternal reward.[23]

There is no other single list of leadership qualities that does a better job of identifying the likelihood of leadership success. All current leadership literature would be strengthened by entering into conversation with Benedict's *Rule*.

Each of these qualities is meant to ensure that the abbot cultivates spiritual wisdom and discretion. But why does the abbot need these qualities? Instinctively, Benedict realized that he could neither legislate morality nor control the future. As a result, his very rule contains within itself the recognition that no one can anticipate all situations that will arise in the future. Hence the need for a leader who possesses wisdom, discretion and insight.

By following *The Rule*, we are able to build a stable community. It is this community that provides the context within which different individuals with varying gifts and abilities can become leaders. By cultivating the spiritual gift of discretion and identifying the qualities most likely to make this occur, Benedict provides one of the most enduring spiritual traditions in all of Christian history.

REFLECTING AND RESPONDING

My first encounter with *The Rule of St. Benedict* puzzled me. How in the world could this slender book (I hold my first copy in my hands as I write this; it is tattered and scarred with its bright red cover falling off) ever cause such a revolution in Christian devotion? I puzzled over this for some time. It is true that for all intents and purposes it was the first written rule for monastic communities, but its instructions are so simple, so practical, so ordinary. There is no great theological paradigm shift here. No shattering philosophical proposal. Just common-sense instruction on how to live together successfully.

Then I understood. In Benedict's day there were vast numbers of roving monks wandering here and there with no real accountability, no real stability, no real spiritual anchor. They even had names, two in particular. The first group of roving monks were called "sarabaites." Benedict said that the sarabaites were "the most detestable kind of monks, who with no experience to guide them, no rule to try them as gold is tried in a furnace (Prov 27:21), have a character as soft as lead."[24] The second group were known as "gyrovagues" and, according to Benedict, they "spend their entire lives drifting from region to region, staying as guests for three or four days in different monasteries. Always on the move, they never settle down, and are slaves to their own will and gross appetites."[25]

Seeing the need for structure and accountability, Benedict went about establishing little community structures of twelve monks with a thirteenth monk who would be their leader and provide oversight and loving accountability for their life together. Further, he saw that these monks needed the discipline of staying in one place, hence a vow of stability.

There is more. They desperately needed instruction in the Christian

way, so Benedict established a "school for the Lord's service." They needed
to learn a practice of careful, prayerful reading and reflection, so Bernard
made *lectio divina* central to their study program. Eventually, Benedict
won the day. Unruly, undisciplined itinerant monks were gathered into
fellowships of nurturing, caring accountability.

Understand, this victory did not come easily. The first group of recal-
citrant monks Benedict gathered together with himself as their abbot tried
to poison him! Ultimately, however, the Benedictine structure of community-based monks (cenobites) become the dominate structure of corporate religious life for better than a thousand years. Quite an amazing
story, really. And that is why Benedict's *Rule* caused such a revolution in
Christian devotion.

We today have something of the same problem Benedict faced. Numerous present-day prophets function without any serious accountability
or training. They come to a city, deliver their "prophecies" and leave for
regions beyond, while local Christian leaders are left to deal with the fall-
out from these often destructive pronouncements. Some are on the elec-
tronic airwaves and so send out their "prophecies" without even meeting
the people about whom they are prophesying.

Please understand, there is a legitimate and even necessary place for
prophesy in the community of faith. But to function with spiritual success, it needs the discipline and structure of the community of faith. Perhaps we need a new articulation of a Benedictine *Rule* for our day!

Benedict's twelve degrees of humility (other translations render it
"twelve steps into humility") is quite profound in its practical effect. We
all know that we cannot attain humility by trying to attain humility. It
simply does not work that way, otherwise we would swell with pride at
our humility! However, as a result of this, many today have assumed that
there is nothing we can do to attain humility of heart. Of course, the
contemporary epidemic of egocentrism and hubris demonstrates the failure of doing nothing.

Then along comes Benedict to remind us that there is indeed some-
thing we are to do. That something, however, pursues humility indirectly.
When we study his twelve steps carefully, we see that they all take up the
Christian discipline of service in one form or another. The first two steps

focus on service toward God and the remaining ten give attention to serving one another. Serve God. Serve one another. It is by means of this sustained attention to service that the grace of humility makes its way into our heart and soul. No longer obsessively concerned about ourselves and our place, we flow easily into a community of mutual, loving service. The wise apostle Paul counsels us, "Love one another with mutual affection; outdo one another in showing honor" (Rom 12:10).

Lord, how simple this life of service is—and how much we need one another to live it. Please, Lord, lead us to someone today that we can serve. Amen.

Gregory the Great

Living the Active Life Contemplatively

My unhappy intellectual soul pierced with the wound of its own distraction,
remembers how it used to be in the monastery in those days. . . .
It thought only about heavenly things . . . but now the beauty of that
spiritual repose is over, and the contact with worldly men and their affairs,
which is a necessary part of my duties as bishop,
has left my soul defiled with earthly activities.

SERMONS ON EZEKIEL

WHEN I ENCOUNTERED GREGORY THE GREAT I realized I had finally found somebody who understood my plight. In 1996 Richard Foster and I were preparing to team-teach this material for the first time. I had been agonizing for nearly twenty years over how to develop a life of prayer and contemplation when my daily responsibilities were filled with "worldly men and their affairs." Encountering Gregory the Great gave me permission to be myself—to live the active life contemplatively. I am forever grateful.

Gregory (540-604) was born to a Roman senator and an aristocratic mother. His status in life afforded him the highest levels of privilege and education. One of the last great church leaders to be trained in the ancient Roman school system, Gregory's raw genius combined with his excellent education provided him a level of unusual skill and preparation as a church leader.

In 573 Gregory was made prefect of Rome, essentially coordinating all church business with the ruling authorities. While serving in this role he came under enormous spiritual conviction, selling all his property in order to establish seven monasteries that thrived for several centuries. As his love and devotion to God deepened, his effectiveness grew. His influence spread throughout the Mediterranean world. In Constantinople, the emperor heard of his tremendous skill and persuaded the religious authorities to send Gregory to his city. Gregory served there for seven years.

Why He Is Gregory "the Great"

In 585, Gregory returned to Rome to assist Pope Pelagius II. His prominence continued to rise and when Pelagius died suddenly of the plague in 590, Gregory was quickly chosen to succeed him. Serving as the bishop of Rome and head of the Western church until his own death in 604, he distinguished himself as one of the greatest popes in the history of the church. His papacy was marked by unprecedented advances and great gains on virtually every temporal and spiritual front. He negotiated landmark treaties with occupying armies, strengthened and spread the role and effectiveness of monasteries and sent missionaries throughout the world.

Gregory's contribution to understanding our life with God is equally robust. While consolidating power in the church he synthesized Cassian, Benedict and Augustine. As he read their work, he often recalled his earlier days when a life of relative calm and modest influence provided a life of ease and rest. It was easy to contemplate God, Gregory mused, when you are not scurrying to meet the avalanche of human needs that confront you as bishop. Although he longed for an easier life and simpler time, he embraced fully God's call for him to be pope and exuded a boundless confidence that the best life is one that simultaneously contemplates God and engages in purposeful activity.

To understand Gregory it is important to keep in mind that he saw every level of the Christian life as beneficial. In his writings he emphasizes that the contemplative life is superior to the active life, but he does not stop at the contemplative life. The contemplative life is surpassed by dynamic interaction between action and contemplation. What follows is a snapshot form of his thought.

Since Gregory rarely speaks about action and contemplation directly, we must deduce his thinking from a variety of sources, including extant books and scattered sermons.[26] Gregory begins with a clear definition of what he believes constitutes contemplation: total regard for God alone.[27] It is to fix our attention on heavenly things. But we cannot sustain pure

Table 6.2. Ordering the Active and Contemplative Life

Disposition of Life	Christian Activity	Source of Growth	Theological Virtues	Source of Tension	Works to Prepare	Role of Scripture	Best Expression of Life
Mystical ascent							Uninterrupted meditation on God
Active and contemplative life	Perfect love of God and neighbor	Christ	Love	Oscillation between the two	Rise above the self to encounter God	Anagoge and tropological	Bishops, rulers, preachers
Contemplative life	Love of God	Holy Spirit as inner teacher producing seven gifts of the Spirit	Hope	Internal state of mind	Review what has been recollected	Allegorical	Monk
Active life	Love of neighbor	Four cardinal virtues	Faith	External activity of the body	Call self to reflect on the self	Historical	Average lay person

contemplation in this life. We can enjoy it for a time, but we always return to our human state. In fact, Gregory compares this tendency to a grasshopper that can leap high in the air for a brief period of time but inevitably falls back to earth.[28]

As you'll notice in the chart above, the motion of the spiritual life proceeds both from bottom to top and left to right. Beginning with the active life and concluding with glimpses of the life to come, we see a concrete progression that absorbs each level in the forward movement toward God until we rest in eternal contemplation of him.

Level One: The Active Life

The active life begins with love of neighbor, which is expressed in concrete acts of service. Whether you teach an illiterate person to read, feed the hungry or clothe the poor, every act of kindness is the beginning point of our life with God.

The source of growth is the cultivation of virtue. The four cardinal virtues are prudence, justice, temperance and fortitude. Together these form the foundation of human character. Each virtue must be present for the other three to maintain their dynamic vitality—in other words, there is no possibility of possessing any of the virtues without possessing all of them. This interconnected nature allows us to increase in virtue gradually over time. It permits us to harness the powers of our mind in order to attend properly to God.

Of the theological virtues (faith, hope, love), the virtue that develops in level one is faith. Faith is the assurance of things hoped for, the evidence of things not seen, as the writer of the Hebrews defines it (Heb 11:1). It is recognizing not the irrational dimension of life and faith but the fact that our Christian beliefs are based on the right use of reason and the integration of every dimension of our human nature.

The focus of our life energy at this point is the external activity of the body. The spiritual work that helps us make headway involves practicing the disciplines of self-reflection, self-awareness, Scripture reading, humility and the cultivation of discretion. Coming to understand who we are and how we operate in relationship to other people is critical for our long-term sustainable effectiveness.

The active life is the life lived by people who are beginning their life with God. Over time our maturity expands and develops and we are able to rise above the active life, but we are never free of it, as we will see. Still, the cultivation of the virtues on this level allows us to discipline our mind and attention in order to rise above all exterior distractions.

Level Two: The Contemplative Life

The second level is the contemplative life. Here we begin to turn inward in a reflective state. Having started with love of neighbor, we now focus on learning to love God as the source of all earthly loves with the Holy Spirit as our teacher. As we turn inward from the outside world, we begin to understand what motivates us, what leads us to God and what takes us away from our deepest longings. The theological virtue of hope develops on this level.

Gregory defines contemplation as "attentive regard for God alone." This is when our spiritual senses reawaken and we begin to learn how to perceive God. The Holy Spirit prompts us to desire him.[29]

After the cultivation of the four cardinal virtues, the Holy Spirit provides us with seven gifts of grace: wisdom, understanding, counsel, fortitude, knowledge, piety and fear of the Lord.[30] These gifts of grace help overcome the impulses that destroy the virtuous life. They turn our gaze inward and calm our sense perception. Here are the gifts of grace that help us combat distractions from our external life:

- Wisdom combats foolishness.

- Understanding combats indifference.

- Counsel combats rashness.

- Courage and fortitude combat fear.

- Knowledge combats ignorance.

- Piety combats hardness of heart.

- Fear combats pride.

Contemplation allows us to dwell in a state of mind and existence as long as we can, even as we recognize that the state of mind cannot last indefinitely. Gregory recognizes that contemplation is possible only with careful training; we cannot enter a contemplative state automatically. We must learn to quiet the senses and empty the mind of all mental images.[31] "Spurn and tread underfoot," Gregory writes, "whatever presents itself to its thought from sign, from hearing, from smell, from bodily touch or taste, so that it may seek itself interiorly as it is without these sensations."[32]

In this same section Gregory offers some of his most astute observations from Scripture. First, he defines the central, primary role of Scripture as working like a "measuring reed" because it measures every action of our life so that we may see what sort of progress we are making. It is also through Scripture that God instructs us both in the active and in the contemplative life.[33] Scripture is a door that affords us entry into the invisible truths that must be understood, a dense forest that shields believers from the cruel heat of the world and a river in which lambs can walk and elephants swim.

He shows us how the active life and the contemplative life are paired throughout Scripture. Beginning with Martha and Mary, Gregory writes, "These two women signify two ways of life. When Martha complained that her sister neglected to help her, the Lord replied, 'Martha, one thing is necessary. Mary hath chosen the best part which shall not be taken away from her' (Luke 10:41-42). Behold Martha's part is not censured, but Mary's is praised so that Martha's too was shown to be good."[34]

Gregory amplifies this teaching with the illustration of Leah and Rachel from Genesis 29. Leah represents the active life, Rachel the contemplative life: "The Blessed Jacob had indeed desired Rachel but in the night accepted Leah because all who are turned to the Lord have desired the contemplative life and seek the quiet of the Eternal Kingdom, but must first in the night of this present life perform the works which they can, sweat with effort, *i.e.* accept Leah in order that they afterward rest in the arms of Rachel."[35]

In explaining this illustration Gregory expands on the interdependence of the active and the contemplative life. "It must be understood," he observes, "that just as a good order of life is to strive from the active to the contemplative, so the spirit frequently reverts from the contemplative to the active, so that the active life may be lived the more perfectly because the contemplative has kindled the mind." Gregory goes on to emphasize that we move in and out of the contemplative and active life just as Jacob would return from his embrace with Rachel to still love Leah because "even after the beginning [in the contemplative life] is glimpsed, the laborious life of good works is not to be wholly abandoned.[36]

Gregory uses a number of additional passages to illustrate his point, the final one taken from Genesis 28, the image of Jacob wrestling with the angel of God.

> There is in the contemplative life much mental struggle, when it rises toward the heavenly, when it stretches the spirit in spiritual things, when it strives to transcend everything which is bodily seen, when it narrows in order to extend. This is well portrayed in the sacred narrative, which tells of Blessed Jacob wrestling with the Angel. For when Jacob was returning to his proper parents he met an Angel along the way with whom he wrestled in a great struggle. Therefore the Angel stands for God, and Jacob, who fights with the Angel, symbolizes the souls of each perfect man who is placed in contemplation.[37]

Just as Gregory reaches the heights of mystical contemplation he returns to the realistic plane of human existence. Because the best expression of the contemplative life is monasticism and because Gregory wanted an understanding of the spiritual life that is for everybody, he could not stop with contemplation as the ultimate ideal of the Christian life. Our earthly thoughts and our human needs always bring us back to our earthly existence. When this happens we are drawn to the even deeper reality that life is a constant oscillation between action and contemplation. Although contemplation is higher than action, the active life always draws us back from contemplation and vice versa. The two work in partnership, not against one another.

Level Three: The Active Life Lived Contemplatively

Thus the third and highest level is a state in which the active and contemplative life work in interdependence. Here we live every day in the experiential dialectic of polar opposites:

- Love/knowledge
- Light/darkness
- Sound/silence
- Exterior/interior
- Joy/fear
- Action/contemplation

It is at this level that we express perfect love of God and neighbor. The theological virtue of love reaches its fullest expression here. Christ is our mediating link as he balances perfectly our inner life and outer world. Just as Adam is the first and foremost contemplative in action but lost his place in the divine order, Christ works to restore it.[38] Contemplation, for Gregory, is always Christocentric. There is no way to return to God except through Christ. "God is our wall within," Gregory states, "but our wall without is the God-man."[39]

The highest virtue is love. Through the creative tension of the active and contemplative life we ascend to a greater height than we can see from contemplation alone. But there are not many who can make this journey. Gregory is very clear: "The active life belongs to many, the contemplative to few."[40] It is at this highest level that we understand both the height and breadth of our love for God. "The broader our love for neighbor," Gregory insists, "the higher our love for God."[41]

Finally, the highest calling of this life, according to Gregory, is not to be an average lay person or even a monk, but to be a bishop or preacher who leads a life of prayer and devotion to God while overseeing the affairs of the local and universal church. The responsibilities to love God and love our neighbor realize their fullest expression at this level. Gregory believes that this state reflects the very life Christ himself led. "When our incarnate Redeemer came, showing both lives, he unified them in himself," Gregory writes. "The mixed life realized in the preachers, who are called both to contemplative devotion to God alone and active love of neighbor, especially in preaching and pastoral counsel, are given the highest rank."[42]

The Grasshopper and Our Life with God

Gregory concludes with an interesting analogy taken from Job 39:20. He uses the image of a locust to illustrate the nature of our spiritual life: "The hopping of the locust is seen as a figure of the alternation between solid practice of charity and bold, if brief, flight into the upper reaches of contemplation."[43] That is to say, our efforts to ascend to God will often plod along on the active plane with brief flights to the contemplative plane.

Through all of this, Gregory provides one of the most enduring understandings of the spiritual life. His relevance remains strong because he captures so well the plight of our life as humans seeking to love God: we are never free of the burdens and cares of this life while experiencing in fleeting moments a taste of the life to come.

REFLECTING AND RESPONDING

What a model for our lives today, this Gregory the Great. It is astonishing that in the sixth century he could see so clearly that the contemplative way by itself was not the *summum bonum* of the Christian life. Rather, he understood that the contemplative life is surpassed by the dynamic interplay between action and contemplation.

Gregory found value in all three levels—action alone, contemplation alone, and the commingling of action and contemplation—but he found the third to be the best. In the active life we learn how to love our neighbor, and in doing this we develop into our character formation the cardinal virtues of prudence, justice, temperance and fortitude. This is no small thing, but it comes only by intention. It is entirely possible to be among people in an exceedingly active life where instead of cardinal virtues we develop cardinal vices of anger, bitterness, manipulation and retaliation. So even here in the active life we learn the lessons of dependence on God to look at others and respond to others in the power of the Spirit.

Gregory views the contemplative life as "attentive regard for God alone." How good for us to find ways to turn from the modern scramble of panting feverishness to see God alone, high and lifted up. Here, Gregory tells us, the graces of wisdom, understanding, counsel, fortitude, knowledge, piety and the fear of the Lord develop. Again this is a great gain, and again it comes only by intention. We all know how easy it is to try to experience a contemplative life and end up deeply confused by the buzzing, buzzing, buzzing of our noisy hearts. We need God's peace to quiet the inner clatter and turn us toward that Center that knows no distraction.

For Gregory, though, the highest level of life comes when we experience the dynamic interaction between a life in the world and a life of prayer. Here the virtue of love is perfected. But not automatically; we need intention. We learn over time and experience how to bring the reality of resting in God into the confusion and busyness of daily life. We learn to work resting.

We learn to live on two levels at once. On the one level we carry on the ordinary tasks of our day. But on a deeper level we live out of inward promptings and whispered words of wisdom. We learn to walk in the light wherever we may be, whomever we may be with and whatever we may be doing.

To be sure, we are working, but we are working resting. There is a rest for the people of God, says the writer to the Hebrews, and we are entering into this divine rest.

There is only one place where I want to take exception to Gregory and his counsel. He finds this highest level of action and contemplation in the bishops and priests as they oversee the life of the church. I certainly hope it is found there. But I also hope it is found in every walk of life and every kind of business. Years later Martin Luther would give us insight into the priesthood of all believers. By this he meant far more than that "the plow boy and the milk maid" could do priestly work, but that the plow boy in his plowing and the milk maid in her milking were doing priestly work.

I have a friend in the Pacific Northwest who paints houses. He tells me he "paints and prays." I believe him, for his life certainly is formed in deep ways into Christlikeness. My mother, Marie Temperance Foster, is another example. She lived an ordinary life as a schoolteacher, piano instructor and homemaker. Throughout her short life she worked with a growing disability from multiple sclerosis. Still, I have not met anyone more godly, more spiritually formed than my mother. The same is true, I know, for business persons, computer programmers and laborers without number.

I'm so glad for Gregory's high Christology regarding the intersection of action and contemplation. No one better understands how to live the active life contemplatively than Jesus. Constantly immersed in crowds, always attending to the deepest of human need, Jesus saw only what the Father saw, spoke only what the Father spoke, did only what the Father did. He is the divine paradigm for conjugating all the verbs of our life.

O Lord, it is so true that we are like the hopping of the locust. Once in a while we catch a glimpse of things above the grasses. But soon we are back down in the thick of things. This is the way our lives run, Lord. But we're not complaining. Only please, Lord, when we need to see the bigger picture of life with you, help us to leap high. Amen.

PATH SEVEN

_____

DIVINE ASCENT

Grow in the grace and knowledge of our Lord and Savior Jesus Christ.

2 PETER 3:18

W e are near the end, but really this is a whole new beginning. Within every one of us is a longing to know and see the way to God. For all our chasing after autonomy and independence, we crave order. Where do we begin? How do we make progress? Where will we end? And will we be satisfied?

Cascading across time is the threefold way of divine ascent. Every path we've examined so far reflects the influence of this timeless approach. All paths embody this spiritual longing to know and to grow.

Buried beneath the history of the church are sterling examples of this threefold way: of a deep, inward transformation that comes about as a result of the purifying of the heart (purgation), the enlightening of the mind (illumination) and the perfecting of the soul (union). We begin with Pseudo-Dionysius (I'll explain his name shortly). He was the key historical figure in the Christian imagination of the spiritual life as divine ascent, and his understanding of how we begin, grow and ultimately experience perfect union with God is quite profound.

We'll follow our examination of Pseudo-Dionysius by looking at a writer whose name has been lost to history but whose book has not. The book, *The Cloud of Unknowing*, has captivated thinkers from John Wesley to Thomas Merton, and we will explore its intriguing take on how we move upward toward God.

Next we will look at Teresa of Avila, who takes the scheme of Pseudo-Dionysius (purgation or purification, illumination, union) and gives it an exquisite beauty of expression in *The Interior Castle*. For a clear delineation of how we progress forward in the spiritual life, Teresa is perhaps our best teacher.

Finally, we will turn to John of the Cross and his "dark night of the soul." As we journey with John through the three stages of divine ascent, we discover that he is guiding us beyond the natural abilities of our senses and passions and even the faculties of memory, intelligence and will. In this way through the "dark night," we are able to move beyond ourselves to discover God and his great love.

Pseudo-Dionysius

Loving God Through the Threefold Way

Moses is first purified, then illumined,
then enters into union with God in the cloud of unknowing.

MYSTICAL THEOLOGY

THE NEWS STAGGERED THE ACADEMIC COMMUNITY. For hundreds of years Dionysius the Areopagite, the celebrated convert of the apostle Paul (Acts 17:34), was the presumed author of four of the most famous and influential texts in the history of Christian spirituality. But in 1895 the charade was up. Scholars successfully proved that the texts that had mysteriously surfaced in 532 were deeply indebted to Plotinus, Proclus and the entire Neoplatonic tradition.[1] Aquinas had intimated a possible connection while Luther claimed a direct influence. Even Erasmus found undeniable parallels, but nobody could muster conclusive proof. Until 1895.

As the dust settled from yet another academic scandal, "Pseudo-Dionysius" became established as the pen name of this mysterious author. Despite the scandal, everyone agreed that the texts had done much good for many people in guiding their walk with God. Their seasoned wisdom ushered these core texts back into a period of visibility and celebrity that continues to this day.

Today the works of Pseudo-Dionysius (ca. 500) provide one of the clearest expressions of how to begin, understand and grow in our life with God.[2] Purification, illumination and union: the threefold way that guides our ascent to God. To capture his main themes, we turn to his four primary works.[3]

Four Primary Works

The Divine Names is the longest of these works. In thirteen power-packed chapters, he defines the nature of "cataphatic theology." Cataphatic theology is incarnational theology; it is seeing how God uses everything in the created order to mediate his presence to us. This means that every part of our spiritual life matters. Our participation in the church, our personal experiences of God, our corporate disciplines, the way we see the hand of God in nature, our understanding of Christian doctrine, even language and the way it is formed becomes a vehicle for helping us understand our life with God.

The Divine Names is an ancient text that teaches us a contemporary lesson: everything we do in life either brings us closer to God or takes us further away. There are no neutral activities. Pseudo-Dionysius helps explain how God lets us know who he is in ways we understand. But eventually a new thought awakens: even when we compile the learning of every person from every age, there is no way we can ever know everything there is to know about God. This recognition inspired his second work, *Mystical Theology*.

Mystical Theology is short and precise. It helps us realize that there is much more to God than we can ever comprehend. Here Pseudo-Dionysius explains "apophatic theology," defining who God is by everything he is not. This, too, is an obscure concept, but it has a profound impact. It forces us to recognize the limits of human knowledge.

Apophatic theology is slightly difficult to embrace. If God is known by everything he is not, how can we be sure this is even relevant learning? The human drive to know brings us to the limits of what is possible to know. And reaching the boundaries of human knowledge results in one of two responses: either we recognize our limits and develop a recognition of revelation, or we say there is nothing more to know and we stop pursuing a deeper life with God.

Dionysius continues by describing how "mystical theology" teaches us about our life with God. "In my earlier books," he writes, "my argument traveled downward from the most exalted to the humblest categories. But my argument now rises from what is below up to the Transcendent, and the more it climbs, the more language falters."[4] Later, he adds, "The supreme cause of every perceptible thing is not itself perceptible."[5] This is why a complete explanation of God is impossible for those who believe in him. Even an explanation of why everything works the way it does eludes our understanding. This isn't a copout or lazy thinking; it is simply an acknowledgment that there is much more to God than we will ever know.

Dionysius covers the earlier stages of the threefold way in his last two works. In *The Celestial Hierarchy* he defines each category of ascent. It is here that Dionysius uses the term "hierarchy" (he actually created the word) and explains the three levels that have guided us through the ages. Purgation, illumination and union: these are the steps that lead us back to God. If we traverse these three levels, we will reach the ultimate end of our human destiny.

The point of Dionysius's work is to teach us that no one is given an instant relationship with God. We must go through a process of learning what it means to live in relationship with him. This process begins with the point of conversion when we first awaken to God, and we follow the threefold path from that moment onward. The first step, purgation, harnesses our misdirected desires so that we can cultivate moral virtue. Unfortunately, too often this is viewed as the final step. In far too many cases we substitute moral piety for ultimate union with God. In other words, most of us end up believing that the moral life is the core and essence of the spiritual life.

This is an unfortunate conclusion. Although Christianity is a moral religion, moral achievement is not God's ultimate intention for us. Rather, our destiny is a life-giving, ongoing interaction with God. Moral virtue is necessary but not sufficient for sustaining ourselves in this life.

Here, *The Celestial Hierarchy* provides the mediating link between earth and heaven. In the ancient world, it was believed that the nine planets of our solar system reflected the nature of heaven. In order to ascend to the highest level of heaven, people thought they had to go through nine distinct stages. Dionysius reflects this understanding when he shows how the nine choirs of angels help us understand how every dimension of the created order can lift us to God. Over and over again, Dionysius wants us to see how God, who is ultimately unknowable, makes himself known through every element of human learning.

For our purposes, this creative scheme helps us see the multiple levels of learning. Often we believe truth is one-dimensional and entirely visible without requiring careful thinking and reflection. Over time we discover that there are depths to every situation, and we often come to appreciate that people and situations have multiple levels of meaning requiring deeper insight. Once we realize this truth, we are able to grow and develop.

In *The Ecclesiastical Hierarchy*, Dionysius follows the same pattern. In a churchless age such as our own, when so many believe they can progress in the spiritual life without participating in a specific community of faith, his claims seem astonishing. For example, he states that we are indebted to the church and to its structure and liturgy in shaping the way we understand God. In his mind, the church literally patterns how we will know God.

What if he is right? What if we literally know God only in the ways our community of faith teaches us about him? What an incredible idea. We would do well to consider more of his thesis as we try to get our minds around this thought.

Table 7.1. Pseudo-Dionysius's Ecclesiastical Hierarchy

Level	Office	Sacrament Performed	Object of Sacrament	Outcome
Highest	Bishop	Anointing with oil	Monastics	Union
Middle	Priests	Eucharist	Baptized	Illumined
Lowest	Deacons	Baptism	Catechumens	Purified

At the lowest level of Dionysius's scheme, deacons work to perform the rituals that usher new believers into the faith. In the ancient world, becoming a Christian was a much longer process than it is today. It did not occur as simply a change of perception or an intellectual ascent. It required a declaration of intent in order to be categorized as a "catechumen." This began a process that could last up to two years, with baptism as the goal. Baptism indicated moral reform and the washing away of the past as the believer prepared to walk with God. Purification, if you will.

Becoming a catechumen is like saying you want to be an engineer. It is specifying a direction or path in life that takes you to your ultimate destiny. But the declaration itself doesn't make you an engineer; it begins the process. In the same way, becoming a catechumen doesn't make us a mature Christian; it just begins the process.

The first level of the hierarchy is purgation or purification, which is guided by the deacons. In the ancient world everyone had a prescribed role. There was an order and a process to life. In a day like our own when so much of life is relational, the equivalent of a deacon would be a caring elder or a loving friend—someone who helps us come to an awareness of God and begin our life with him. One of the main movements of the twentieth century has been described as "relational theology." The whole movement is predicated on our relationship to one another mimicking our foundational relationship with God.

The next level of the hierarchy is illumination, which is guided by the priests. If we were living during this period, had confessed faith in Christ and had successfully completed our time as a catechumen, we would be allowed to enter the church through baptism. Once baptized, we would be initiated into an elaborate process in preparation for our first Eucharist. The Eucharist indicated our acceptance of Christ and solidified our relationship with the church. The notion that we could enter into a relationship with Christ without entering into the life of the church was unthinkable. It is through our participation in the life of the people of God that our mind is raised to God and our understanding is illuminated.

We have to remember that this was an age that believed every spiritual activity and process had to be mediated. Direct, immediate knowledge of God was believed to be reserved only for mystics who had devoted their entire life to prayer. Even though this idea seems arcane and outdated in our own time, it reminds us that we often short-circuit an opportunity for deep knowing by believing every spiritual channel is instantly available to us. But there is simply no way our minds can absorb all there is to know instantly. As much as we want to believe that our minds handle information and ideas like digital processors, both our mind and our morality develop over time. We become more and more like what we think and do.

On the highest level of Dionysius's hierarchy, the bishop works to bring

us into union with God. For Dionysius, this level was restricted to monastics. And today this level is almost totally neglected. Ultimately, Dionysius
wants us to realize that our return to God must include participation in
the life of the church. We need its teaching, its liturgy and its patterned
life. We need its community. We need its language. We need its symbols.
We need its enduring presence as the one institution created by God to
bear witness to him.

Every community ultimately produces what it values. If you are in a
community that values intimacy with God, then it will cultivate a level of
understanding that leads to intimacy with God. In this Moses is our role
model. Borrowing from Exodus 19 and 20, Dionysius uses Moses' encounter with God on Mount Sinai as the archetypal experience for each
one of us. His ascent into God's presence on the mountain is our ultimate
destiny. If we decide to ascend our own Mount Sinai, we can anticipate
our own profound relationship with God. Nevertheless, as great as it is, it
is incomplete. No matter how well we know God, he is ultimately beyond
any understanding we can have of him.[6] The chart of Dionysius' thought
gives a summary in outline form.

Learning from Ancient Wisdom

Why should we even bother with this ancient wisdom? The reason we
need Dionysius is that he tells us about ourselves in ways we seldom hear
today. He states succinctly and clearly that we cannot grow into a deeper
life with God without the guidance and support of the Christian community. We cannot grow in our life with God without a deeper connection through worship. Ultimately, Dionysius teaches us that we cannot
grow in our life with God without a deliberate coordination of our life
with others.

The unfortunate message from many religious leaders is that the spiritual life is an individual quest. They treat our life with God as strictly
individual and consider the role of others as an afterthought. But different
religious communities convey the essence and meaning of the Christian
life differently. Some do it well, while others do it poorly. And it shows.
It shows in the levels of Christian maturity we realize.

Table 7.2. Dionysius's Thought

Levels	Faculty of Judgment	Level of Spiritual Reality	Types of Knowing	Types of Spiritual Insight	Theology	Key Texts	Outcome
Highest	Will	God	Intuition	Spiritual vision	Apophatic mystical theology	*Mystical Theology*	Perfect union with God
Middle	Intellect	Angels	Interpretation-driven	Spiritual knowing	Cataphatic	*Divine Names*	Illumination
Lowest	Senses	The church	Percept and concept	Spiritual experience	Symbolic	*The Celestial Hierarchy* and *Ecclesiastical Hierarchy*	Purification

REFLECTING AND RESPONDING

I find Dionysius genuinely helpful. To begin with, he gives us the concepts of the cataphatic and apophatic approaches to the knowledge of God—and we do need both. The words are strange to our ears, but the ideas are clear enough.

In cataphatic theology we come to understand how God mediates his presence to us through the physical world. Everything in creation—the cathedral elm and the Christmas rose, hummingbird and moose, sun, moon and stars, bread and wine—opens us to a life that is in back of and beyond the physical world. How good of God to use the physical world we understand so well to lead us into realities we can barely comprehend and need so badly to experience.

In apophatic theology, on the other hand, we learn that in our life with God we face massive limitations. God is far beyond us. We can know only a fraction of the whole. We are in way over our heads and it behooves us to recognize this fact.

In cataphatic theology, God is near to us, or "immanent," as we say. In apophatic theology, he is beyond us, or "transcendent," as we say. Both are true and both are essential to a clear understanding of an experiential life with God. We have Dionysius to thank for setting forth these matters in such a clear and understandable manner.

Another thing I am glad for is this word Dionysius gave to the world: "hierarchy." Now, I know this isn't a concept we are thrilled about in today's egalitarian mindset. But we need to understand that Dionysius is using this word in a thoroughly positive way. He is making it clear to us that there is a right ordering of the universe. He is underscoring the importance of place in our world. When, for example, we speak of refugees as "displaced persons," we mean more than that they have had to leave their homes. We mean that all their roots have been torn up, that their whole sense of identity as persons has been shattered.

Many today have rejected the very idea of place because they find themselves oppressed by their place. And we should reject oppressive places, for they represent a severe disorientation in the right ordering of the universe. However, we cannot be "placeless." As long as we are finite human beings we need a place, a role, a function in life. Placeless human beings are among the most miserable in our day.

In the Hebrew world, there is a proper place for the aged, the orphan, the widow, the sojourner. The New Testament describes the church as a set of places. The gifts of the Holy Spirit are a way of describing the place of the various members of the body of Christ. There is a place—a proper function, a proper role—for the apostle, the prophet, the evangelist, the pastor and teacher, and all the gifts of the Spirit. So I'm glad Dionysius has helped us to think carefully about place. It helps us see why we cannot live this life of discipleship to Jesus by ourselves. We need the community of faith to be the person we are called to be. And there is a place—a proper function or role—for every one of us within this community.

Now, of course, the heart of our thinking in this chapter is the threefold way of divine ascent: purgation, illumination and union. We will work on other aspects of this threefold progression as we get into the other representatives of this teaching. For right now we pause to think about the second of the three: illumination.

Illumination means, very simply, our growth in the practical knowledge of God. By it we are learning to love God with all our mind. This is why the priest oversees this stage of the divine ascent. The idea is that the pastor/priest informs our mind with a lived knowledge of God. We listen carefully and prayerfully to the sermon, for example, for in it we hope to receive knowledge of God that informs our living. When we receive the Eucharist, we take in knowledge of God in a different way. We study the Scripture—or in the case of the sixth century, if we cannot read we receive a passage from the pastor/priest to memorize—and knowledge of God increases in our mind. Simple . . . and so very essential.

All three aspects of this progressive ascent work hand in hand, and so it is a little artificial for us to focus only on the second of the three here. Even so, we can begin now to experience aspects of illumination, especially as it comes to us through the cataphatic path—through the physical world of the senses and the mind. For example, perhaps we take a day to watch the created order—really watch it. Or maybe we take a day to soak in the book of Jeremiah or Romans—really soak in it. Or perhaps we take a phrase of Scripture and let it fill our mind for an entire day—really fill our mind. These simple exercises, and many others like them, are ways of beginning to love God with all our mind.

O God who is First, O God who is Last,

*   O God who is one Substance, O God who is three Persons:*

*   We come humbly and bow before you. The world we live in has taught us to short-circuit our relationship with you. We're taught to expect an instant relationship, instant answers to prayer, instant growth in grace, instant spiritual maturity.*

*   O God, truly merciful, forgive us our sins. Forgive our impatience. Forgive our arrogance. Forgive our impetuousness. O Lord, our Lord, forgive.*

*   Teach us to take one step at a time. Teach us contentment in growing into your life little by little. Teach us the humility of unanswered prayer. In the name of the Father, and of the Son, and of the Holy Spirit. Amen.*

The Cloud of Unknowing
The Sharp Darts of Longing Love

If you are to experience God or see him at all,
insofar as it is possible here it must always be in this
"Cloud of Unknowing" and in this darkness.

THE CLOUD OF UNKNOWING

THE FOURTEENTH CENTURY OPENED AS A brewing cauldron of religious and social dissent. Embroiled with France in what would become the Hundred Years War (1337-1453), England experienced the utter collapse of its political and cultural life. The social disruption intensified as the bubonic plaque ravished the English Isles, striking first in 1348 and then again in 1361, killing a third to half of the entire population. As the institutions of medieval life crumbled, the working poor organized, first for sheer survival and eventually to engage in some of the earliest efforts at collective bargaining.

With these calamities running wild it is little wonder that the fourteenth century spawned some of the finest spiritual literature in Christian history. Along with the author of *The Cloud of Unknowing*, three other distinguished writers produced classics: Richard Rolle, Walter Hilton and Julian of Norwich. As the garment of faith unraveled, these writers provided attractive and provocative guidance for our life with God.

The authorship of *The Cloud of Unknowing* remains a mystery, but wide speculation abounds. Included in the work are many parallels with Walter Hilton's fine writings from this same period. It is unknown why the author preferred anonymity. It may be that he never dreamed it would have a wide readership. Or, even more possible, it may have been a woman whose very life would be threatened if she were perceived to be writing without the sanction of the church. Of course, many devout believers of this era valued anonymity in much the same way our society values celebrity. Perhaps the author will be discovered some day, but for now we are left to ponder its great message and its invitation to a deeper life with God.

Sharp Darts of Longing Love

For our purposes, *The Cloud of Unknowing* can be summarized in chart form.

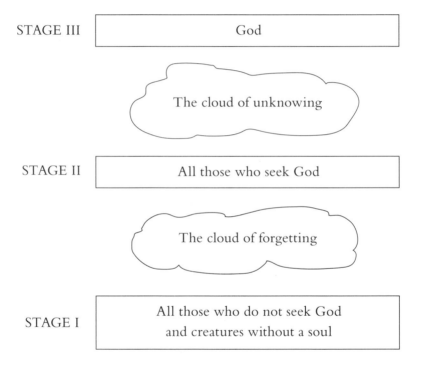

STAGE III — God

The cloud of unknowing

STAGE II — All those who seek God

The cloud of forgetting

STAGE I — All those who do not seek God and creatures without a soul

Between levels I and II and between levels II and III there are two important realities: "the cloud of forgetting" and "the cloud of unknowing." "The cloud of forgetting" shields us from the power of our former life of sin. As we move into level II, we learn to live in the power of God, leaving behind all elements of our life lived without any knowledge of him.

In a similar fashion, "the cloud of unknowing" stands between our life as a fully devoted follower of Christ and our ultimate destiny to live eternally with God. Instead of forming a shield that blocks our memories of a life we no longer want, this cloud ushers us into the presence of God. It is as "the sharp darts of longing love" are shot heavenward that our life is drawn into the eternal power that originates in God alone.

"The cloud of unknowing" is not a physical cloud but a darkness of understanding, a privation of knowledge.[7] Our mind helps us understand that we lack knowledge and also that we will not penetrate the cloud with our mind but with our heart and the sharp darts of longing love. The cloud can be penetrated only when we quiet our mind and suspend our compulsion to prove everything rationally. The greatest temptation we face is to spend more time showing off our intellectual prowess than learning how to love God. The combined power of our intellect and pride becomes the greatest barrier to our life with God.

The Active and the Contemplative

The Cloud then raises an interesting issue: which is the highest expression of the Christian life? Gregory the Great made a compelling case that the active and contemplative life together is the highest expression of our life with God. The author of *The Cloud*, on the other hand, returns to the ancient teaching that the highest expression of a devotional life is a dedication to prayer and contemplation.

Here is how *The Cloud* makes its case. In stage I, the active life, as commonly assumed, is the lowest expression of our life with God. This is where moral virtue is cultivated and moral vice is crushed. This is also the level where we engage in works of love of neighbor and develop deeper thoughts and love for God.[8] But we really don't know God in any sort of sustained way.

Stage II is what the author defines as "the higher part of the active life and the lower part of the contemplative life." He is quite specific as to what occurs here: good spiritual meditations and earnest considerations of our spiritual state apart from Christ lead us into a deeper life with God. We do not come to full knowledge of God at this level, but we make tremendous progress. We are in a transition period where we still rely on external aids for our spiritual life, but we are moving to a deeper place where prayer becomes increasingly significant and external aids to worship become less helpful.

In many respects, *The Cloud* articulates a reality that is obvious today: people are at different places in their walk with God and so need different forms of worship and study to facilitate their growth. No two people mature at the same rate or in the same way, but we do seem to cluster around forms of worship that minister to us. When this happens we gather into groups with others at a similar place in their spiritual journey. Ultimately, though, we are not to stop here.

The highest level, the contemplative life, consists entirely in learning how to live in the presence of God. There is darkness here, but it is not a darkness of absence, but rather a darkness of incomplete knowing. We are carried into the "cloud" by love and sustained in it by gazing on God alone. We shut out every other source of stimulation—sensual, intellectual and reflective—in order to focus on God alone. At this level, we even move beyond our thoughts of God in order to dwell in his presence without thought or distraction.

Of course, no one in this life can sustain this highest level of concentration for long. Even the noblest monks who had the greatest opportunity and the fewest distractions could not sustain this life. But our calling is not to sidestep the opportunity but to recognize our own limits. Our goal is to be knit together with God at the very core of our being. The fact that our groping for this higher life falls short does not dismiss us from the reality that our longing for peace and contentment always leads us back to God.

Like Gregory before him, the author borrows from the wonderful story of Mary and Martha found in Luke 10. Martha exemplifies the active life, while Mary embodies the contemplative life—attentive regard for God alone. The two cannot understand each other. Mary stands for all contemplatives who send forth impulses of love. She is so occupied with the life of the spirit that she has little understanding and even less desire to please others. Martha, by contrast, stands for all actives who engage in meaningful activity but never stop long enough to know and experience the depth of God.[9]

Awakening a Curiosity

Inevitably, every one of us reaches a point when we recognize we will die. When we reach this moment, it awakens a curiosity about whether this life is all there is and, if there is something more, how we prepare for it. When we have settled our questions about the existence of God and come to believe in him, we realize the only sustainable force in life is following God and trying to become like him. This realization doesn't happen quickly or instantly but matures over time if we engage in the right thoughts and disciplines.

When we embark on this path we begin to reflect on the times in our life when we have failed to express the love of God or experience his presence in a compelling way. This makes us wonder about the things that distract us from this goal and especially the harmful thoughts and attitudes that originate in our own behavior. Inevitably, we come to think about the seven deadly sins and how they ruin our opportunity to enjoy the love of God. In *The Cloud*, the author gets very specific about the seven deadly sins and shows how they awaken and how they can be eradicated. Here is how he helps us understand ourselves.

Anger or wrath awakens when our desires are frustrated—when we are unable to control our response when a goal or desire goes unmet. Wrath is simply the result of realizing that we cannot control our world in the way we desire.

Envy is one of the most pervasive sins in the community of faith. It often exists between churches and within denominations. On an individual level, it demonstrates an inability to accept the gifts God has given us and grow in our understanding and expression of them. As a result, we are unable to embrace the gifts of others.

Sloth is a weariness of life and repugnance for physical and spiritual work. In other words, laziness. The Bible makes it clear that all of us are to work. Work is how we participate in restoring the fallen world. God also says that we find meaning through our work. It is through work that we engage with others and make a meaningful contribution with our life.

Pride is a result of an inordinate pleasure in a natural ability or intellectual talent. One of the greatest discoveries in life is to recognize that no matter how gifted we are in a particular area, there are others who are equally or even more gifted. When we realize this, it is the first step to true humility and the ability to embrace the gifts God has given us in ways that matter to him.

Covetousness or greed results from failing to learn that whatever level of wealth we enjoy, our possessions are merely tools to help us along the way. They are not the reason for the journey but aids to it. In the West, covetousness has been a perennial problem, and not just for the rich. The poor also must learn the proper place of wealth.

Gluttony seduces us into believing that satisfaction in life can come from sources other than God.

Lust typically manifests as unbridled sexual activity. Through the centuries Christianity has received a bad rap for being against sex. However, the Christian faith has never been against sex, only against sex outside the covenant of marriage. The entire tradition of Christian teaching recognizes that unbridled sex brings ruin to our life. We simply cannot sustain ourselves physically, spiritually or emotionally when we engage in this level of intimacy with multiple partners and no sustaining commitments.

The main point we need to learn from these seven deadly sins is that our ongoing participation in any or all of them will destroy our soul.[10] But how do we overcome such strong forces?

Learning "the Exercise"

For the author of *The Cloud*, the only way to eradicate the deadly sins is to continue in "the exercise." Now this term may evoke for some of us the ancient practice of self-flagellation, but this is not what *The Cloud* is referring to. The exercise is not a physical activity but a mental effort to express attentive regard for God alone. Advanced research teaches us that physical exercise is good for the heart, helps strengthen our circulation and renews our mind. In the same way, spiritual exercise helps destroy vice and cultivate virtue.

To develop the virtues that overcome the vices, we must engage in deliberate efforts that follow a clearly defined path. A virtue, according to *The Cloud*, is nothing other than an ordered and controlled affection that has God as its object and focuses on him alone.[11] The first and chief virtue is humility. Humility involves understanding ourselves as we really are and becoming aware of the way others experience us.

This is tough. In fact, it seems almost impossible. Because we often justify our own behavior and question others' intentions, we have difficulty recognizing our strengths and limitations. *The Cloud* teaches us that true humility develops only when we recognize one of two realities: our own foolishness or how incredible it is to be loved by God. While I have most certainly experienced my own foolishness, my awareness of being loved by God is fleeting. Still, here is what I have come to understand in those brief moments.

When I have experienced a true knowledge of God's love, nothing else in life has mattered. I haven't wondered how I'm doing at work. I haven't wondered if I'm going to miss an opportunity. I haven't wondered about my bank account. I haven't even wondered about my wife and kids. I have been aware only of God. Filled with this awareness, I have been able to see that what really matters in life is love. Love for God. Love for my family. Love for others. Love for life. It is this love that beats against "the cloud of unknowing." It is this love that takes us beyond our thoughts and experiences to a fuller knowledge of ourselves and a truer knowledge of God.

Eventually, as we continue to pursue the cloud of unknowing, we find that we are encumbered by thoughts and experiences from our past. Some of these memories are noble. Others are not. Regardless, both types of memories distract us. In order to move beyond these distractions, we must live above "the cloud of forgetting." When we live above "the cloud of forgetting," we are able to cultivate attentive regard for God alone in such a way that we experience a stability in life found nowhere else. We can engage life. We can commit ourselves to friends and ministries. We can even sustain interest in worthwhile contributions that once annoyed us. But the stability that makes this possible is born out of living in such close proximity to God that we are drawn by his radiant love.

Steps to Life with God

The Cloud teaches us that if we want this life, we find it by following seven essential steps.[12] First we confess our sins. Every step forward requires an acknowledgment of our past. It doesn't require that we linger in it but that we simply recognize the times we have lived away from God and the harm we have done to others.

Second, we develop humility. We seek to achieve attentive regard for

God alone. This requires concentration. It is genuinely hard work, especially in cultures such as our own where we are bombarded every day
with an endless array of sensual stimuli. But the cultivation of humility
and the ability to concentrate on God produces the spiritual reflexes that
over time make it easier and easier to respond to our circumstances with
the same spirit as Jesus.

Third, we submit to those in authority over us. One of the most obvious realities in life is how many of us lose important opportunities because
of a rebellious spirit. I have found that the discipline of submission to authority is one of the most significant in determining whether a person will
be a good employee. When we have learned how to submit to God, we
also learn how to submit to those who have authority over us, whether it
suits us or not.

Fourth, we cover all thoughts and impulses with "the cloud of forgetting." This idea is one of the most interesting, since it reflects our need to
put the past behind us. Obviously, short of the onset of dementia, this is
impossible to do completely. But it is possible to put behind us the energy
and power wielded by the past. It is my sense that the more we focus on
God, the less we feel victimized by our past. The people in our society
who are unable to move beyond devastating experiences from their past
often live with a sense of affliction; they are unable to receive the love of
God in a way that restores them. It is not that they lack faith but that their
suffering has been so great that they cannot progress beyond it. The concept of the cloud of forgetting can be helpful to these people.

Fifth, we learn to use the spiritual disciplines of reading, reflecting
and praying in order to grow in God. Over time, I have come to realize
that I feel depleted if I don't read every day. I don't think this is true of
everyone, but I know it is true of me. Most of my energy on most days
is spent determining what I should do and solving problems that would
keep me from doing it. My prayer life is often a combination of what I
have been reading in the Bible, what I am reading from the subjects
I enjoy and what is going on in my personal and professional life. Often
I find that reading in these three areas awakens in me a deeper understanding of my life and a deeper commitment to walk with God. I don't
experience these elements as diversions so much as complements to the

meditation and reflection that complete the work of spiritual ascent.

Sixth, we learn to align our will and desire with the will and desire of God. But how can we be sure this is occurring? Over the course of my life, I have had the opportunity to make decisions that determined my life's destiny as well as the destiny of my family. These have always been difficult experiences, but there are guideposts along the way that have helped me. Years ago, I learned to ask the following questions regarding life decisions:

- Is it consistent with Scripture?

- Is it morally good?

- Do the people who love me most and know me best think this is the right thing to do?

- Does it seem to me like the right thing to do?

- Do I have a growing burden that I should do it?

- Do I have the energy and commitment to see it through?

I would later discover that these principles were similar to other writings on the subject,[13] but the important thing for me was to recognize that God makes his will known to us through a variety of sources. And it is at the point that we understand the will of God that we are able to make progress toward him.

Seventh, we learn to rest, especially in the presence of God. This is the hardest one for me to do well. I am at a period of my life where everything around me says I need to be doing, not being. And yet I have a growing appetite to spend more time in prayer, more time with my family and more time on projects unrelated to "productive" work. My best consolation is the teaching of Scripture that advocates six days of work, one day of rest. I have found that without a legitimate weekend I am less productive the next week at work. Without rest we simply cannot sustain ourselves over time. The unremitting pressure of work takes an obvious and subtle toll on us.

This is why *The Cloud* repeatedly reminds us to practice "the exercise" in which we are always learning attentive regard for God alone. This is the only way to root out the tendency to sin. The author takes this principle from Christ himself, who told Mary and Martha that only one thing is necessary—that God be loved and worshiped above anything else (Lk 10:42).[14]

To be one with God, we need to live in the truth and depth of our spirit.[15] We learn to resist being distracted by our senses. Further, we exercise discernment in order to see how our thoughts can be aligned to think properly of God. Ultimately, both our body and our mind help us recognize our need for God and the fact that we cannot satisfy this need on our own. The key is to sustain ourselves in a spirit of devotion. This brings all the energy of our life into alignment with God's will and desire for us. We can know we are in the will of God by the inward testimony of the Holy Spirit that confirms in our spirit his love and presence.

REFLECTING AND RESPONDING

I have always had a love-hate relationship with *The Cloud of Unknowing*. It is, of course, a book on contemplative prayer of a very high order. It invites us to seek God not through knowledge but through love. "On account of pride, knowledge may often deceive you, but this gentle, loving affection will not deceive you. Knowledge tends to breed conceit, but love builds. Knowledge is full of labor, but love, full of rest."[16]

The love language in *The Cloud* truly is appealing, especially for those of a postmodern sensibility. "Beat upon the cloud of unknowing with the hammer of your love."[17] "Lift up your heart with a blind stirring of love."[18] "Pierce the cloud of unknowing with the arrow of your love."[19] "Humility is subtly and perfectly contained in this little blind impulse of love as it beats upon this dark cloud of unknowing."[20] Few books radiate such an infectious love of God.

At the same time, the author's almost allergic reaction to any kind of knowledge or understanding of God gives me pause. Even though we cannot know everything about God, we need to know something. Love simply cannot flourish in a vacuum.

But, then, at the very moment I am ready to dismiss *The Cloud* as unabashed anti-intellectualism, it comes up with this notion of "the exercise," this bringing of the mind, heart and affections into a disciplined attentiveness toward God. In *The Cloud* we read, "the essence of this exercise is nothing else but a simple and direct reaching out to God for himself."[21] So you see my puzzle.

The Cloud's emphasis on "the exercise" arises out of a concern about how we actually free ourselves from the seven deadly sins and cultivate the seven godly virtues. It is here that we discover something of the wisdom of *The Cloud*. Most modern readers are likely to find this section dull and boring, but that is because we do not take the idea of purifying the heart with much seriousness today. We are captivated by the love language of *The Cloud*, but all this moralizing seems a bit much. Such thinking only stunts our spiritual growth.

The writer, of course, is working with us on the first stage of the threefold way: purgation. How important it is for us to deal with the deeply ingrained habits of sin. And to cultivate deeply ingrained habits of virtue. Without this double purifying of heart, mind and spirit, we can never truly enter the mystical way of love. So I urge us to give sustained attention to this middle section of *The Cloud*. It may lack the euphoric flights of ecstasy we often crave, but it is rock-solid guidance for a moral life. A disciplined attentiveness toward God is a deep need in our day.

In point of fact, however, the efforts of "the exercise" are purely and simply a practical outflow of our love for God. So, in reality we discover that the two experiences—our disciplined attentiveness toward God through "the exercises" and our piercing the cloud of unknowing with short darts of longing love—actually flow into one reality. The author of *The Cloud* reminds us that "in this exercise God is perfectly loved for himself."[22]

So then, how do we secure a handle on the life of pure love commended to us in *The Cloud*? I think it is best for us to start with this first and most basic level of purgation. Purifying the mind. Purifying the heart. Purifying the soul. But we go about it with this difference. We hold our lives into the light of God's presence by means of love and for the sake of love. Every action, every thought, every imperfection is held up into the light of God's love. We are surrounded by love and baptized in love. In this way we experience forgiveness and acceptance and affirmation. In this way we rise above the cloud of forgetting. And in this way, in God's time, we too will be able to shoot short darts of longing love into the cloud of unknowing.

O God of mystery and of love, we do want to love you more fully and we sense somehow that "the exercise" of The Cloud *is critical to this end. O, to always have an attentive regard for you alone. O, to have an ordered and controlled affection that is always God-directed. O, to have a heart and mind and spirit that always swing like a needle to the polestar of the Spirit.*

May we, dear Lord, grow in our practice of thinking your thoughts after you. Amen.

Teresa of Avila

Entering Christ's Mansion

Consider our soul to be like a castle made entirely out of a
diamond or of very clear crystal in which there are many rooms.

THE INTERIOR CASTLE

THE SIXTEENTH CENTURY WAS ONE OF the most spectacular periods in the history of Christianity. It was filled with calamity on every front. The social cohesion of Europe was blowing apart. The long decline of the Roman Catholic Church was culminating in the Protestant Reformation, and monasteries all across Europe were closing. Political alliances never dreamed possible were forming. Some of the most profound prose and poetry in world literature surfaced in this period. Whole new economic industries developed, and entire social empires collapsed. And all of the tensions ravaging Europe were present in the church.

Luther, Calvin and Zwingli captivated the underclass and gave meaning and direction to the longings of many to be free of religious oppression. Ignatius of Loyola countered with some of the most profound global initiatives in modern Christian history. Together these countervailing forces created the fertile seedbed from which sprung fresh new advances in the spiritual life.

Eventually, the warring factions settled their differences and entire countries entered into new religious alliances. Sweden and Norway became Protestant, England became Anglican, while France and Spain remained staunchly Roman Catholic. In the midst of this uproar, Teresa de Cepeda y Ahumada was born in 1515, just two years before Luther launched the Reformation. She would die in 1582 as Teresa of Avila after catapulting the threefold way onto the world stage and displaying her own religious genius.

Teresa's work is best understood from three key texts. Her *Life of St. Teresa* is considered the finest spiritual autobiography written in the time period between Augustine's *Confessions* and Merton's *Seven Storey Mountain*. Her second work, *The Way of Perfection*, deals with the life of prayer in the context of community and amplifies how we live out of the highest state of the spiritual life: the life of union or perfect communion with God. Her final major writing, *The Interior Castle*, plots our road map for the spiritual life.[23] Its rare ability to explain the nature and destiny of our life with God makes it an especially important work.

The Genius of Teresa

The genius of Teresa's writings is her ability to conceptualize the different phases of the spiritual journey. Her works define seven distinct stages or "dwelling places" in our life with God. As Teresa notes, the ultimate goal of this journey is spiritual intimacy with God.[24]

The Interior Castle follows the threefold order of Dionysius,[25] using the analogy of a castle—we enter the inner chamber of our soul to experience enduring intimacy with Jesus Christ. The first, second and third dwelling places focus on the elements of purgation or purification. The fourth dwelling place transitions to illumination. The fifth, sixth and seventh dwelling places focus on union and perfect communion with God. For Teresa, this union is not a matter of intellect but of a life committed to the love of God. As we progress through each mansion or dwelling place, we achieve unbroken momentum as our soul is united with Christ.

The First Dwelling Place: Entering In

Teresa begins by focusing on the beauty and possibility of every human soul. The destiny of each one of us is to live eternally with God. By effort, we can enter into this life and make great progress if we so desire. "There is nothing comparable to the magnificent beauty of a soul and its marvelous capacity," Teresa writes. "Indeed our intellects, however keen, can hardly comprehend it just as they cannot comprehend God."[26]

As we enter into this life, we begin to see the radiant majesty of God's invitation and our glorious opportunity. "Let us consider that this castle has many dwelling places; some up above, others down below, others to the sides; and in the center and middle is the main dwelling place where the very secret exchanges between God and the soul take place."[27] To arrive at the center room requires that we enter the castle and the doorway to this whole remarkable adventure through prayer. In fact, every level requires a different type of prayer as we move deeper in our life with God.

But the main point initially is to decide to enter. To leave the world behind is to choose to embrace life with God. It is to turn away from external preoccupation. Eventually we will see the proper place of the external life, but for now it is an impediment to our life with God.

Teresa wants us to understand this perspective. "There are souls so ill," she observes, "and so accustomed to being involved in external matters, that there is no remedy. They are now so used to dealing with the insects and vermin that are in this wall surrounding the castle that they have become almost like them."[28]

It is in the first dwelling place that we entrust our soul to God. We realize we are created in his image and must recover our fallen nature. This requires that we turn our back on seeking happiness and contentment in the ways of the world and seek to find it in God. As a first step, we cultivate virtue.

Unfortunately, not everyone who enters the castle continues their journey with God. Many start, but few finish. Teresa tells us why. "During the period of a month they will sometimes pray, but their minds are then filled with business matters that ordinarily occupy them. They are so attracted to these things that they are not able to proceed correctly."[29] But those who persevere experience enough of the presence of God to be drawn toward the second dwelling place.

The Second Dwelling Place: Continuing On

Our entry into the second dwelling place comes through perseverance. Even after we begin the spiritual journey, we can still succumb to the temptation of believing that the world provides the contentment we seek. In this case we are like the seed sown on hard soil that sprouts but quickly withers because it cannot take root (Mt 13).

In the second dwelling place, external aids to God's grace increase our power to resist the ways and distractions of the world. Sermons, edifying conversations with other Christians, spiritual disciplines and verbal prayer are only a few of the aids that strengthen our resolve and ground our life in God. These aids fill our mind with thoughts of God and help us obey and follow him.

To remain in the second dwelling place requires determination. Having discerned the correct path, we have to decide to continue in it. Our natural faculties war within us. Reason persuades us that the pleasures of this life will satisfy our eternal longings. We must remain strong in our choice to progress forward and upward in the spiritual life.

We are assisted in this process in the second dwelling place when we realize both the strengths and limitations of our natural faculties of memory, intelligence and will. Memory helps us remember the great saints of the past who lived this life and give us confidence that it ends as we hope. Our will is motivated to love as we experience love, and as we enter into the communion of saints, we choose to enjoy fellowship with them. Finally, our intellect helps us see that we will not find a more hopeful destination. This convinces us that the upward path will lead to enduring intimacy with God. It is here that we conclude that our highest goal in life is to bring our will into perfect conformity with the will of God.[30]

The Third Dwelling Place: Learning Respect

When we enter the third dwelling place, we learn to fear and respect God. It is here that we practice love of neighbor as an act of obedience to God.

Teresa is mindful that we are never free of venial sins—those sins that arise in our mind and cause normal disruptions. But she does believe we can move beyond the power they wield over us. The third dwelling place is where this process begins. We begin to recognize that forsaking the things of the world is not enough. We must develop humility. True humility awakens when we recognize how strong our desire is for God and yet how distant our goal and how often we are unable to attain it.[31]

Humility also develops as a result of being in relationship with other people. At its core, humility is a recognition that for all the gifts God has given us, we still do not have them all. We are then able to recognize the gifts God has given to others. Humility is the recognition of our own limitations.

The Fourth Dwelling Place: The Majesty of God's Love

Moving from purgation to illumination, we develop a new awareness of God as we enter into contemplative prayer and experience a deeper reality of God's love. This is the point of God's grand entry into our spiritual journey. Our longing and desire for God gives way as his power overwhelms us with the majesty of his love.

We desire to please God. The outward disciplines that have dominated our life yield to inward disciplines of prayer and devotion. In Teresa's mind, it is at this point that we no longer need discursive reason. We have found enough reason to believe. Now we accept the truths of God as we discover them and begin to gain a deeper understanding of the ways of Christ.

As we seek God we begin to experience his presence in real and profound ways. Our spiritual experiences of God are now on a completely different order. They are like an underground stream that fills a bottomless well.

Teresa offers a wonderful analogy at this point. Our spiritual experiences come either from God's aqueduct through elaborate disciplines and ardent effort, or from a spiritual reservoir deep within us that is directly supplied by God alone. Either way, water is always flowing from the stream of God's eternal supply. Both water from the aqueduct (effort) and water from the reservoir (God alone) sustain us in our spiritual journey.

How then can we access this living water? We begin, as mentioned above, by cultivating true humility and recognizing all God has done for us that we do not deserve. Next, we move beyond the knowledge we obtain from our senses and our faculties. This is not easy. We have become so accustomed to trusting our senses that moving beyond their power is nearly impossible. Think about how often we enjoy worship because it "ministers" to us. What we mean is that something has stimulated our senses in a way we enjoyed—a mark of a spiritual dilettante.

Still, it is genuinely difficult to move beyond reliance on our natural faculties. Our disposition to trust memory, intelligence and will is so strong that we can barely conceive of not relying on them. Yet we must throw off their power if we are to make progress in our life with God. Essentially, our senses and faculties have developed habits that keep us from loving God fully. Breaking these habits is necessary if we are to move into a deeper life with God.

Fortunately, God does not hold our wanderings against us. He invites us back and draws us close over and over again. Through prayer, we begin to experience God's presence in new and profound ways. As our life with God deepens, we recognize the right use of all our natural capacities. We begin to recognize how God works.

The work God performs on our soul is easy and light (Mt 11:28-30). It is meant to lead us into greater understanding. It utilizes the intellect but moves beyond it, recognizing its natural limits. Ultimately, God draws us beyond the power of our own selves and into his loving embrace.[32]

The Fifth Dwelling Place: The Prayer of Union

At this point a critical change occurs. The fifth dwelling place moves beyond our natural senses and faculties and relies on our spiritual understanding. Teresa emphasizes that at this level we are no longer capable of human understanding.[33] We are entering the territory where our intuitions of God exceed the limits of our rational thoughts of him—where, as Pascal notes, "the heart has its reasons which reason cannot know."

Here we glimpse our first tangible understanding of union with God, but we are not able to articulate it. We do, however, enter into a deeper life of prayer and contemplation, experiencing a closeness to God that manifests itself in a deeper love of our neighbor. None of our natural faculties—memory, intelligence or will—work any longer.[34] We recognize that union with God will satisfy us in a way nothing else in this world can.

But how can we be sure we are in a deeper place? We know because God provides the inward testimony of his Spirit. As we move beyond our natural senses and faculties, our capacity for inward knowing illumines our life with God. Teresa shows how we move beyond the prayer of recollection and the prayer of quiet into the prayer of union. It is through the prayer of union that we develop a longing to be joined eternally with

God. She borrows from the life of the silkworm to make her point.

Our soul grows from all the good work of the community of faith: by confession, reading good books, listening to provocative sermons and observing the lives of the great saints that have gone before us. But like the silkworm, our soul is destined for something more. Just as the silkworm must change into a butterfly, so our soul must change in order to be united with God. As this metamorphosis occurs, we prepare to make the last significant push in our spiritual journey.

The Sixth Dwelling Place: Inward Hearing

Next we realize that our ultimate goal is perpetual communion with God. We are so deeply touched by God's love that we feel inward pain when we are not in his presence. We long for perfect union but are not yet able to sustain it. Teresa admits that it took her forty years to arrive at this place.[35]

In the sixth dwelling place our soul experiences inward hearing—we recognize the voice of Christ speaking to us directly. What we are hearing is Christ calling to us from the seventh dwelling place, encouraging us to keep coming toward him so that we can fully embrace him.[36]

We now begin to experience a longing that Teresa describes as a "loving pain."[37] As we hear Christ's voice and experience this pain, we also become vulnerable to being led astray. How then do we tell when something is from God and when it is not? In one of the most fascinating sections of the entire work, Teresa offers clear guidance in how we can distinguish the voice of God from that of the devil or our imagination.[38]

When the leading is from God, Teresa writes, it comes through words that are very different from our common speech. Leading from God comforts us and restores community. It lingers a long time and becomes an ever more weighty concern. When the leading is from God it also brings a sense of certitude, peace and inner delight. It produces a profound breakthrough and fresh new insight. Our Spirit-led, trusted friends confirm the leading, and our thoughts surrounding the leading dwell on God alone.[39]

Ultimately, we know our leadings are from God when we experience a higher spiritual experience of ecstasy.[40] Although most of our spiritual experiences occur over time, we occasionally have moments of instantaneous rapture. This is when God comes to us immediately and in ways that exceed all human thought or expression. And this instantaneous experience of rapture confirms our spiritual leadings.

The final result of a leading from God is expressed in several profound ways. First, we cease to esteem anything earthly as having lasting significance or value. Next, we develop a level of self-knowledge that leads to true humility. We are particularly mindful that a creature as low as us is being given attention by such a great God. Finally, we are able to see the real grandeur of God and are overwhelmed by it.

The Seventh Dwelling Place: Perfect Peace

Finally we enter into perfect union with God. We undergo complete transformation and experience a state of ultimate peace. Echoing earlier mystics who emphasized *apatheia,* Teresa sees complete peace as the right ordering of every thought, desire and action—a rare state realized only near death. At this point we experience complete release from all striving. All our faculties, all our senses and all our passions are satisfied. Teresa notes that she herself has experienced this state only once for four hours, but even this brief glimpse set off a perpetual longing that has never ceased.

The seventh dwelling place is also where we enter into a permanent relationship with Christ. Our commitment is now irrevocable. The soul experiences spiritual marriage with Christ that can never be undone. The Lord visits the center of our soul.[41] We recognize that our entire existence is joined to him, and a radiant beam shines forth from the center of our soul where Christ dwells. Christ in us is a force so powerful that every sense and faculty is overwhelmed. The radiant beams shining forth casts a completely different light on our entire existence. It is at this point that we achieve a stability of purpose and a constancy of virtue that we enjoy at no other level.[42] This new realization helps solidify our confidence in Christ and the Christian life.

Although the seven dwelling places distill an arduous process and years of spiritual growth, Teresa never envisions this life as happening apart from the people of God. When we love both God and neighbor, we live with an awareness of the necessity of balancing the active and contemplative life. After all, Mary and Martha must walk together. The union we enjoy with Christ keeps us focused on what is essential in our life day by day.

REFLECTING AND RESPONDING

Teresa was an astonishing woman, and her book, *The Interior Castle*, even more so. This book is one of the premier writings on prayer from the Christian tradition, and it grew out of what Teresa called a "second conversion" experience.

For twenty years Teresa had faithfully lived out God's call on her life. But they were years of spiritual dryness. A Sahara of the heart, if you please. Then one day upon entering the church her eyes fell on a statue of Jesus that had been brought to the convent in preparation for a celebration. It depicted Jesus covered with wounds from the crucifixion. As she gazed on the statue, something moved within the deepest part of her spirit. She could do nothing but fall at Jesus' feet as she contemplated how much he had suffered and how ungrateful she had been toward his love. While lying at the feet of the statue, she begged Christ to give her the strength never to offend him again.

This "second conversion" had dramatic results. After her encounter with the absolute holiness of God, Teresa began to experience a deep and abiding pain associated with her own sense of distance from God. Teresa experienced the holiness of God in such a profound way that she was propelled to commit every ounce of her being into becoming more holy herself, into becoming more like Jesus, into drawing nearer and nearer to the heart of God. *The Interior Castle* ultimately became an autobiographical description of her deepening experiences of entering into the inmost regions of the "palace where the king lives."

The Interior Castle positively dances with metaphor, an extended metaphor really, picturing the soul as a crystal or a diamond castle. Nothing quite compares to its galvanizing, almost erotic description of communion with God. The soul is a paradise where the Lord says he finds his delight. The body is the outer walls of the castle. Self-knowledge is a room in that castle. In the final dwelling places, we come to the ultimate arrival of spiritual intimacy between God and ourselves—union. Here Teresa turns, as if inevitably, to the metaphor of marriage. Not marriage as a modest, domestic arrangement. Oh, no. This is marriage as the passionate union of the beloveds where "God carries off for Himself the entire soul, and, as to someone who is His own and His spouse."[43]

There are three supreme values to *The Interior Castle* that I want to mention. First, it fills us with an almost overwhelming appreciation for the splendor, nobility and vast reality of the human soul. Teresa urges us to "visualize your soul as vast, spacious, and plentiful." What a refreshing corrective this is to the modern trivializing of the soul. We today so easily shrink the person down to a consumer—or even a commodity. How much better to attend to Teresa and her sense of the enormous value of the person: "I don't find anything comparable to the magnificent beauty of a soul and its marvelous capacity."[44] Clearly, Teresa's vision is far closer to the divine estimation.

Second, Teresa does better than just about anyone I know at showing us a clear progression forward in the spiritual life. And she does so without the deadly legalism that characterizes most efforts in this direction. Utilizing the threefold scheme of Dionysius she carefully and beautifully invites us through the purifying fires of God's forgiveness and the illuminating graces of God's wisdom into the perfecting union of God's immense love. The journey simply takes our breath away.

Finally, Teresa's description of union is as good as we will find anywhere. This is no small trick. She is confined to human language, which can give only an abbreviated approximation of an experiential reality that extends beyond words. Also, she is trying to describe to us a life in God that most of us can see only from a distant shore.

I believe her success here is due to her multiple use of metaphors, piling one on top of the other. In doing so she gives us something understandable to hang on to as we try to grasp things we do not fully understand. One example: "Let us say that . . . union is like the joining of two wax candles to such an extent that the flame coming from them is but one, or that the wick, the flame, and the wax are all one. But afterward one candle can be easily separated from the other and there are two candles."[45] The whole of *The Interior Castle* is worth Teresa's efforts to describe for us the landscape of union, even if we are visiting this landscape only as foreigners and sojourners.

Frankly, I am at a loss to give you practical handles for entering the experiences Teresa describes in *The Interior Castle*. More often than not I feel like I'm wandering through some of the side halls that are above and below. Teresa also describes "lovely gardens and fountains and labyrinths, such delightful things that you would want to be dissolved in praises of the great God who created the soul in His own image and likeness."[46] Maybe that is where I am, delighting in sun and sky, trees and flowers.

Perhaps the best guidance I can give is to encourage you to read this book for yourself. Begin with a weekend when you can read it from beginning to end nonstop, seeing the work as a whole and capturing its basic themes. Then you can spend the next year or so reading meditatively, dwelling on key passages and phrases. All the time, request "His Majesty" to bring you into the life for which you are ready, just as he did for Teresa. If you will do this faithfully and quietly you will, I am sure, find that the crystal castle of your own soul will begin to glow with divine love.

Teresa was a lover of God and a lover of souls. Perhaps it would be good to end with what is often called Teresa's bookmark. It received that name because it was inserted into the prayer book she was using at the time of her death. Listen:

> Let nothing disturb you,
> Let nothing alarm you.
> While all things are passing;
> God is unchanging.
> Be patient and you will gain everything.
> With God in your heart nothing is lacking.
> God alone suffices.[47]

Lord Jesus, Teresa is certainly a wise guide in the life of prayer. We need this so much because so many today utterly trivialize prayer. Or turn it into a mechanical exercise that deadens the spirit. We really do need someone who has gone beyond the superficialities of our modern culture. Thank you that Teresa is one such person.

Many of us, Lord, feel like we are only at the beginning stages of prayer: perhaps room one or two, if that. Some of us even feel like we are still out on the front porch! Help us, Lord. Draw us in gently. May we see what a good thing it is to enter into a conversational life with you. May Teresa's life and writings be a source of inspiration for us. And more than inspiration—life-giving action. Teresa is clearly a leader in the life of prayer. Teach us, Lord, to follow her lead. Amen.

John of the Cross

Illuminating the Dark Night

This dark night is an inflow of God into the soul that
purges it of its habitual ignorances and imperfections, natural and spiritual,
and prepares the soul for union with God through love
by both purging and illumining it.

THE DARK NIGHT

SMALL AND STARVING, JUAN DE YEPES (1542-1591), later known as John of the Cross, struggled every day of his young life. His home in Fontiveros, Spain, was modest and poorly furnished. Although wealth ran liberally throughout his extended family, none of it had trickled down to his own father. To compound matters, his father died when Juan was just three, leaving the family destitute. Fortunately, Juan was bright.

By the time he was a teenager, the Jesuits were in charge of John's education. His big break came in 1568 when Teresa of Avila invited him to join the Carmelite order in order to bring it to men. He agreed and, despite his small stature, made a huge impact. Eventually he became Teresa's most ardent supporter and closest confidant. He is remembered to this day for his able interpretation of her work.

Although a huge gap in age separated the two (twenty-seven years), in matters of the spirit age is insignificant. John's rare abilities and brilliant pen helped catapult Teresa's works onto the religious stage. His efforts were widely recognized and drew both praise and ire from all factions of the church. Eventually he became the focal point of various and enduring controversies, and after twenty-three years of faithful service he was literally tortured to death in 1591.

The Dark Night

John's three pivotal works are *The Ascent of Mount Carmel*, *The Living Flame of Love* and *The Dark Night*.[48] Both *The Ascent of Mount Carmel* and *The Living Flame of Love* document the trials we must overcome in order to arrive at a state of perfect union with God. This perfect union with God goes beyond our ability to experience or comprehend him. But *The Dark Night* lays out this process most specifically. It teaches us how to understand the ultimate challenges we face in order to live the spiritual life fully.

Before I had read *The Dark Night* I always thought John's phrase was an allusion to the most intense experience of God's absence. But the book is not only about God's absence; it is also about our ignorance, the absence of knowing God. *The Dark Night* illumines how little we can know of God on our own. In order to know him we must "annihilate and calm our faculties, passions, and sensual appetites and affections."[49]

Moving Beyond Our Faculties, Passions and Appetites

John outlines his understanding of our nature as humans by identifying our essential faculties, our dominant passions and our sensual appetites. The essential faculties are memory, intelligence and will. Our dominant passions are joy, hope, fear and sorrow. Our sensual appetites are simply our five senses that allow us to taste, touch, see, hear and smell. The faculties, the passions and the senses together form our natural capacity to order our thoughts and experiences into a meaningful whole. John is concerned that we build structures of meaning and that we understand how these structures are created. This becomes especially important when we realize that despite all our natural ability, the "dark night" takes us beyond our innate capacities and places us on a whole new plane of spiritual understanding.

The Dark Night expects that we will eventually crash into our natural limits. When we do, the light of God's Spirit will draw us into a whole other dimension. John speaks of our will becoming divine. When we are united with God as an expression of divine love, we move beyond the limits of our natural strength and encounter the strength and purity of his Holy Spirit.

How then should we understand the "dark night"? The dark night is an experience both of deprivation of knowledge and absence of experience. First, God's wisdom is simply too great for us to comprehend. Second, because our soul is so impure, we initially experience the radiant beams of God's light as darkness because our soul is so contaminated it cannot reflect any of this light back.[50]

Also, the light of Christ that shines forth from God is so far beyond our natural capacity to understand that we become confused. The confusion is a result of having no developed categories in which we can receive and understand these experiences. The result is pain, affliction and discomfort.[51] The troubling experiences associated with this entire event lead to overwhelming affliction. We become saturated with the knowledge of our own inability to understand. We are confronted by our pitiful weaknesses in our natural, moral and spiritual capacities.[52]

John goes on to demonstrate how the divine ray of contemplation strikes the soul with overwhelming light. Because it darkens the natural light of our reason, it darkens and deprives us of our natural light. In this state we are not only ignorant but also empty. But this purgation is necessary.[53] Without it, we would be unable to experience the satisfaction of all the abundant spiritual delight that comes when we move to a new level of spiritual understanding.

The reason we feel empty is that the dark night sets aside every natural means of experiencing happiness. We simply cannot rely on our natural faculties anymore. Equally difficult, however, is the fact that we have not yet experienced the inner contentment that comes from God alone. We must recognize our need for a twofold peace.

The Refining Fire of God's Light

By twofold peace, John means our need for both sensory peace and spiritual peace. This is achieved only by the refining fire of God's light. God's rays of light affect us in the same way fire consumes a log. Before transforming the soul it purges it of all contrary qualities. This transformation causes blackness and darkness as the soul's ugliness is burned away.[54]

There are several important things we need to understand in this process. First, the soul will be transformed only by this purging, so we must

learn to submit to it. Second, the experiences of suffering that result from
the dark night do not come from God but from our own lack and imperfection. Third, our sins will be destroyed through this process. Fourth,
the destructive aspect of the fire blinds us to its purifying effect. Fifth, this
consuming fire destroys both external imperfection and internal dispositions that are against God. Sixth, we need to be patient in the midst of all
this purification since all we can see is our misery. And finally, we must
recognize the distinct difference between the internal and external purging so that we realize what is purified and illumined and what still requires additional help.[55]

Ultimately, all three levels of the threefold ascent require that we complete each step in order to move forward in our ascent to God. In other
words, on the level of purgation, we experience purgation, illumination
and "perfection of purgation" before we can move to the next level of illumination. The same process is necessary on the level of illumination if
we are to ascend to the final level of union. On the level of illumination
we come to see reality accurately by purging our old perceptions, illumining our new perceptions and uniting with God, sharing his perspective of
the world. It is only after we have undergone this development at both of
the initial stages that we are able to ascend to final union with God.

The Rhythm of the Spiritual Life

John teaches us how to recognize the rhythm of the spiritual life. Our life
with God fluctuates between active and passive insights of sense and spirit.
During the passive nights, the absence of presence is not the loss of God
but only a transition period when our natural faculties have been surpassed and our spiritual capacities are not yet developed. This is a critical
transition point where many of us cease to move any deeper in our life
with God. We hit a wall of unknowing and stop rather than persevering
and discovering a new dimension in our relationship with him.

In the ancient world, the ultimate goal of the spiritual life was defined
as *apatheia,* a state in which all our thoughts, desires and ambitions are
ordered perfectly. John does not intend for us to live without passion, but
he does want us to recognize that our only experience of joy and happiness in life comes when we channel every aspect of human nature prop-

erly. To channel our desires and passions appropriately, the right thoughts and the right dispositions ultimately lead us to God. It doesn't happen quickly and it doesn't happen accidentally, but if we persevere we realize the presence of God at a higher, more complete level.

REFLECTING AND RESPONDING

I liked John of the Cross immediately when I learned how short he was: four foot eleven inches tall. When Teresa of Avila first met John she exclaimed, "I have just met half a friar!" Of course, she also knew that she had encountered a giant of a soul.

I also like the fact that John was such a fun-loving person. A great storyteller and an engaging conversationalist. People reported that when on horseback with a group, John would regale everyone with his lively stories. John, we are told, loved picnics and would arrange weekend jaunts for the friars.

And then I love the way John was able to lift the burden of anxiety from people. Folks would come to him for confession filled with guilt and an oppressive religiosity, and John would tenderly bring them into the love and care and acceptance of God. It was said that John was able to cure people of "the illness of scrupulosity." So I find John of the Cross immensely appealing and interesting.

For our purposes we are focusing on how John developed the threefold structure of purgation, illumination and union. At the heart of his book *The Dark Night* (and his other writings as well) are poems John composed while he was imprisoned in Toledo, Spain, for nine months in a room ten feet by six feet. Because he had no pen or paper he composed these poems solely in his head, committing them all to memory.

The heart of John's work is expressed in his now famous phrase "the dark night of the soul." This centers on his teaching of detachment—*nada* in Spanish. The idea is that nothing is important except for God. We are stripped of every attachment and entanglement in order to be utterly simple and naked before God. We are not even to cling to mystical experiences of one kind or another. Nada!

John's poetry, even in translation, is quite captivating. Listen:

One dark night,
Fired with love's urgent longings
—Ah, the sheer grace!—
I went out unseen,
My house being now all stilled . . .[56]

Now, this image of the "house being all stilled" is a reference to the stilling of the human senses: the faculties, the passions, the sensual appetites. There is, John teaches us, the need for a silencing of all humanly initiated activity if we are to be truly attentive to God alone. This even includes all the religious activity we use to respond to God. All of our normal ways of acting and responding are to be stilled; as John puts it in *The Ascent of Mount Carmel*, "Nothing, nothing, nothing, and even on the Mountain nothing." Nada! Listen to another snippet of his poetry:

O living flame of love
That tenderly wounds my soul
In its deepest center! Since
Now you are not oppressive,
Now Consummate! If it be your will:
Tear through the veil of this sweet encounter!
O sweet cautery,
O delightful wound!
O gentle hand! O delicate touch
That tastes of eternal life
And pays every debt!
In killing you changed death to life.[57]

Of course the "flame of love" is the purifying work of the Holy Spirit. And, note, this is a purifying that wounds the heart: "O sweet cautery, / O delightful wound!" Purity of heart does indeed leave its mark.

The "union" material in John of the Cross is quite moving. Consider this from *The Living Flame of Love*: "Oh, how happy is this soul that ever experiences God resting and reposing within it. Oh, how fitting it is for it to withdraw from things, flee from business matters and live in immense tranquility, so that it may not even with the slightest mote or noise disturb or trouble its heart, where the beloved dwells."[58] Or, consider this from

The Dark Night: "Only the love of God, which is being united to the soul, imparts the heat, strength, temper, and passion of love."[59]

Perhaps it would help you to understand John of the Cross if I share briefly one period that could be thought of as a "dark night" for me. By every outward standard things were going well. Publishers wanted me to write for them. Speaking invitations were too numerous and too gracious. Yet through a series of events, it became clear to me that God wanted me to retreat from public activity. This was an action that some would see as professional and literary suicide. But that was a matter I had to leave in hands greater than mine. I had heard the *kol Yahweh*, the voice of the Lord saying, "Be still!" And so I did.

I stopped all public speaking. I stopped all writing. And I waited, silent, hushed, hidden. No doubt God had important things to teach me. Things that would go deep into the subterranean chambers of my soul. Things that demanded extended periods of stillness and attentiveness. Things that could not be learned while I was distracted by the blare of human adulation . . . and criticism.

At the time this began, I did not know if I would ever speak or write again—I rather thought I would not. As it turned out, this fast from public life lasted about eighteen months.

I waited in silence. And God was silent too. I joined in the psalmist's query: "How long will you hide your face from me?" (Ps 13:1). The answer I got? Nothing. There were no sudden revelations. No penetrating insights. No spiritual ecstasy. Not even gentle assurances. Nothing. Absolutely nothing. Nada.

It was as if all feeling, all emotion, all human responses had gone into hibernation. I was being stripped of dependence on all exterior and interior results. I became dead to all the busyness, self-promotion and superficial drives of the world around me. I was learning trust in God alone. It was as a good friend put it: "You are learning to 'lay low' in the Lord." And so I was.

This discipline of silence ended finally and simply after eighteen months with gentle assurances that it was time to reenter the public square. The "dark night" had come to an end.

Now, it is important for you to know that this was a one-time event.

Never before nor since have I sensed any similar guidance. Apparently, God is not interested in repeat performances.

O God of darkness and of light, you have promised light for the way. All we see right now is utter darkness. Still, we believe. In your time and in your way please turn our darkness into your glorious light. Amen.

Conclusion

As a deer longs for flowing streams,
so my soul longs for you, O God.
My soul thirsts for God,
for the living God.

PSALM 42:1-2

OUR WORLD TODAY CRIES OUT FOR A theology of spiritual growth that has been proven to work in the midst of the harsh realities of daily life. Sadly, many today have simply given up on the possibility of growth in character formation. Vast numbers of well-intended folk have exhausted themselves in church work and discovered that this did not substantively change their lives. They find that they were just as impatient and ego-centric and fearful as when they began lifting the heavy load of church work. Maybe more so.

Others have immersed themselves in multiple social service projects. And while the glow of helping others lingers for a time, they soon realize that all their Herculean efforts left little lasting imprint on the inner life. Indeed, it often made them much worse inwardly: frustrated and angry and bitter.

Still others have a practical theology that will not allow for spiritual growth. Indeed, they just might see it as a bad thing. Having been saved by grace these people have become paralyzed by it. To attempt any progress forward in the spiritual life for them smacks of "works/righteousness."

If they have a theological bent they will know to watch out for all such efforts as likely "semi-Pelagianism" . . . or worse. Their liturgies tell them that they sin in word, thought and deed daily, and so they conclude that this is their fate until they die. Heaven is their only release from this world of sin and rebellion. Hence, these well-meaning folk will sit in their pews year after year without realizing any movement forward in their life with God.

Finally, there is a cultural malaise that touches us all to one extent or another. I am referring to how completely we have become accustomed to the normality of dysfunction. The constant media stream of scandals and broken lives and mayhem of every sort elicits from us hardly more than a yawn. We have come to expect little else—even from our religious leaders . . . perhaps especially from our religious leaders. This overall life dysfunction is so pervasive in our culture that it is nearly impossible for us to have a clear vision of spiritual progress. Shining models of holiness are so rare today.

Echoing Through the Centuries

And yet there is, echoing through the centuries, a great company of witnesses telling us of a life vastly richer and deeper and fuller. In all walks of life and in all human situations they have discovered a life of "righteousness and peace and joy in the Holy Spirit" (Rom 14:17).

They have found that real, solid, substantive transformation into the likeness of Christ is possible. They witness to a character formation that is nigh unto amazing. They have seen their egocentric passions give way to such a selflessness and humility of heart that it astonishes even them. Rage and hate and malice are replaced with love and compassion and universal goodwill. All this is a deep interior work of the heart, not surface show. The inner life has been molded and shaped into something new, something beautiful. To be sure, this has not happened overnight. This vast throng of witnesses all tell of ups and downs, of detours and reversals. But they also tell of genuine progress forward.

All the men and women we have written about in this book have entered into this deep, character-forming life with God in profound ways. Some were more fully formed than others, perhaps, but all were substantially changed in the interiority of the soul. Each and every one experienced a life flowing with love and joy and peace and patience and kindness and generosity and faithfulness and gentleness and self-control (see Gal 5:22-23). All were unique personalities and all came at the spiritual life from vastly different angles. In this book we have described these various angles as "paths of Christian devotion."

We discussed seven of these paths:

- The Spiritual Life as the Right Ordering of Our Love for God
- The Spiritual Life as Journey
- The Spiritual Life as Knowledge of God Lost in the Fall
- The Spiritual Life as Intimacy with Jesus Christ
- The Spiritual Life as the Right Ordering of Our Experiences of God
- The Spiritual Life as Action and Contemplation
- The Spiritual Life as Divine Ascent

These "paths," of course, are not exclusive of one another. No one path is "right" and the others "wrong." Indeed, they overlap and intertwine and mingle with each other. Likely, we will all find ourselves on one path or another at different seasons of our life.

Longing for the Heart's True Home

So, you see, it really doesn't matter which of these paths we are on or what stage of our spiritual development we are at or the extent of our knowledge and talents. Only one thing is essential for us to move forward in this life with God. This one thing is purely and simply a "longing" for this life with all our heart and soul and mind and strength. Psalm 42:1 evokes for us a powerful image to express this "longing" of the heart. It sets before us the image of a deer that longs for flowing streams. This image, says the psalmist, is the icon for our soul panting and thirsting and longing for God.

Now, we are not here speaking of a longing that we might have, say, to go skiing or to eat chocolate ice cream. Oh no, this is a longing that drills down deep to the very core of our being. It is a longing that sweeps up all our emotion and desire and hope into one great yearning for God. It is, in fact, the longing that God has created deep within our heart for its true home. This is the longing we hoped to convey to you when we gave this book its title: *Longing for God*. This God-crafted longing calls out to us beyond the noise and hurry and crowds. Quietly, persistently, it reminds us of those things we value the most. Lovingly, urgently, it calls us to peace and wholeness and affirmation.

Oh, friend, do you long for this kind of life? Do you? Do you have a burning craving for utter heart purity? "The pure in heart shall see God," say the Scriptures (Mt 5:8). Even more, when we see God we long for purity of heart with all the energy of our soul. Oh, to have a flaming vision of a God-saturated life! Oh, to experience the searching, persuading, compelling reality of the Hound of Heaven! Oh, to have an insistent, heart-felt longing that will not let us go until we at last feast on what Thomas Kelly calls "the real whole-wheat Bread of Life!" Like the deer longing for flowing streams so our soul longs for God, for the living God.

Is this what you long for? Is this what I long for? If so, the invitation is open wide to one and all to come home, home to where we belong, home to that for which we were created. "Come to me," says the living Christ. "Come to Me all you who labor and are heavy laden and I will give you rest. Take My yoke upon you and learn of Me, for I am gentle and lowly in heart and you will find rest for your souls, for My yoke is easy and My burden is light" (Mt 11:28-30 NKJV).

Appendix 1

Pre-Christian Influences on Our Life with God

"To an unknown god."
What therefore you worship as unknown, this I proclaim to you.

ACTS 17:23

As I read Plato, he plainly, of all the pre-Christian philosophers, is seen to
exhibit the Father and Son from the Hebrew Scriptures. And in his writings I
understand nothing else than the Holy Trinity to be implied.

CLEMENT OF ALEXANDRIA

LONG BEFORE THE BIRTH OF JESUS, several streams of eternal longing joined together to provide insight into the "unknown God." These writers helped to bring about a more complete understanding of God. We are not always sure what to make of pre-Christian and non-Christian religions. Yet Scripture itself teaches that writings and personalities beyond Scripture contribute to our knowledge of God. Paul writes that in the fullness of time God sent forth his Son (Gal 4:4). Before Jesus, Scripture affirms the pivotal role Jews and non-Christians played in our knowledge and understanding of God. Cyrus the Persian (2 Chron 36), Artaxerxes the King (Neh 2) and Ruth the Moabite (Ruth 4) are but three examples that make this point clear. A fourth and notable example comes from Acts 17 where Paul praises the Athenians for their partial discovery of God.

The convergence of these multiple streams formed many impressions of God, but none served this cause more powerfully than the dominant periods of Jewish life and the golden age of Greek philosophy.

In the same way, the early days of the Christian community witnessed a huge controversy over the right and proper use of higher Greek culture, the legitimacy of its poets and philosophers in providing general revelation of God's truth, and the role of non-Christian literature in the confirmation, construction and teaching of Christian doctrine. As the first theologians sifted through Greek thought, they attempted to discern what was appropriate for Christian understanding. During this early period, three key life philosophies influenced early Christian thinking and continue to play a role in our understanding today: (1) Stoicism, the most widely held philosophy, (2) a highly spiritualized form of Platonism, and (3) the Christianized philosophy of Aristotle.

The Role of Providence and the Right Use of Reason: The Influence of Stoicism

Stoicism had an enormous influence on early Christian thinking. The influence came in two primary ways: (1) their view of providence, and (2) their emphasis on reason disciplining the passions and emotions. This influence is felt right up to our present time and is helpful for our life today when we discern the nature of this influence.

Prior to the first Christians, the Jewish people stressed God's providence by emphasizing his active role in the course of history, even the history of other nations. They celebrated God's faithfulness in carrying out his promises, including his intervention in times of trouble and his judgment for their lack of faithfulness.

The Stoics, however, did not think of providence in this way. As far as they were concerned, God's providence is apparent in the marvelous order of the universe, in the way things fit together so well. The universe is good as a whole and in every part. It is governed by a single principle that is rational and immanent, vitalizing and directing all things. This principle is manifest as organism in plants, appetite in animals and reason in people. As a result, we carry the possibilities for our well-being in our own hands. Because this orderly cosmos is our dwelling, we should be governed by its laws. Morals, human laws and customs should conform to the unwritten laws of nature. Such a view of providence is one in which God has already provided all we need in order to live well, rather than the Jewish view of God intervening in the course of history to punish or save us. Still, there was enough of the Jewish understanding of the goodness and order of the universe for Christian theologians to complement the Stoic understanding of God's providence with the Hebrew view of history.

For the Stoic, life governed by reason means we should exercise our reason to control our passions and emotions. We realize our true nature and achieve freedom from the domination of our passions when we are guided by our reason. Otherwise, if we do not allow our reason to govern us, we become a slave of our passions and cannot deal with the horrible events that destroy our wealth, erode our social position and even take our life. When we become free from the power of our emotions, we are able to enter the ideal state of *apatheia*, the state of existence in which all thoughts, desires and actions are ordered properly. Thus the "ideal" sage is utterly indifferent to all external realities and completely free of the motivating force of affections.

The Stoic notion of *apatheia* motivated the early desert fathers to pioneer the ascetic practices of Christian spirituality. These monks, who withdrew to the Egyptian wilderness, believed they must resist the devil in the same way Jesus did in order to prove their total devotion to God. One of their richest legacies is the teaching that in order to control the passions, or the "eight deadly thoughts" (gluttony, lust, avarice, self-pity, anger, sloth, vainglory and pride), we must follow the path of trial and temptation that connects us directly with the trials and temptations of Jesus.

According to these monks, once we are converted, we are assailed by these deadly thoughts, just as Jesus was tempted in the wilderness after his baptism. These disruptive appetites and passions threaten to control us. They hinder the work of God so we are unable to love either our neighbors or God as Jesus taught us to do.

This can be illustrated by the deadly thought of avarice. Evagrius of Ponticus (345-399) said:

> Our need for material goods suggests to the mind a lengthy old age, the
> inability to perform manual labor (at some future date), famines that are
> sure to come, sickness that will visit us, the pinch of poverty, the great

shame that comes from accepting the necessities of life from others, and much more. Thus, the urge to give to others in need, which comes to us spontaneously since the Holy Spirit at work in us is generous, is hampered and even choked to death by these fears.[1]

Not only is the general purpose of controlling the passions similar to the Stoics but the monks even used the stoic term *apathy* to describe their goal. But (and this is an important but) however much the monks were influenced by the Stoics, they had a very different purpose in mind. Unlike the Stoics, who sought to become independent and autonomous, the monks sought to become free of the control of their passions in order to follow God. For them the goal of apathy was not to become unfeeling but to have the blessing Jesus promised his followers, purity of heart, so that they could love freely and be unhindered. In fact, the Stoic goal of autonomy was seen by the Christians as the deadly thought of pride.

God's Favorite Pre-Christian Philosopher: The Influence of Plato

The second significant pre-Christian influence is Plato. Plato illustrated to the early Christians that misplaced desire and disordered love are the two greatest challenges to our life with God. Like Stoicism, Plato and a highly spiritualized form of Platonism were used by early Christians to defend themselves against their opponents. This Neo-Platonism is influential even up to our present time.

The first Christians pointed to various ways in which Plato agreed with their outlook. He, like Jesus, turned from the material world as the center of ultimate reality to emphasize an eternal realm, which for Plato was the realm of ultimate ideas. He, like Jesus, believed that this world was the handiwork of a power greater than ourselves and above and beyond our comprehension, emphasizing that this world is neither our home nor our ultimate destiny. Plato, like the Jews and first Christians, has a story of the Fall. Although he has various aberrant ideas (including his belief in the transmigration of the soul, the movement of the soul at death into another body, and his emphasis not on marriage but on communal living) many of Plato's most compelling insights were appropriated for use in Christian theology and spirituality.

At the heart of Plato's work is his belief that we always desire, but we do not always desire properly. How then do we direct desire to its proper satisfaction in order to fulfill the meaning and destiny of our life. In *The Symposium*, for example, love, as a spiritual force, is the mediating link between earth and heaven. Love cultivates desire. It longs for knowledge. It leads to understanding. But love disordered by misplaced desire destroys knowledge and understanding.

Immediately you can see how critical this notion is for us today. The disordering of love by misplaced desire is ruinous for the human soul. We desire food to eat and clothes to wear. We desire sexual satisfaction. We desire to exercise our gifts and abilities in order that we can make a unique contribution to the quality of our community. But when these desires become disordered, we seek their fulfillment in ways they were never intended to be satisfied. The satisfaction of a desire contrary to its original intent disorients us from the habits and patterns that produce meaning and purpose for our life.

Of course, desire itself is not evil. It is the inappropriate satisfaction of an appropriate desire that becomes evil. And the result is a ruined soul.

The influence of this idea on early Christian spirituality is impossible to overstate. It illustrates that misplaced desire and disordered love are the two greatest challenges to our life with God. At the heart of Plato's *Symposium* is the belief that love is the spirit that leads us to a deeper desire for the transcendent good. For Christians, when love is disrupted, our capacity to know and serve God is disrupted as well.

In another work, *Phaedrus*, this theme is extended. In several key passages Plato identifies themes that will become hallmarks of Christian thinking: the nature of the soul, the competition between reason and desire, the role of reason and the progressive unfolding of wisdom and insight.

The right use of reason is the culminating principle of *Phaedrus*.[2] The higher elements of the mind guide us into the highest expression of life. Here permanence, happiness and contentment overcome the debilitating gravity of evil. When we are overcome with the power of goodness, we gain self-mastery, inner peace and lasting contentment. In this way, we are able to direct desire to its proper satisfaction.

In one of the most famous passages of *Phaedrus*, Plato uses the analogy of two horses and one charioteer to expand his treatment of the human soul.[3] Here Plato demonstrates the role of reason in the spiritual life as we learn how to discipline our mind appropriately in order to attend to God properly. Reason can prove neither the existence of God nor the reliability of intellectual virtue. What reason can prove is the way specific human actions lead to the appropriate or inappropriate satisfaction of human desire.

Phaedrus attempts to illustrate how "will" (the white horse) and "desire" (the black horse) can be contained through "reason" (the charioteer). The implication, of course, is that reason is supreme, and when understanding is present, reason can guide will and desire to their appropriate end. The chariot, as the vessel carrying human life, only arrives at its appropriate end when all three human powers are coordinated appropriately.

Finally, in *The Republic*, Plato captures the goal and destiny of human life. The central unifying theme is articulated in the "Allegory of the Cave," where the dynamics of human transformation are placed in dramatic relief. The story begins with mindless slaves shackled to a horrible existence of endless and meaningless activity. Although everyone has succumbed to a slave mentality, one bold individual begins to think and decides to discover the nature of the reality behind the shadows. This thought gives rise to desire, which in turn gives rise to action. As a result, the desire to know causes him to turn from his mindless existence in the cave to pursue understanding of the ultimate nature of all reality. (This is precisely the image that C. S. Lewis uses in his book *The Silver Chair*.)

What is important—and particularly useful in later Christian thinking—is the emphasis on the change of perspective that begins with a turning or a conversion. As this turning progresses, deeper levels of knowledge and understanding unfold. This is not instantaneous knowledge but a progressive unfolding that leads to profound insight.[4]

The significance of Plato's thought to Christian spirituality comes in three dramatic forms. First, this idea of turning or converting is pivotal to Christianity. Coupling this idea with the teaching that no one ascends to full knowledge of God without going through a laborious process became a hallmark of monastic spirituality. The second contribution is Plato's emphasis on how hard it is for those who are enlightened to return to their former existence in order to assist others in turning from the shadows to encounter the reality of the transcendent good. Early Christians quickly realized that once an individual has ascended to the heights of divine insight and illumination, the obligation to return and assist others in this journey must be tied to rigorous discipline and Christian devotion. Finally, Plato's understanding of the soul helped to shape the view of the capacities of the human soul as memory, intelligence and will. This triad dominated Western Christian spirituality for centuries to come.

The Ordering Power of Habit and Wisdom: The Influence of Aristotle

After Plato the key themes he first introduced were amplified. In the writings of his greatest student, Aristotle, the disordering effect of runaway desire was replaced by the ordering power of habit and wisdom. Beyond Plato no other non-Christian influence on Christian thinking has been greater than that of Aristotle. Of particular significance is Aristotle's emphasis on habit, the way in which it is cultivated, its central role in the development of virtue and the role of virtue in the acquisition of wisdom.[5]

For Aristotle, the goal of the spiritual life is eternal contemplation of the "unmoved mover." In order to attain this goal, we must cultivate virtue. Virtue is not easily attained, but ascends through two levels. First, moral decency directs our bodily appetites to their proper satisfaction. Then, after satisfying our physical desires, we are able to concentrate on the higher-order activities of the mind. Habit and virtue are dual elements of human character. Without the satisfaction of our desires and the development of moral virtue, the ability to think and develop intellectual virtue is impossible. The foundation of intellectual virtue is the ability of the moral virtues to harness the desires of the flesh and channel these desires into their proper avenues of satisfaction. Even more, virtue is understood as good habits we can rely on in order to make our lives function well.

Although the full thrust of Aristotle's influence would not be felt until the thirteenth century with the rise of Thomas Aquinas, the significance of his teaching on wisdom and habit and its influence on early Christian spirituality is staggering. Habit works to satisfy our innate human desires in a way that orders human life. Without good habits we are not able to satisfy the yearnings of the human heart in a way that is consistent with the goal and destiny of our life. Habit becomes a second nature as powerful as our first nature and helps to shackle the disorienting power of misplaced desires. If we do not develop sound moral habits then we will not be able to develop the intellectual habits that cultivate wisdom and lead us to God.

This second aspect, developing wise and proper thoughts that lead to God, is the benchmark for measuring the strength of our habits. The power of the human mind to concentrate on God is directly tied to the ability of human passion to be quiet. If our passions are not quiet, then we are disrupted and our ability to attend to God is disrupted as well.

Aristotle, like Plato before him, has a huge body of literature, which casts a long shadow over Western civilization. His role in elevating habit and the necessity of developing moral virtue in order to cultivate intellectual virtue laid the groundwork for his enduring contribution to Christian spirituality.

Searching for One Fixed Point: Scripture

In addition to the influence of several streams of early Greek philosophy, the first Christians relied heavily on their Jewish heritage. Of particular influence is the centrality of the Hebrew Bible as both the formative and authoritative text of the community. This development was absolutely essential to early Christians—and to us today.

Subsequent to the Jewish loss of the land and the first temple, the pressing question arose as to how an individual and a community could find God. Through a variety of developments, Jews and then the first Christians, came to the startling insight that God could be experienced apart from any specific time or place.[6]

As the focus shifted from a static time and a specific place, the Jews, and then the first Christians, gravitated to the biblical text and their interpretation of it as the one fixed point that could guide their understanding and experience of God. In this context the importance of the Bible as the bearer of divine meaning is central. As a result, the first Christians embraced the authority of Scripture and captured the deeper spiritual meanings concealed in the written text.

Jewish mystical thought at the time of Jesus amplifies themes consistent both with ancient Jewish teaching and the contemplative ideals of Plato. These ideas include: one transcendent God, a cosmos ruled by providence, a definable moral order, the ultimate foundation of all of life is beyond this life, and our daily experiences in life are influenced by the ultimate reality beyond our earthly existence.[7]

In this context Jewish exegesis teaches that the written Word of God reveals the complete will of God. Thus Scripture plays an integral role in our awakening to our life with God. It is also in this context that the partial and incomplete understandings of Plato and the Greek contemplative tradition take on greater significance as written Scripture joins with Greek philosophy in forming the integrating center for all truth and value.

The perfect embodiment of this early development was Philo (20 B.C.-A.D. 50), an Alexandrian Jew who synthesized the Greek contemplative ideal with the monotheistic faith of the Hebrew Bible. Philo utilized the levels of reality identified by Plato, but introduced his own unique understanding, suggesting that we progress through the stages of body, intellect and soul in our quest for God. He emphasizes, for example, the allegorical, deeper reading of Scripture, while introducing a method that captures the way language-forms help us know and experience God. The most significant deficiency in Philo, however, and one which the first Christians worked hard to counter, was his lack of focus on the importance of a sustaining community as the context within which we establish and nurture our life with God.[8]

The Fall of Judah: The Rise of Scripture Following the Destruction of the First Temple

The role of Scripture in the development of early Christian spirituality is significant and legendary. Following the Babylonian captivity (sixth century B.C.), Jewish self-consciousness underwent two significant transitions. First, the loss of the temple forced the Jews to look for new ways to find and encounter God. Then, following this loss, a shift in emphasis toward the correct interpretation of Scripture became primary. These two developments motivated the earliest followers of Jesus to lay down priorities that endure to this day. At the very center of these priorities is Scripture as the formative and authoritative guide for all believers. As a person reads Scripture and seeks guidance from the Spirit of God, its deeper meaning (the mystical or allegorical sense of Scripture) is made clear to the believer.[9]

Jesus as the Central and Integrating Force

In this matrix, where the forces of Jewish faith and Greek philosophy collide, Jesus becomes the central integrating force for all Christian spirituality. His life and work become the dynamic center of what it means to become a Christian and to gain intimate knowledge of God. Despite certain efforts to undermine the integrity of the New Testament witness, the accounts of Christ's life (the Gospels) and the interpretations of these events (the Epistles) have defined the way believers measure their progress in the spiritual life. As these first communities formed around the living witness to Jesus Christ, they effectively mediated his presence to all subsequent generations.

The life of Jesus becomes the paramount example of one who realized the perfection of the love of God in his earthly life. For the Christian community, Jesus exists to connect every generation of Christian believers to the life with God we long for and seek. Through consistent participation in the community of faith we can make progress in our spiritual life by identifying with the life of Jesus and embodying in our own life the perfect love and holiness that God intends.

The Immediate Impact: Peter, Paul and John

This focus on the life of Jesus is amplified by the written testimony of his first disciples. In the writings of the earliest New Testament texts, Peter, Paul and John began to interpret the meaning of Christ's life to the first Christians. The commitment of the first Christians to modeling their life after the life of Christ gave shape and force to the earliest Christian understandings of our life with God. Combining ecclesiastical concerns and sacramental practices, the first Christians practiced a form of scriptural interpretation that would dominate Christian spirituality for twelve centuries.

In this context the goal of reading Scripture is to recreate an awareness or consciousness of Christ as articulated by the original New Testament writers. By reading, meditating and praying the Scriptures, and basing this activity within the broader context of the worshiping community, believers are able to understand the life and work of Jesus Christ and appropriate this understanding for their own life. Thus the goal of Christian spirituality is to find God present and active in his written Word.

Beyond the scope of the life of Jesus presented in the Synoptic Gospels (Matthew, Mark and Luke), two other sections of the New Testament play a prominent role in the shape and force of Christian spirituality. The writings of Paul and John both serve constructive roles in shaping the Christian understanding of our mystical union with God.

Throughout Paul's writings, an emphasis is placed on contemplation and the way it leads us to a perfection of the image of God (Acts 9; 1 Cor 12:12; 2 Cor 3:17-18; 12:1-6). At the core of this perfection is the goal to have our life identify so intimately with Jesus Christ that we become like Christ. To amplify this process, Paul uses the term *in Christ* 164 times in placing a central accent on our life being united with Jesus so that we can become like him.[10]

Extending Paul's thought and placing Jesus in the center as the Enlightener of all life, the apostle John demonstrates how our life in Christ provides new levels of understanding. Throughout his writings John consistently demonstrates the way our identity in Jesus Christ produces an immediate identity with God. In this context the goal of the Christian life is not simply to imitate Christ's activities but to develop a consciousness of union with God that fulfills all the longings of the human heart.

As we look back at each of these early influences on the shape and force of Christian spirituality, they help us understand the way the Christian life begins, evolves and takes on ultimate meaning in each successive age. They also help orient us to the enduring aids we need in every stage of Christian devotion.

Between the close of the first century and the dramatic unfolding of events subsequent to Constantine conquering the Roman Empire in the fourth century, Christians endured ten of the most pernicious waves of persecution in the history of civilization.[11] Although these campaigns of persecution waxed and waned, they left an indelible mark on the Christian community and the Roman Empire. Of particular consequence was the need to show the relevance and reality of our life with God while enlisting passionate followers into the way of Christ.

Appendix 2

Christian Women and Spirituality

IT WOULD SEEM THAT THERE ARE BOTH similarities and differences in the spiritual lives of men and women. It is sometimes understood that "spirituality" represents a primary experience of God that precedes formal theological reflection. Until recently, most women were not allowed to be educated. Those who were educated usually came from rich and noble families who hired tutors for their gifted wives and daughters. These women made fantastic contributions, but in many cases they did not have the intellectual preparation or social position for their work to be received readily. As a result, their authority to write came from the authenticity of their religious experiences and not the status of formal education or the normal processes of receiving sanction from the church.

Many of the women we will consider are well known to historians of the church. In almost every case the women from the first nineteen hundred years of the church fit best into path 5, the right ordering of our experiences of God. They could not have done otherwise. It is only recently that we have begun to see contributions spread across all seven approaches. The accompanying list is not intended to be exhaustive but gives an overall sense of the many women who gave eloquent witness to their life with God. In each case, we have sought to highlight the unique expression of Christian fidelity of each of these good and holy women. They continue to give light to our path and guidance for our life with God today.

Saint Photini (c. 50)

Photini, the Samaritan woman at the well, is first identified in John 4:5-42 as the woman who was given water to drink by Jesus. At Pentecost Photini was baptized along with five sisters and her two sons. She then began a missionary career after having a dream of Jesus directing her to go to Rome along with her entourage. There she caused a stir because she reportedly preached Christ with great boldness. This attracted too much attention, and she learned that Nero was looking for her, but in her boldness she and her son went to him first. Photini told him, "We have come to teach you to believe in Christ." Nero asked whether they all had agreed to die for the Nazarene, and she defiantly told him they would gladly die. She and others were then beaten and thrown into jail. Later they were brought back to him and he tempted them with wealth and much gold. Nero asked his daughter Domnina, along with her slave girls, to try to persuade Photini and her sons to give up their faith for the wealth.

However, Photini catechized Domnina and her hundred slave girls and baptized them all. Nero's daughter then ordered that all the tempting gold be sold and the money distributed to the poor. Nero was furious and ordered that they all be burned. Tradition holds that the fire did not destroy them, nor later poison. All except St. Photini were then beheaded. Her death is not recorded; however, it is known that she sang hymns and blessed God in the prison, for she drank of the "living water."

Saint Eudokia of Heliopolis (d. 107)

Eudokia of Heliopolis was a Samaritan woman who became a devout follower of Christ. As an ascetic nun she ministered to many people who came to receive assistance at her monastery near Baalbeck, Lebanon. The conversion of so many people to Christianity under her influence brought her to the attention of authorities who had her beheaded in 107.

Saint Tatiana (c. 200)

Tatiana, who was indifferent to her family's wealth, came to love the spiritual life, including prayer and good works. She tended the sick, visited jails and helped the needy. During the reign of Roman terror she was thrown into the arena at the Coliseum to be ravaged by a lion. However, she caressed the lion, who then left her alone, so she was tortured again and beheaded.

Xenia, Deaconess of Rome (c. 220)

Xenia, deaconess of Rome, though the daughter of a Roman senator, chose to live as an ascetic and she led a community of virgins. She was well known for her spiritual life, charity, humility and virtuousness. Tradition teaches that she often spent days and nights standing in prayer and fasting. When she died, a wreath of stars appeared over her monastery, shining brighter than the sun.

Saint Mary of Egypt (c. 344–421)

Saint Mary of Egypt had lived as a prostitute for seventeen years when she found herself in Jerusalem for the Feast of the Exaltation of the Holy Cross. On coming to the church that held the cross, she was unable to enter because a force was repelling her. In the churchyard she was overcome with shame about her ill-spent life. After her prayers of repentance, she was indeed able to enter the church, where she again prayed for guidance regarding her future course. A voice told her to renounce the world and cross the Jordan River. Tradition holds that she lived alone there in the desert areas, engaging in prayer and thanksgiving. Priests who brought her the sacraments claim that she walked across the waters of the Jordan to receive them, without wetting her feet. Tradition holds to many other tales of her virtue and devotion. She is also the best example of what often happened to prostitutes who came to faith: since they had no husband and had been abandoned by their family they had nowhere to go and were in need of a community. As a result, they found their best option to be the formation of convent-like communities where they could have their physical needs met while they pursued their life with God.

Saint Hildegard of Bingen (1098–1179)

Hildegard of Bingen was a woman of genius and is considered by some to be the instigator of the flowering of German mysticism. At an early age she began to report having visions and was placed with the Benedictines at the age of seven. Her family considered that move as a tithe since she was their tenth child. By the time Hildegard was thirty-eight she had become abbess of the monastery.

Hildegard wrote medical and scientific treatises, poetry, music and plays, and did illustrations to clarify her visions. Within the security of the Benedictines she had the opportunity for intellectual growth and development. Some of her visions and writings criticized those in power, of whom she was not afraid. Then, as she matured and grew in confidence, she saw her role as one speaking for God, and that her role in the process of salvation was to share with those around her, enhancing their spiritual elevation. She never saw the visions as something for herself, but they were like gifts to be spread out to those even in distant places. In her writing she elaborately described the visions in glorious detail and then commented on their meaning. Sometimes the visions included music sung by angels. She explained that the meanings of her visions had layers that were literal, moral, allegorical and anagogical (as interpretive of Scripture), reminiscent of the fourfold sense of Scripture.

Her writings include three books: *Scivias*, *The Book of Life's Merits* and *The Book of Divine Works*.

Saint Elisabeth of Schonau (c. 1129-1165)

Elisabeth of Schonau became a Benedictine at the age of twelve. From her youth she followed the *Rule of St. Benedict* and practiced acts of mortification, which were expected during that era. At about the age of twenty she experienced various kinds of ecstasies and visions. These seemed to happen on Sundays, holy days or after reading the lives of saints. Sometimes Elisabeth would see representations of the passion, resurrection or ascension of Christ, as well as other scenes from Scripture. She began to write what she saw and heard on instructions from her superiors. From these writings developed three books of "visions," the first being simple and the later two with theological terminology, perhaps from collaboration with her brother, Egbert, who was a priest.

In one writing, *Liber viarum Dei*, Elisabeth speaks to all classes of people, including the clergy. She gives prophetic threats against priests who might be unfaithful leaders, against the worldliness of some monks who only lightly take their vows of poverty, against the vices of laity and against bishops who might be lax in carrying out their responsibilities to the church. She also wrote other revelations that sometimes seemed exaggerated. The church has never examined or passed judgments on her writings, and she was never canonized, though her name often is seen with the title of saint.

Christina the Astonishing (1150-1224)

Though there is much distrust of accounts of the Middle Ages, and especially bizarre mystical phenomenon and ascetic feats, Christina the Astonishing is still a good example of one who sought a deeper life with God. Her biographer, Thomas of Cantimpre, claimed that Christina had visited heaven and was sent back into the world to become a living example of the necessity for forgiveness of sin to avoid punishment. At the same time, she is portrayed as one who had been resurrected and was already enjoying a continual vision of God.

As was still common in that era, Christina practiced the usual penances, as well as extreme asceticism (such as food deprivation) along with incredible feats, (such as standing in the river for days in winter), and other odd physical challenges. In everything, her body was never harmed in any way. Along with the ascetic acts, it was claimed that she could levitate, sing heavenly music of wonderful harmony, and prophesy.

Clare of Assisi (1193-1253)

Within two years of her death, Clare was canonized (in 1255) by Pope Alexander IV in recognition of her holy life and broad influence. Born the third of five children in 1193, Clare grew up in a moderately wealthy family with keen religious sensitivities. The details of her early life are sketchy, but on March 18, 1212, Clare accepted the "Palm Branch" from the bishop of Assisi, symbolizing her entry into the Christian life and her commitment to follow Christ even unto death through martyrdom.

There are many nuances to her life, but four distinct contributions stand out. First, she was the first woman to write a Rule or order for the religious life. Then, in contrast to Francis, she emphasized a complete material separation from the world. As a result, she emphasized not penance (as Francis did), but total poverty as the gateway to the spiritual life. Finally, she emphasized the role of our religious community in achieving sanctification.

Although she wrote little (one Rule and four letters to Blessed Agnes of Prague), she is remembered as a formidable intellect who has significantly enhanced our understanding of Franciscan spirituality and our life with God.

Mechthild von Magdeburg (1207–1282)

Mechthild von Magdeburg was a mystic, social critic and prophet in an age where such gifts in a woman were considered heretical. This German woman had a courtly upbringing. By the age of twelve she was having religious visions. She left home at the age of twenty-three and joined a house of beguines (a lay religious order not under any human authority) and only later entered a Cistercian convent. Her house of beguines strove to live a life of evangelical perfection through poverty, chastity, prayer and some ascetic practices. Their primary effort was social work.

Translations of her work *The Flowing Light of the Godhead* may be unreliable because she wrote in a medieval low German. Later eighteenth-century scholars classified Mechthild as a "Romantic," part of a movement which felt that the Enlightenment had emptied human life of much of its richness and diversity. These mystics were viewed with suspicion because they seemingly opposed the church's function as the necessary link between God and humanity. Mysticism, of course, by its very nature strives for an experience and vision of the Almighty that is immediate. Some have felt that she was a precursor to the Reformation, because she boldly criticized the moral depravity of some clergy and some of her visions dealt with the decline of the church.

Rose of Viterbo (1233–1252)

Rose of Viterbo, as with many other women in the history of the faith, had a deep spirituality that resulted in her stepping outside traditional roles for women in the church and society. From an early age Rose was remarkable for her holiness and miraculous powers. Rose's primary foci were prayer and preaching. In her early life she began to preach to groups of women, usually outdoors. Though she had no license to preach, she walked through the streets of Viterbo, Italy, carrying a cross and exhorting large crowds of followers to live virtuously. Rose also urged them to develop a rich prayer life, and there were times when she would prophesy.

She became a third-order Franciscan and reformer. Though she defended the church and its doctrines, she exhorted the clergy to also live a moral and saintly life. There were reports of healing after she prayed over people, and particularly for a blind girl who recovered her sight. In one of her street sermons she found herself in an argument with a heretic, who even after a long discussion refused to come to faith. In desperation Rose flung herself into a bonfire, then walked out unscathed. On that the heretic announced he would accept the faith. Her notoriety and preaching did lead to problems, so others drove her and her family out of the city, stating that women should not be preaching, let alone in the streets.

Hadewijch of Antwerp (mid-thirteenth century)

Hadewijch of Antwerp was a Dutch mystic and poet. Born into the aristocracy and well-learned, she was a beguine, or lay member of a sisterhood. Little is known of her life except what can be gleaned from her writings. She was known for her descriptions of visions, which were earthy and embodied descriptions of her encounters with Christ, the divine Bridegroom. In all things she considered love as an overriding theme that leads to ecstasy and joy. She stated that "love is meant to be explored and experienced in all its many moods and forms rather than be defined and categorized."

Her writings included *Letters (Brevien)* and also *Poems in Stanzas*. When she wrote about love, she described its advanced stages, from band and chain to light (such as enlightened reason, a live coal, or how all contradictory behavior is set afire and extinguished by the madness of love), dew (or what is left after the fire of love has burned up everything in its violence) and living springs (which is the great river flowing endlessly from God and hell, signifying the terror of those lost in the storms of love). Her other writings contain great descriptions of her visions, which are often quite exotic for the modern reader.

Saint Bridget of Sweden (1303-1373)

Bridget, a celebrated saint of Sweden, was born into a wealthy and educated family. She was married at thirteen to Ulf Gudmarson, and they had eight children. Her saintly and charitable life made her well known throughout the country. After one pilgrimage with her husband, he died on their return.

Bridget had experienced spiritual visions as a child, and upon the death of her husband she began to have them more frequently. She founded the Order of St. Savior, also called the Bridgettines. She had no qualms about challenging authority and prevailed upon Queen Blance to take life more seriously. In 1350 she traveled to Rome, partly to pursue her mission to elevate the moral tone of the age. Her visions and spiritual inspirations led her to continuously challenge and admonish the popes on spiritual issues. She remained in Rome for some years, living austerely and looking after the poor and the sick. Bridget made herself universally beloved in Italy through her kindness and good works. She dictated a book of revelations about the sufferings of Christ.

Julian of Norwich (1342-1416). See path five.

Saint Catherine of Siena (c. 1347-1380)

From the age of seven Catherine of Siena had visions of Christ and was determined to live a life devoted to him. She began to live a conscientious and pious life, then at the age of fifteen announced to her family that she would refuse to marry. Though she lived at home, she began to live a solitary and ascetic life, eating only once a day. Shortly after, she became a tertiary Dominican, a layperson who lives at home.

Catherine became known locally for her visions, asceticism and patient service to the poor and sick. Often her days were spent guiding people toward a path to God. Along with the practical work, she spent time in contemplation or raptures and studying. Knowledge spread about how she spent the day in prayer, sometimes extending into the night. She remembered the names of all those who came to her, and when asked how she remembered them replied, "When a servant of God is filled with devotion and a burning desire for the salvation of sinners, and when she prays to the Eternal Majesty, he rewards her with a mental eye with which she sees all those for whom she is praying." Catherine also experienced ecstatic emotions after taking communion; her face would glow and she would break out with words of jubilation. During the scourge of the plague in Florence, she ministered to the sick, and many reported being healed after she interceded for them.

Catherine occasionally became involved in some church political struggles. Other than her letters, her main thoughts on our life with God are contained in *Dialogues*, which has been translated into English.

Margery Kempe (1373-1440)

Margery Kempe, a mother of fourteen children, was an English mystic whose autobiography is one of the earliest in all of English literature. After she was finished bearing children, she began a series of pilgrimages to places such as Jerusalem and Rome. Apparently illiterate, she dictated *The Book of Margery Kempe* to two clerks. This book was translated into modern English in 1940. The writing describes her journeys and also religious ecstasies, which often included crying spells.

From a literary standpoint her writing is considered more an autohagiography than autobiography. She pictured herself as a saint and described her life and visions accordingly. The central focus of *The Book* is a spiritual treatise, including religious drama, accounts of conversations with Jesus and other possibly questionable material.

Saint Catherine of Genoa (1447-1510)

Catherine of Genoa, along with her husband, worked and lived among the poor in Genoa, Italy. They lost a fortune through bad circumstances, and in the process Catherine turned to the contemplative life. During their work in a hospital her husband died, but she continued her efforts, becoming the matron of the hospital.

Catherine's efforts and personal life did not go unnoticed, for her spirituality ran deep. She is noted for her writings, but they do not rise higher than her reputation for acts of charity. Her best known works are *Life and Teachings* and her *Dialogues*. These describe her knowledge of the pure love of God and the struggle to accept that pure love, sometimes through renunciation of self. She writes, "Take a piece of bread and eat it. . . . [I]ts substance goes into you to nourish the body and the rest is eliminated because your body no longer needs it. For the body is more important than the bread: it was created as a means, but it is not to remain forever with us. Likewise, we must remove all evil inclinations from our bodies, they cannot live on within us, lest we die" (from *Life and Teachings*).

Saint Teresa of Avila (1515-1582). See path seven.

Margaret Fell Fox (1614-1701)

Margaret Fell Fox was one of the earliest and most effective Quaker leaders in the seventeenth century. Initially married to Judge Thomas Fell, eleven years after his death (in 1658) she married the founder of the Quaker movement, George Fox (in 1669), whose ministry had led to her own spiritual awakening. She is best remembered for her legendary courage, her tenacity in the face of persecution and her profound Christian life. She also articulated one of the earliest and finest defenses of the right of women to preach, *Women's Speaking Justified*. She did not shrink in the face of opposition and used her broad social connections to advance religious liberty, even taking her concerns directly to the king. She was instrumental in getting legislation passed that protected the rights of dissenting religious groups to gather and worship as they chose. Her life of virtue and holiness, and her commitment to the right of every person to love God and express their gifts fully, are enduring hallmarks of her legacy.

Madame (Jeanne-Marie Bouvier de la Mothe) Guyon (1648-1717)

Madame Guyon was forced into an arranged marriage at an early age (16) to a man more than twenty years her senior (Jacques Guyon, age 38). Born at the end of the Thirty Years' War (1618-1648), she suffered mightily throughout her life, including frequent illnesses and early widowhood (at age 28). She was a controversial figure, advocating daring religious practices when French society was in upheaval and the Roman Catholic Church was in reaction.

Her books and writings all emphasize a detachment from the sensible world in order to know Christ directly and to gain union with God. She calls us to abandon ourselves wholly and completely to God, working to free ourselves from all thought and emotion. Her quest to find the pre-reflective relationship with God is a mark of all great mystics. Guyon characterizes her position this way: "Perfect poverty by total privation of everything that was mine, both inward and outwardly. Perfect obedience of my will to the will of the Lord and submission to the church."[1]

She also advocated a life of prayer that transcended reason. "May I hasten to say," she begins, "that the kind of prayer I am speaking of is not a prayer that begins in the heart. It is a prayer that comes from the heart and is not interrupted by human thinking."[2]

Unfortunately, her approach lacked balance and she succumbed to opposition and even persection throughout her adult life. In 1688, through a variety of circumstances, including a seven-month stay in jail on heresy charges, she became a friend and talking companion of François Fénelon. This marked Madame Guyon's official entry into the Quietist Movement and her role as one of its more outspoken enthusiasts. Fénelon's response to Guyon was mixed. He recognized and appreciated the originality of some of her positions, but her overall approach and especially some of her more outlandish ideas eventually led Fénelon to distance himself from her.

Her works were eventually published in 1704 in the Netherlands. Her ideas gained popularity, especially among the English and German pietists. She died in 1717, believing herself to be a member in good standing in the Roman Catholic Church and an ardent follower of Jesus Christ.

Saint Elizabeth Ann Seton (1774-1821)

Elizabeth Ann Seton, a modern American saint, began as a well-educated, married Episcopalian. Her Protestant years were the foundation of her spiritual life, as she was devoted to the reading of Scripture, felt the importance of the sermon in liturgy, and was eager to be guided by clergy in matters of doctrine. Following the death of her husband, however, she became a Catholic and lived another sixteen years.

Elizabeth patterned her spiritual life after Teresa of Avila. Her primary characteristics were confidence in God, prayer, joy in any circumstance and concern for those in pain and facing death. Her longing for relationship with God was grounded in love for the Almighty and the Eucharist. Elizabeth established a religious community as well as a school for girls in Baltimore, Maryland, which was the first free Catholic school in America. The three crucial tests in her life were (1) her indecision about conversion,

(2) being the head of a religious community, and (3) the death of her daughter. During this time she suffered from tuberculosis, but continued to guide the children and the sisterhood, and established two orphanages and another school. She was the first native-born American to be canonized by the Catholic Church, which transpired on September 14, 1975, and is considered the patron saint of widows, those near death, and teachers.

Elizabeth Gurney Fry (1780-1845)

Elizabeth Gurney Fry, an English Quaker, was born into a family of high social class and privilege, but spent the best years of her adult life helping the poor and oppressed. She came from a large family (the fourth of twelve children) and had eleven children of her own. In 1799 she had a profound spiritual awakening and embraced strict religious practices. In 1813, under the influence of Stephen Grellet, she visited Newgate Prison and was appalled at the conditions under which women and children lived. She began working to improve their lives, helping to organize the women into working groups and coordinating a school for the children.

In 1818 she was invited to address the House of Commons on the issue of prison conditions, and subsequently became a symbol of social reform throughout the English-speaking world. Her own efforts motivated other Quakers to initiate reforms that led to the abolishment of slavery, the promotion of Native American rights and the improvement of conditions in mental hospitals.

Hannah Whitall Smith (1832-1911)

Hannah Whitall Smith, a Philadelphia Quaker, wrote *The Christian's Secret of a Happy Life,* which became a classic after it was published in 1870. Written from the perspective of Quaker simplicity and practicality, the book is a great encouragement to those who want to live a more joyful and fruitful life. Smith's secret to a happy life is to trust implicitly the promises of God. Through that trust the average man or woman can elevate the level of their lives to a higher degree of consecration.

As seen in the lives of the many women described here, Christian service seems to flow naturally from the dedicated Christian. Hannah Smith's writing reminds us that service often begins as a joy and ends up a burden.

However, if we really want to do God's will, and his will is written on the heart of the believer, the earnest Christian will want to follow him. Again her counsel is that the spiritual foundation must be built before the edifice of Christian service can flow from the individual. Thus Hannah urges us to turn our will over to Christ completely in order to find complete joy in service to him.

Saint Thérèse of Lisieux (1873-1897)

Thérèse of Lisieux suffered throughout her life, eventually dying of tuberculosis. As a child she claimed she was instantly healed when a statue of Mary smiled at her. She became a Carmelite nun at the age of fifteen. As she developed her spiritual life, she proclaimed that her vocation was love, and this was lived out through her burning love for Jesus, which she expressed through constant prayer. Thérèse's motto was "Love is repaid by love alone." She was simple, humble, trusting and prayerful, even while suffering with disease.

This humble woman practiced virtues that became known as St. Thérèse's "Little Way." The focus of this lifestyle made love and trust in God the center of one's life. In her twenty-four years of life, she did nothing extraordinary, but that was her unique quality. As a "modern" saint she is a great example of a loving and simple life dedicated to God. As her health declined, she wrote her autobiography, *The Story of a Soul*, in which she encouraged others to follow her simple journey.

Catherine Booth (1829-1890)

Catherine Booth is part of the long history of devout and spiritual women of the church who spoke fervently against evil in society and sin in individuals, who defended and tended to the weakest of society and who made lasting contributions to righting systemic ills within the societies of their era. Catherine was British and the product of a Christian upbringing. She read her Bible through eight times by the age of twelve! By fourteen she was writing articles that denounced the plague of alcoholism.

At the age of twenty-three Catherine married William Booth, a Methodist minister, and began a long ministry together with him. Over time their ministry focused on the struggle against alcohol, and their work resulted in the Salvation Army, first in England and then throughout the world. William spoke to the ragged and poor, while Catherine spoke to the wealthy in an effort to raise funds for their mission.

Catherine Booth could also be called a feminist, in the best connotation of the word. While working with the poor in London she found women and children working in poor conditions for long hours for much less money than men doing the same work. She and others in the Salvation Army attempted to shame employers into paying better wages for the women, along with improving working conditions.

Catherine also found that she could speak to large groups. Her preaching was met with outrage by the established churches and especially by women who considered her leadership inappropriate. But women were considered as equals in the Salvation Army, largely due to her influence. Her speaking ability, along with activity among the poor, established her reputation as an extremely capable and spiritual woman. Once again the spiritual journey of a devout woman led to action and the Christian witness of benevolence.

Evelyn Underhill (1875-1941)

Evelyn Underhill is a noted modern writer on spirituality. This brilliant woman combined scholarship with spiritual insight, and her writings are treasured among those who study spirituality. Her best known writing is *Mysticism: A Study of the Nature and Development of Spiritual Consciousness.* In *Mysticism* she exalts the spiritual life as a profound spiritual love affair between humans and God. That writing is divided into two sections. In the first, "The Mystic Fact," there are seven chapters that attempt to define the phenomena of mystical experience, especially in relation to the total human experience. In the second section, "The Mystic Way," Underhill expounds on the historic evidence for mystical experiences, taken from writings of both the East and the West.

Underhill practiced a devotional life with fervor and thus wrote from personal experience and insight. She was much sought after as a spiritual director and became a well-known conductor of retreats among the Anglicans.

Simone Weil (1909-1943)

Simone Weil, a French philosopher, social activist and mystic, resided on the periphery of traditional Christian belief. Simone grew up in an agnostic household of Jewish lineage; her father was a doctor. Throughout her life she suffered from headaches, sinusitis and poor physical condition. Simone had limited ability with social interactions, probably due to her ascetic lifestyle, introversion and eccentricity, not to mention her brilliant mind. She was active in many political movements of her era and wrote about them with insight.

While visiting Assisi and Italy in the spring of 1937, she had a profound religious experience in the same church where Saint Francis had prayed. This led her into prayer for the first time in her life. A year later she had more powerful revelations, and from that point her writings became more mystical and spiritual, though she always maintained a focus on social and political issues. During World War II she was active in the French resistance to such an extent that her health deteriorated and she contracted tuberculosis. Simone developed an obsession with discovering more about God and what his will might be for her life. In one mystical experience she stated that "Christ himself came down and He took me." Following her experiences, her biographers state that she spent the rest of her life searching for God's will and writing about the intellectual consequences of her mystical experiences.

Though she became attracted to Catholicism, she declined to be baptized until the end of her life, as she wrote in *Waiting for God*. In this book she explains how she thought Plato related to the Christian faith. Though she felt herself primarily attracted to Christianity, she had a great interest in other religious traditions as well. Simone came to believe that some of these other religious traditions were valid paths to God, but she was totally opposed to any syncretism, feeling that it would destroy the value of individual religious traditions.

Dorothy Day (1897-1980)

Dorothy Day, like so many Christians through the ages, spent her early years in rather pagan circumstances, including two common-law marriages and an abortion. After the birth of her daughter, Tamar, she began a spiritual journey and awakening, which led her to embrace Christianity as a Roman Catholic. She had her daughter baptized first because "I did not want my child to flounder as I often had floundered. . . . I wanted to believe, and I wanted my child to believe, and if belonging to a Church would give her so inestimable a grace as faith in God . . . then the thing to do was to have her baptized a Catholic."[3] Then Day herself was baptized at the age of thirty.

Living in New York City, she became involved with the Catholic Worker movement, which had laid out a path of neutrality and pacifism in the turbulent 1930s. That movement expanded into a hospitality house in the slums of New York, then a series of farms for communal living. By the start of World War II, there were many such communities throughout the United States and in ten other countries. At one point Dorothy became disgusted that communists were parading for the rights of the poor instead of Christians. "I offered up a special prayer, a prayer which came with tears and anguish, that some way would open up for me to use what talents I possessed for my fellow workers, for the poor."[4]

Though Day had a rather progressive attitude toward social and economic rights, she still claimed an orthodox and traditional sense of Catholic morality and piety. She was awarded the *Pacem in Terris* (Peace on Earth) in 1972 by Pope John XXIII. She was proposed for sainthood in 1983.

Mother Teresa (1910-1997)

From the small country of Macedonia, Teresa lived to become one of the best known Christian women of the twentieth century. Again we see a woman who at a very young age felt the call of God on their life. For her the call was to the mission field. She joined the Sisters of Loreto at the age of eighteen and was already in India by the age of twenty-one, where for seventeen years she taught at St. Mary's High School in Calcutta. Drawn to serve the poor and suffering outside the convent, she received permission to begin a work in the slums of Calcutta, at first with an open-air school for children. Voluntary helpers and financial aid would follow. By the age of forty she had permission to begin her own order, The Missionaries of Charity.

The sisters primarily took care of those for whom no one else cared, often the victims of disease and of AIDS. As the order grew and spread around the world, it did include both "active" and "contemplative" groups of men and women. Thus the work included those longing for God through a variety of streams. By 1990 there were over a million coworkers in more than forty countries. Mother Teresa received the "Pope John XXIII Peace Prize" in 1971 and the Nobel Peace Prize in 1979.[5]

To keep this famous woman in a human perspective, in her private letters, *Come Be My Light*, Mother Teresa divulged that for several decades she experienced spiritual dryness and a profound sense of being disconnected from God. Those that knew Mother Teresa called her a clear illustration that time devoted to God in prayer not only does not detract from effective and loving service to our neighbor, but is in fact the inexhaustible source of that service. Does the fact that she persevered indicate that she had great spiritual depth? It should be noted that John of the Cross, Martin Luther and Oswald Chambers confessed to feeling the same spiritual challenges. Mother Teresa eventually embraced this long period of spiritual dryness by noting, "I have come to love the darkness." Eventually, she experienced a special encounter with God's grace that seems to have reassured her in her life mission. She said, "Before you speak, it is necessary for you to listen, for God speaks in the silence of the heart." Whether this visitation removed all doubt, turmoil and despair remains unclear. What is clear is that she never stopped loving God and serving humanity.

Further Reading

Armstrong, Christopher J. R. *Evelyn Underhill: An Introduction to Her Life and Writings*. Grand Rapids: Eerdmans, 1975.

Bauerschmidt, Frederick Christian. *Julian of Norwich and the Mystical Body Politic of Christ*. Notre Dame, Ind.: University of Notre Dame Press, 1999.

Beer, Frances. *Women and Mystical Experience in the Middle Ages*. Rochester, N.Y.: Boydell Press, 1992.

Chervin, Ronda De Sola. *Prayers of the Women Mystics*. Ann Arbor, Mich.: Servant, 1992.

Furlong, Monica. *Thérèse of Lisieux*. New York: Orbis, 1987.

Glasscoe, Marion, ed. *The Medieval Mystical Tradition in England*. Exeter Symposium IV. Suffolk: St. Edmundsbury Press, 1987.

Hindsley, Leonard P., ed. and trans. *Margaret Ebner: Major Works*. New York: Paulist, 1993.

Kelly, Ellin, and Annabelle Melville, eds. *Elizabeth Seton: Selected Writings*. New York: Paulist, 1987.

Kienzle, Beverly Mayne, and Pamela J. Walker, eds. *Women Preachers and Prophets: Through Two Millennia of Christianity*. Berkeley: University of California Press, 1998.

Lehmijork-Gardner, Maiju, et al., ed. and trans. *Dominican Penitent Women*. Classics of Western Spirituality. New York: Paulist, 2005.

Marshall, Sherrin. *Women in Reformation and Counter-Reformation Europe*. Bloomington: Indiana University Press, 1989.

Mazzoni, Cristina. *The Women in God's Kitchen*. New York: Continuum, 2007.

McLellan, David. *Simone Weil: Utopian Pessimist*. London: Macmillan, 1989.

McGinn, Bernard. *The Flowering of Mysticism: Men and Women in the New Mysticism—1200-1350*. Vol. 3 of The Presence of God: A History of Western Christian Mysticism. New York: Crossroad, 1998.

Nava, Alexander. *The Mystical and Prophetic Thought of Simone Weil and Gustavo Gutiérrez: Reflections on the Mystery and Hiddenness of God*. New York: State University of New York Press, 2001.

Scott, David. *A Revolution of Love: The Meaning of Mother Teresa*. Chicago: Loyola Press, 2005.

Tobin, Frank. *Mechthild von Magdeburg: A Medieval Mystic in Modern Eyes*. Columbia, S.C.: Camden House, 1995.

Warren, Nancy Bradley. *Women of God and Arms: Female Spirituality and Political Conflict, 1380-1600*. Philadelphia: University of Pennsylvania Press, 2005.

Windeatt, Barry, ed. *English Mystics of the Middle Ages*. Surrey, U.K.: Cambridge University Press, 1994.

Appendix 3

The Contribution of the Eastern Orthodox Church

Most of us tend to be more familiar with Western Christianity (Roman Catholic, Anglican and Protestant) and its saints, writers, theologians and leaders in the field of spirituality, mysticism and spiritual formation. This appendix is written to provide a brief orientation to the rich tradition and great minds of the Eastern Church, the Orthodox. Some of the early subjects were of course part of the "Great Tradition before the Schism" (pre-1054). Though the early church in the East could boast of its brilliant theologians and leaders, over time it became more distinct from the Western Church through its focus on light versus darkness, life versus death, spirit versus matter and the limitations of reason. It also preserved one of the most original and beautiful theologies of iconography, the belief that the presence of God is mediated by objects and art forms that elevate us to the Almighty.

The Orthodox would be in agreement with Pascal, for example, in recognizing the limitations of knowing God through reason. Their theology still notes the profound difference between knowing about God and knowing God. The Eastern Church emphasizes a great reverence for mystery coupled with a distrust of reason. In contrast to the Western Church, with its fascination and interest in the intellectual heritage of Aristotle, the East asserts that theologians first should know God through prayer, contemplation and spiritual disciplines, and then build their theology from intimate communion with him.

The Orthodox also resonate with the "spiritual life as journey" (see path two). They view our salvation as a journey of not just being "saved" but as *continually* being saved as we move toward the goal of *theosis,* or becoming like Christ. It should be noted that for the Orthodox, all aspects of our spiritual life are united. We cannot separate our participation in the

liturgy of the church from our theology, or our spirituality from our
spiritual formation and devotion. All of life is a sacrament lived for God.
The Orthodox model of the unity in the triune God is also the Orthodox
all-encompassing model for living the Christian life.

Saint Paul of Thebes (c. 227-c. 341)

Paul of Thebes was orphaned at a young age, became a hermit and lived
in a cave for over ninety years. Tradition holds that he prayed incessantly
and lived on dates and bread, which were brought to him by a raven. In a
vision, St. Anthony the Great was told that this hermit was a great servant
of God and that he should visit him. They conversed through the night,
and Anthony learned about the feeding by the raven. In the morning the
raven brought enough bread for the two of them.

Paul told Anthony that he knew he would soon die and instructed Anthony to return to bury him with a cloak received from Athanasius. When
Anthony returned, he beheld the soul of Paul surrounded by angels,
prophets and apostles, shining like the sun and ascending toward God.
Anthony had forgotten to bring a shovel, but two lions came up from the
wilderness and dug a hole with their claws. Thus he died at the age of 113
years. He is not noted for great deeds but was held up as an example of
extreme devotion by the early monks and hermits of the desert.

Saint Anthony the Great (c. 251-356). See also path two.

Anthony has been called "the Father of Monasticism," though this form
of spirituality was already being practiced in the deserts of Palestine and
Egypt. Anthony was an Egyptian born to wealthy parents. On the death
of his parents he gave the money from selling their properties to the poor,
forsook his status and became the disciple of another hermit. Thus he was
an early ascetic who retired to isolated desert locations and focused his life
on devotion and prayer.

On writing Anthony's biography, Athanasius stated that the devil
fought Anthony by afflicting him with boredom, laziness and fantasies
that he overcame by the power of prayer. It was further claimed that the
devil was so angry with his failure to tempt Anthony that Satan literally
beat him physically and warred against him with phantoms of snakes and

wild animals. But Anthony laughed at them scornfully and told them that God gave him victory over anything the devil could send on him.

Over time Anthony's legend grew and he was threatened by governments that disliked his preaching. His fame even reached Emperor Constantine, who asked Anthony to pray for him. In 338 he was also asked by Athanasius of Alexandria to help him refute the heretical teachings of Arius. But Anthony left no writings, though his sayings were spread by some of his disciples, like Serapion. His sayings were included in various collections of sayings of the desert fathers. He asked that he be buried in an unmarked grave lest his body become an object of veneration. Thus his life became an example of devotion, humility, care for the less fortunate and attention to prayer.

Saint Pachomius (c. 298-348). See also path two.

Abba Pachomius is the recognized founder of cenobitic (religious orders living in community) monasticism. He became attracted to Christianity while serving in the Roman army and becoming a captive, because Christians brought food and necessities to the captives. Though he began his calling as a hermit, he learned about communities that had been created by Macarius. Following this example, Pachomius began to organize these cells into formal organizations. From his initial monastery, the concept spread, and by the time of his death it is estimated that three thousand monasteries were spread across Egypt. With the assistance of Basil of Caesarea, the formal rules for ascetics, *Ascetica,* became the rule and is still used by the Eastern Orthodox Church, a rule comparable to the *Rule of St. Benedict* in the West.

Pachomius never allowed himself to become a priest. During his forty years with the monks he was a zealous defender of orthodoxy against Arianism. His reputation as a holy man has endured the test of time and continues to this day.

Saint James, bishop of Nisibis (early fourth century)

James, also known as Jacob, grew up in the city of Nisibis on the border of the Persian and Roman empires. He became a hermit who devoted his time to prayerful conversations with God, living always an ascetic life,

usually under the open sky, dressed in goat skins. On moving into the city
to learn more from the Christians of the community, he was soon recognized for his strict and pious life. The church of the city elected him as
their bishop in about 314.

James was revered for his great miracles and his gift of clairvoyance. His
desperate prayers during an attack on the city by the Persian Sopor resulted in the enemy being attacked by hordes of flies and mosquitoes,
which drove them away. Later he was numbered among the Fathers at the
Council of Nicaea in 325, and was also a defender of the faith against
Arianism. His thoughts were written into a discourse of eighteen chapters
about faith, love, fasting, spiritual warfare and the resurrection of the dead.

Saint Athanasius of Alexandria (293-373). See also path two.

The importance of Athanasius to Christian theology cannot be overstated.
He is revered as a saint by the Oriental Orthodox and Eastern Orthodox,
Roman Catholic and Eastern Catholic churches and is regarded as a great
leader by Lutherans, Anglicans and most Protestants in general. He is
counted as one of the four Great Doctors of the Eastern Church.

Athanasius is recognized as the first to identify the twenty-seven books
of the New Testament that are in use today. His polemical writings against
theological opponents are extensive, including *Orations Against the Arians*,
and his defense of the divinity and person of the Holy Spirit (*Letters to
Serapion* and *On the Holy Spirit*). His most-read book, a biography of Anthony the Great, *Vita Antonii*, has served as inspiration to monastics of
both the East and the West.

Saint Ephraim the Syrian (306-373)

Ephraim was a prolific hymnographer (writer of hymns) and theologian
in the fourth century. He also wrote homilies in verse and biblical commentaries. These were works of practical theology to instruct the church
in troubled times. His works are free of Western influence. Having a
reputation for humility and for being totally surrendered to God, Ephraim's
focus was often the importance of repentance. It is said that he had a great
gift of wisdom, and grace flowed from his mouth. He was a disciple of
James, bishop of Nisibis.

Saint Cyril of Jerusalem (c. 315-386)

Cyril of Jerusalem is venerated as a saint by both the Roman Catholic and Eastern Orthodox churches. He was present at the Council of Nicaea and always gave a thorough adhesion to the Nicene doctrines. Cyril wrote twenty-three catechetical lectures, delivered while he was a presbyter, containing instruction on topics of faith and practice. The lectures, which were prepared for catacumens coming into the church, were based on texts of Scripture with an abundance of biblical references.

Cyril emphasized freedom of the will. To him sin is the consequence of, but not a natural condition of, freedom. The body is not the cause but an instrument of sin. His remedy was repentance.

Saint Gregory of Nazianzus (329-389)

Gregory was an itinerant young man, with a great yearning for knowledge. He was a fellow student and also a friend of Basil the Great at Basil's monastery in the desert. Gregory, as with so many early fathers, had great humility, thinking himself unworthy to be a priest and fearing that his faith would be tested by the responsibility. He was an active opponent of Arianism.

Later he served as bishop of Constantinople from 381-389. He hated the city and its politics, but was known as a peacemaker who tried to bring Arians back to the faith. Gregory was a noted preacher on the Trinity. He is revered also by the Western church as both father and doctor of the church. (To be a doctor of the church, one must be noted for both eminent learning and recognized sanctity.)

Saint Gregory of Nyssa (c. 335-395). See also path two.

Gregory was married and a brother of Basil the Great. He was another defender of the church against Arianism. Some of his writings have survived and are known for surpassing the other Cappadocian fathers in the depth and richness of both his theology and philosophy. One of his mystical writings is *From Glory to Glory,* recently published in 1963.

Evagrius of Ponticus (c. 345-399). See path two.

Saint John Chrysostom (c. 347–407)

John of Constantinople, later called John Chrysostom (or the "golden-mouthed" for his reputation as a master orator), was a child of a fervent Christian mother. Early in life he became a monk. After some years in the monastery he returned to the church, first at Antioch, and began to preach, which led to some fame. At the age of fifty he was made bishop of Constantinople, a city given to luxurious living. After living a life of solitude and poverty, John was unable to tolerate the way the Christians of this city wed the gospel to their own lives of luxury.

First he reformed the clergy, denouncing those who lived in wealth and ordering the priests to live an austere life. The luxurious items that adorned the bishop's palace were sold, with the proceeds given to feed the poor. And he thundered against the laity who were not living in accordance with the gospel.

Of course Chrysostom learned that the powerful and wealthy do not appreciate being called down, and he was involved in various political intrigues. His only aim was to expound the Scriptures so that the laity would fully understand the lessons and fully grasp their practical applications. Thus his entire life was a battle against evil and for the integrity of the church in its call to service. John Chrysostom's life is a prime example of the contemplative life leading to action.

Saint Macarius the Great of Egypt (c. 330–390)

Married and widowed early in life, Macarius led a life not uncommon for monastics of the early church. He was well educated while still following ascetic principles of prayer, fasting and penitence. The humility of the saint is shown by his unwillingness to be ordained at an early age. Great spiritual battles ensued, with demonic attacks in which he reportedly had discussions with demons. At about the age of thirty he sought out Anthony the Great, father of Egyptian monasticism, and lived with the elder saint for a number of years. By the age of forty, Macarius was made the leader of desert monks. On the death of Anthony, Macarius received Anthony's staff, and it was reported that he also received a "double portion" of his spiritual power.

Macarius performed many healings and was often sought out for help and advice, which disturbed his solitude. It was reported that through his prayers, the Lord even raised the dead. His endless conversations with God often sent him into states of spiritual rapture. His inner passion, though, was always exhibited through his life of action. During the Arian controversies he was exiled to an island of pagans, and the inhabitants of the island soon were baptized as Christians. His writings survive in "Fifty Spiritual Homilies" and seven "Ascetic Treatises."

In his teachings he emphasizes that the inner actions of the Christian usually determine his or her grasp of divine truth and love, that one acquires salvation through grace and the gift of the Holy Spirit, and that we inherit eternal life as much by grace as by truth. Macarius died at the age of ninety.

Saint John Cassian the Roman (c. 360-435). See path six.

Saint Cyril of Alexandria (c. 378-c. 444)

Cyril was the pope of Alexandria at the height of its importance in the Roman Empire. He was also known as "the Pillar of Faith." This learned saint was tutored by his uncle, Theophilus, who was the pope of Alexadria prior to him. Later he was a central figure in the First Council of Ephesus (431), which discussed the various problems with Nestorianism, among other issues.

Cyril regarded the presence of God in the person of Jesus to be so mystically powerful that it spread from his body into the rest of the human race, even promising immortality and transfiguration to believers. Nestorius, by contrast, held Jesus to be primarily a moral and ethical example to the faithful.

Cyril was scholarly and a prolific writer, reflecting accurate thinking, precise exposition and great reasoning skills. Among his writings are commentaries on John, Luke and the Pentateuch; treatises on dogmatic theology; letters and sermons.

Saint Euthymius (378-473)

Euthymius was recognized as a leader among monks in early Palestine. He taught other monks the principles of leadership in monastic communities, and as a result many of the monasteries that were founded could be traced to his influence. Most of what he taught he learned from monks who had fled Egypt due to persecution. Such customs as having a probationary period were passed on through his teaching. The functional organization of monasteries seemed to be his expertise, and this was highly important in the later survival of these new institutions. His personal advice and guidance to young monks proved fruitful, as numbers of them became bishops, patriarchs and superiors in monasteries.

Saint Romanos the Melodist (c. 450–c. 500)

Romanos was Greek, born in Syria of Jewish parentage. He was made a deacon early in life and was noted for his ascetic lifestyle of perpetual prayer and fasting. At one point he prayed fervently for a better voice and for skill in hymn writing. Tradition holds that he experienced a vision and soon possessed a marvelous voice and the ability to write hymns of profound theology. Romanos was also known for his humility, even after composing over eight thousand hymns and becoming revered as a great melodist.

Saint John Climacus of Sinai (c. 525–606)

John Climacus became a monk early in life and received an excellent education, and later was called Scholasticus. Though highly educated, he always taught that human wisdom could lead to conceit. Again, the grace of humility was present in him as in the lives of so many Eastern saints. John lived for many years as a hermit and was reported to have received the gift of tears and continual prayer. He was often sought out by other monks for spiritual guidance, which interrupted his prayer life. When he was made abbot of the monastery at Mount Sinai, tradition holds that many saw the prophet Moses giving commands to those who served at the celebration table.

His writing includes a book of thirty homilies dealing with various virtues, from holy and righteous activity to divine vision. *The Ladder of Divine Ascent* identifies the thirty steps we ascend in our spiritual life as we move toward God, while it also warns of pitfalls and dangers. The book is revered among the Orthodox.

John Moschus (c. 550–619)

John Moschus was a monastic living near Jerusalem. He wrote *Pratum*

Spirituale (The Spiritual Meadow), containing stories and directions regarding monastic life. His prose is recognized as some of the most beautiful writing to come out of that era.

Saint Maximus the Confessor (c. 580–662)

Maximus was born a nobleman in Constantinople. He was best known as a theologian and the author of many christological and ascetic works. Maximus defended orthodoxy against the monothelite heresy, which asserted that there was only one will in Christ. He insisted on the dual nature (human and divine) of Christ, each having its own will. For his stand he had his right hand cut off and his tongue cut out, and he was exiled. Thus he was unable to preach truth. Later his theology was affirmed by the Sixth Ecumenical Council. Many of his writings are found in the *Philokalia*.

Saint Peter of Damascus (late seventh and early eighth centuries)

Writing in the *Philokalia*, Peter of Damascus pointed out that the gifts of God were sometimes situations that made our lives more pleasant but often were challenges that developed deeper spirituality. He noted that poverty is a gift we can endure with patience and gratitude; in sickness we can earn a crown of patience; weakness and ignorance are given so we can turn our backs on worldly things and live in stillness and humility.

Saint John of Damascus (c. 676–749)

This Syrian monk and presbyter was raised in Damascus. He was known as a polymath, whose fields of interest and contribution included law, theology, philosophy and music. John was also an administrator for the ruler of Damascus. He entered the fray of arguments regarding icons and wrote *Apologetic Treatises Against Those Decrying the Holy Images*. These writings influenced the Second Council of Nicaea. Having become involved in the politics of the discussion, he later was accused wrongly of other writings, which turned out to be forgeries. The caliph of Damascus ordered John's hand cut off so that he could write no more. According to a tenth-century biographer, his hand was miraculously restored after fervent prayer. John lived out the rest of his days in the monastery of Saint Sabas, near Jerusalem, where he continued to write commentaries, hymns and apologetic writings, including *An Exact Exposition of the Orthodox Faith*.

Saint Photius the Great (c. 810–c. 895)

Photius is better known for his efforts at peacemaking between the Eastern and Western churches than for his writings. He is recognized as the standard-bearer of the church in its disagreements with the pope of Rome. Thus he was involved in various issues, such as articulating why the filioque clause ("and the son") should not be inserted into the original Nicene Creed, the popes' claims of supremacy, and jurisdictional questions over churches in Byzantine areas. On a personal level he was recognized for the virtue of his life and his political genius along with intellectual aptitude.

Saint Symeon the New Theologian (949–1022)

Symeon the New Theologian is so called to distinguish him from John the Evangelist (called John the Theologian in Greek) and also Gregory of Nyzanius, also called Gregory the Theologian. These are the only three men in the Eastern Orthodox Church to have been given the title Theologian.

Symeon was well educated and his family expected him to go into politics. However, at about the age of twenty he was overcome with an ecstatic state in which he experienced God as a living presence of radiant light. Though he continued for a time in his family's wishes and became an imperial senator, his continuous mystical experiences were not compatible with a public life. He became a monk at twenty-seven.

In his writings he stated that humans could and should experience God directly. He urged not only monks and ascetics toward that experience, but also those involved in normal activities of the world. The small hermitage under his direction became a full monastery. There he wrote *Hymns of Divine Love*, a collection of poems describing his mystical experiences.

Saint Gregory of Sinai (c. 1290–1346)

Gregory of Sinai lived in the spirit and teachings of the early desert fathers. For the last twenty-five years of his life he lived on Mount Athos in Greece, the center of monasticism for the Orthodox. He provides us with some of the most practical wisdom and direction regarding our lives in Christ.

Having received the spirit of Jesus Christ by means of a pure prayer of the heart, he teaches us to communicate mystically with the Lord. But not understanding the greatness, honor and glory resulting from grace, and not caring about our spiritual growth through the keeping of the commandments and reaching true contemplation, we are careless and throw ourselves into the abyss of insensitivity and darkness.

Thus we are dead in the Spirit, alive—but not in Christ—and not in accordance with the conviction that what is born of the spirit should be spiritual. However, what we have received through our baptism into the life of Jesus Christ is not destroyed but is only buried. Wisdom and grace demand that it be revealed and brought into the open. But how? Two methods can lead us to this actualization.

First, this gift is open to the one who keeps the commandments; and to the degree that we keep the commandments, we experience light and wisdom. Second, we can acquire this gift through ceaselessly calling on the Lord Jesus, or through constant awareness of God's presence.

Saint Gregory Palamas (c. 1296-1359)

Gregory Palamas was the archbishop of Thessaloniki. His theology held to three centralities: knowledge, prayer and divine vision. Gregory noted that there is a natural knowledge of God, but it is different to know *about* God than to actually know God. This is still a central truth in Orthodoxy. Gregory was a strong defender of the reality of a monk's experiences in prayer. He asserts that God has an unknowable essence but knowable "energies." (This can also be called a neo-Platonic paradigm of an infinite and perfect being, by definition ineffable to finite beings.) Thus for Palamas, God's grace was part of God, and those energies were knowable and were what monks were seeing during their prayers.

Gregory called philosophy, which should further our knowledge of God, a "fallen" state of knowledge when it is misused and turned, in effect, into God. He did not support the view that soul and body were distinct and separate in the larger scheme of human life, nor did he accept that the soul was good and the body evil. Matter could not be in essence evil, for it is the creation of God. He saw that apart from sin, nothing is wrong in the present life, not even death, but everything can lead to evil.

He defended the concept of the divine vision and supported those who claimed to have seen the Divine Light with their own eyes. He felt that the divine vision was not a charismatic gift but rather the fruit of inspired prayer. He also wrote that the passions, when properly focused and directed through prayer, have the ability to draw up the flesh to a dignity near to that of the spirit, and in this state the Spirit gives the body experiences of divine things. He asserted that when the apostles Peter, James and John were observers of the transfiguration of Jesus at Mount Tabor, they were actually seeing the uncreated light of God, and that it is possible for others to be gifted to see that same uncreated light of God with the assistance of spiritual disciplines and contemplative prayer, though not in any mechanistic manner. Thus one observes in Palamas's theology a holistic view of humanity and a dynamic conception of faith, bound up in a spirituality of sanctification and transfiguration.

Some of the writings of Gregory of Palamas can be found in the *Philokalia*.

Saint Nicholas Cabasilas (1319-1391)

Nicholas was a Byzantine layperson and mystic well-educated in theology, astronomy, law and rhetoric. He was a poet and also wrote prose on issues such as hesychasm, usury and other social issues. The major writings of Nicholas include his *Commentary on the Divine Liturgy* and *The Life in Christ*. In that writing we discover Plato's experience where the ultimate object of our memory has been transformed by our Christian experience. Nicholas says, "When men have a longing so great that it surpasses human nature and eagerly desire and are able to accomplish things beyond human thought, it is the Bridegroom who has smitten them with this longing. It is he who has sent a ray of his beauty into their eyes. The greatness of the wound already shows the arrow which has struck home, the longing indicates who has inflicted the wound" (*The Life in Christ*, bk. 2, chap. 15).

Saint Michael of Klopsk Monastery (c. 1385-1453)

Michael took on the role of "fool-for-Christ," to avoid the praise of men, and preferred the garb of rags. Tradition holds that he was a fervent student of Scripture as well as the lives of the saints. Michael became an example for the monks in their spiritual struggles. It is said that he wore out his body in work, vigils and care for others. As he gained the gift of clairvoyance Michael denounced the vices of the people, including the wealthy and powerful. He foretold the birth of Prince Ioann III and his conquests. He also denounced Prince Shemyako for blinding his brother.

In Saint Michael's final days his prayers resulted in the granary of the monastery not experiencing decrease, despite the fact that grain was dispensed to the poor. He also foretold the place of his death and burial and died in 1453.

Saint Basil the Blessed Fool-for-Christ and Wonderworker of Moscow (c. 1488-1557)

Basil was born during the reign of Czar Ivan the Terrible. As a youth in Rostov he took on the role of foolishness by wearing chains formed into heavy iron crosses. On his head he wore a large iron cap. Those working with Basil began to notice extraordinary occurrences, such as a time when in tears he told a man not to worry about wearing out his shoes. Within days the man died.

On moving to Moscow at sixteen, Basil walked barefoot through the streets in burning heat and winter cold. He began to denounce quietly injustices that he observed in the streets, and his reputation grew, with the population calling him Blessed Basil. As he walked in his bare feet, he preached mercy for the poor. At the same time he was harsh on those who gave alms for selfish reasons. He preached in taverns and was seen clutching the corners of such buildings in tears as he prayed for those within. Basil prophesied great sorrows for Russia, which included an invasion by Poland. It is said that he reproached Ivan the Terrible in a worship service because through prayer he realized the czar was thinking about building a palace. Basil was recognized as a man of prayer, for his communion with the divine and for his compassion. By the time of his death he was revered by both the clergy and the populace of Moscow.

Saint Nicodemos of the Holy Mountain (c. 1749-1809)

Nicodemos was a hesychast monk and author of Christian writings on prayer and asceticism. He is best known as the compiler of Orthodox writings into the *Philokalia*.

Saint Seraphim of Sarov (1759-1833)

Seraphim lived as a hermit and ascetic monk, once living for sixteen years in a forest, growing vegetables for food, studying the Bible and the writings of the fathers, and praying continuously. After physical deterioration due to being beaten by robbers, Seraphim moved into a small room of a monastery and lived as a recluse. However, during that time he became well known for his spiritual direction, his spiritual and prophetic gifts and healing miracles. Thus Seraphim became one of Russia's best known and beloved saints and leaders.

Bishop Ignatius Brianchaninov (1807-1867)

Bishop Brianchaninov is noted for being an ascetic writer, usually on issues regarding one's spiritual life. His primary work is *The Arena*.

Saint Silouan of Mount Athos (1866-1938)

Silouan was a Russian monk at Mount Athos. It was said that he had the gift of unceasing prayer, though at one time in his life it was taken from him. His diaries had great influence on Christian spirituality in the twentieth century. A stanza from his writings, found in *The Life and Teachings of Elder Silouan* by Bishop Alexander, follows:

> O Lord, grant me tears to shed for myself,
> and for the whole universe,
> that the nations may know Thee and live eternally with Thee.
> O Lord, vouchsafe us the gift of Thy humble Holy Spirit,
> that we may apprehend Thy glory.

Alexander Schmemann (1921-1983)

This brilliant writer and theologian was dean at St. Vladimir's Orthodox Theological Seminary in New York. Schmemann was a brilliant author. One of his most noted works is *The Eucharist*, which uses the Eucharist as an explanation of the meaning of the Christian life and spirituality.

John Meyendorff (1926-1992)

Father Meyendorff received his education at the Orthodox Theological Institute in Paris and also at the Sorbonne. At St. Vladimir's Orthodox Theological Seminary, New York, he was professor of church history and patristics; at Harvard he was lecturer in Byzantine theology; and then at Fordham he served as professor of Byzantine history. He also had various positions at Columbia University and Union Theological Seminary. His publications include *Gregory Palamas, Byzantine Theology* and a number of other theological writings on the Orthodox Church, Orthodox and Byzantine theology and relations between the Orthodox and other Christians.

Kallistos (Timothy) Ware, Bishop of Diokleia (1934-)

Bishop Ware is possibly the best known modern interpreter of Orthodoxy for this era's non-Orthodox. He has taught at Oxford and has translated a number of liturgical texts and the *Philokalia*. He has been a prolific contributor to the understanding of Orthodox spirituality in the English-speaking world. Perhaps his best known writings are *The Orthodox Church* and *The Orthodox Way*.

Acknowledgments

EVERY BOOK IS A COMMUNITY EFFORT. We are especially grateful to our students over the years who were the original recipients of this material. Their interaction with key figures and core ideas helped clarify our own thinking.

We are also indebted to many who helped in the preparation of the manuscript. Brad Sydow served for twelve years as Gayle's assistant at two different institutions and has played a key role in this entire work. He has read the manuscript multiple times and offered many helpful suggestions and insights. He also played a central role in the preparation of the "Christian Women and Spirituality" and "Contribution of the Eastern Orthodox Church" appendixes as he has spent the past several years exploring this latter trajectory of the Christian faith.

Andrew Winckles and Jeremy Norwood served two different periods as research assistants, tracking down obscure articles and finding key texts. Jeremy is now a professor in his own right and Andrew is preparing to become one. Thanks, guys.

Damon Seacott of Spring Arbor University and Nancy Town of Westmont College have provided able assistance throughout this entire project. The encouragement of Carolynn Foster throughout has been exceedingly helpful. Special thanks to Chris Simpson, who read the entire manuscript and made valuable comments. Cindy Bunch, senior editor at InterVarsity Press, has supported this effort throughout. We thank her.

Finally, there is no better supportive critic than Gayle's wife, Pam. She carries a long-running interest in the practice of the disciplines and especially our life of prayer, and she has read every chapter as we have prepared it. She is the educated layperson who has often said, "Help me know why I should care about these individuals; make me want to read them for myself." We trust her prodding will bear fruit in your reading habits . . . and your life.

Notes

Introduction

[1]This has been argued at length by such distinguished thinkers as Charles Taylor in *Sources of the Self*, Lezsek Kolakowski in *Modernity on Endless Trial*, and Robert Bellah in *Habits of the Heart* and *The Good Society*.

[2]This literature includes Dallas Willard's *Hearing God*, *The Spirit of the Disciplines* and *The Divine Conspiracy*; Richard Foster's *Celebration of Discipline*, *The Challenge of the Disciplined Life*, *Prayer: Finding the Heart's True Home* and *Streams of Living Water*; Eugene Peterson's *A Long Obedience in the Same Direction*, *Leap Over a Wall*, *Subversive Spirituality* and *Christ Plays in Ten Thousand Places*; Henri Nouwen's *The Way of the Heart*; John Ortberg's *The Life You've Always Wanted*; and Diogenes Allen's *Three Outsiders*, *Christian Belief in a Postmodern World* and *Spiritual Theology*.

Chapter 1: Path One

[1]For more, see Origen, *Selected Works*, trans. Rowan A. Greer (Mahweh, N.J.: Paulist, 1979). Origen is reported to have written more than two thousand books, many of which were destroyed or lost to history. This number is widely disputed, but nobody questions that he was highly prolific.

[2]See *The Works of Philo*, trans. C. D. Yonge (Peabody, Mass.: Hendrickson, 1993); also "Sifra," trans. Karlfried Froehlich in *Biblical Interpretation in the Early Church* (Philadelphia: Fortress, 1984).

[3]Origen, *Selected Works*, pp. 245-70.

[4]Ibid., p. 250.

[5]Ibid., pp. 252-54.

[6]Ibid., p. 254.

[7]Ibid., p. 258.

[8]See Numbers 33:9ff. Note: our Bibles translate "Helim" as "Elim." Origen spells the same location as it is presented here.

[9]Origen, *Selected Works*, pp. 261-63.

[10]See Plato's *Republic*.

[11]Origen, *Selected Works*, pp. 231-36.

[12]Ibid., pp. 231-32.

[13]Ibid., pp. 233-34.

[14]See, for example, Augustine, "The Teacher," *Philosophy in the Middle Ages*, ed. Arthur Hyman and James J. Walsh (Indianapolis: Hackett, 1978), pp. 20-33.

[15]See Augustine *Confessions*, trans. J. G. Pilkington (Peabody, Mass.: Hendrickson, 1994), pp. 45-208. Also see Augustine's *City of God*, trans. Marcus Dods (Peabody, Mass.: Hendrickson, 1994), pp. 1-511.

[16]Two key texts by Augustine that articulate these thoughts are *On the Holy Trinity*, trans. Arthur Haddan, in *On the Holy Trinity; Doctrinal Treatises; Moral Treatises,* Nicene and Post-Nicene Fathers, series 1, vol. 3 (Peabody, Mass.: Hendrickson, 1994), pp. 1-228, and *On Christian Doctrine*, trans. D. W. Robertson Jr. (Indianapolis: Bobbs-Merrill, 1958).

[17]The two really go hand-in-hand as J. P. Moreland *(Loving God with Our Mind)*, Alister McGrath *(Intellectuals Don't Need God and Other Modern Myths)* and others demonstrate.

[18]Augustine *The Enchiridian* and *The First Catechism*, trans. S. D. F. Salmond, Nicene and Post-Nicene Fathers 3 (Peabody, Mass.: Hendrickson, 1994), pp. 237-314.

[19]Augustine *Confessions*, bk. 8, chap. 5, trans. by R. S. Pine-Coffin (New York: Penguin, 1961).

[20]Ibid., bk. 3, chap. 1.

[21]Ibid., bk. 8, chap. 12.

[22]One telling example from the history of literature is noteworthy. In Dante's *Divine Comedy*, Virgil is Dante's guide through the Inferno and Purgatory. But Virgil, as the image of human reason, cannot enter Paradise. Thus, as Dante enters Paradise, he is accompanied first by Beatrice. Then, as he prepares to enter the highest levels of Paradise, where Beatrice is not yet prepared to go, Dante is handed off to an old, white-bearded man who turns out to be Bernard of Clairvaux. Bernard, as the image of perfected wisdom and godliness, is the poet's supreme and final guide in the spiritual life.

[23]Bernard of Clairvaux, *Selected Works*, trans. G. R. Evans, Classics of Western Spirituality (Mahweh, N.J.: Paulist, 1987), pp. 15-19.

[24]Ibid., pp. 99-100.

[25]Ibid., pp. 99-143.

[26]Bernard of Clairvaux, "On Loving God," in *Selected Works*, pp. 173-205.

[27]Ibid., pp. 194-95.

[28]Ibid., pp. 195-97.

[29]Blaise Pascal, *The Pensées*, frag. 12, trans. Thomas Krailsheimer (New York: Penguin, 1965).

[30]Ibid., frag. 24.

[31]Ibid., frag. 44.

[32]Ibid., frag. 45.

[33]Ibid., frag. 418.

[34]Ibid., frag. 149.

[35]Ibid., frags. 117, 121-22.

[36]Ibid., frags. 132-37.

[37]John Steinbeck, *Cannery Row* (New York: Viking, 1945).

[38]Pascal, *Pensées*, frag. 308. The Jansenist movement was named for Cornelius Jansen, bishop of Ypres, who published *Augustinus*. His ideas were popularized by seventeenth-century clerics who enjoyed his focus on Augustine's understanding of grace and its sufficiency for salvation.

[39]Pascal, *Pensées*, frag. 308. The graphic presentation here was originally developed by Diogenes Allen and is presented here by his permission.

[40]Blaise Pascal, *Love Aflame: Selections from the Writings of Blaise Pascal*, comp. Robert E. Coleman (Wilmore, Ky.: Asbury Theological Seminary Publications, 1974), p. 3.

[41]Ibid., pp. 14-15.

Chapter 2: Path Two

[1]Thomas Kuhn, *The Structure of Scientific Revolutions* (Chicago: University of Chicago Press, 1966).

[2]See *The Renovaré Spiritual Formation Bible* (San Francisco: HarperCollins, 2005), esp. fifteen section introductions and the general introduction.

[3]Bernard McGinn, *The Foundations of Mysticism: Origins to the Fifth Century* (New York: Crossroad, 1993), pp. 144ff.

[4]The faculty that includes our reasoning capabilities and our ability to make discerning judgments.

[5]The order presented here is altered slightly from Evagrius's original order. His original order is as follows: gluttony, impurity/lust, avarice/greed, sadness/melancholy, anger, acedia/sloth/indifference, vainglory/envy, and pride. Over time, Evagrius's order has shifted slightly as later writers attempted to address the way in which the deadly thoughts and the godly virtues expressed various levels of our faith development. For a more contemporary treatment of these issues see Seward Hiltner's *The Seven Deadly Sins*, and Donald Capps's *Life-Cycle Theory and Pastoral Care*.

[6]Evagrius Ponticus, *The Praktikos and Chapters on Prayer*, trans. John Eudes Bamberger (Kalamazoo, Mich.: Cistercian, 1981), p. 17.

[7]Ibid., p. 18.

[8]Ibid., p. 17.

[9]Ibid., p. 20.

[10]Ibid.

[11]Ibid., p. 19.

[12]Ibid., p. 17.

[13]For a more extensive treatment see the entire work of *The Praktikos and Chapters on Prayer*. Evagrius's basic framework of the eight deadly thoughts is discussed in sections 6-14. His amplification of each of these deadly thoughts and how to treat them and respond is found throughout sections 15-56.

[14]Ibid., p. 25.

[15]Ibid., sections 63-90, pp. 33-39.

[16]Ibid., p. xxxvi.

[17]Diogenes Allen, *Christian Belief in a Post-Modern World* (Louisville: Westminster/John Knox, 1989); C. C. Gillespie, *The Edge of Objectivity* (Princeton, N.J.: Princeton University Press, 1960), and Michael. Polanyi, *Personal Knowledge* (Chicago: University of Chicago Press, 1958).

[18]George Herbert, *The Country Parson; The Temple,* ed. by John N. Wall Jr. (New York: Paulist, 1981). For vices, see poem 64, p. 203; poem 88, p. 232; for virtues, see poem 43, pp. 182-83; poem 48, p. 186; poem 66, p. 206; poem 83, p. 225.

[19]Ibid., poem 165, "Love (III)," p. 316.

[20]Ibid., poem 51, p. 190.

[21]Ibid., poem 41, p. 181.

[22]Ibid., poem 47, p. 186.

[23]Ibid., poem 32, p. 174.

[24]Ibid., poem 107, p. 255.

[25]Ibid., poem 116, pp. 266-67.

[26]George Herbert, *The Temple*, Classics of Western Spirituality (New York: Paulist, 1981).

[27]Northrop Frye, *The Secular Scripture* (Cambridge, Mass.: Harvard University Press, 1976).

[28]John Bunyan, *The Pilgrim's Progress in Modern English* (Gainesville, Fla.: Bridge-Logos, 1998), p. 211.

[29]Thomas Merton, *The Seven Storey Mountain* (New York: Harcourt, 1948). *The Seven Storey Mountain* covers his life only up until he enters the monastery. *The Journals* encompass the entire expanse of his life right up to the day of his untimely death.

[30]According to all sources, Merton is believed to have accidentally electrocuted himself with a faulty fan while traveling in Thailand for a conference on religion and spirituality in the East and West. When releasing the Japanese version of *The Seven Storey Mountain* in 1966, here is what Merton says about his classic: "Perhaps if I were to attempt this book today, it would be written differently. Who knows? But it was written when I was still quite young, and that is the way it remains. The story no longer belongs to me."

[31]Thomas Merton, *The Intimate Merton* (San Francisco: HarperOne, 1999), p. 23.

[32]Ibid., p. 47.

[33]Ibid., p. 199.

[34]Ibid., p. 299-302.

[35]Ibid., p. 94.

[36]Ibid., p. 176.

[37]Thomas Merton, *Mystics and Zen Masters* (New York: Farrar, Straus & Giroux, 1967), pp. 91-112.

[38]Thomas Merton, *Life and Holiness* (New York: Image/Doubleday, 1963), p. 9.

[39]Esther de Waal, *A Seven Day Journey with Thomas Merton* (Ann Arbor, Mich.: Servant, 1992), p. 26.

[40]Merton, *Seven Storey Mountain*, pp. 40-41.

[41]Thomas Merton, *Contemplative Prayer* (New York: Doubleday, 1971), p. 11.

[42]De Waal, *Seven Day Journey*, p. 26.

Chapter 3: Path Three

[1]*The Imitation of Christ* is generally ascribed to Thomas à Kempis, although its exact authorship has never been determined.

[2]Maurice Merleau-Ponty, *Phenomenology of Perception*, trans. Colin Smith (London: Routledge, 1989).

[3]Thomas Aquinas *Summa Theologica* 1.2.1.

[4]Thomas Aquinas *Compendium of Theology*, trans. Cyril Vollert (St. Louis: Herder, 1947), p. 208.

[5]Thomas Aquinas *Summa Theologica* 1.79.9.

[6]Ibid., 1.12.12.

[7]Ibid., 2.2.1.3.

[8]Ibid., 1.1.8.

[9]Thomas Aquinas *Summa Theologica*, Q.82, pp. 1528-31.

[10]Ibid., Q.180, pp. 1923-33.

[11]Ibid., 2.2.Q.83.a.1.c.

[12]Ibid., I.Q.82.a.4.

[13]John Goldingay, "The Logic of Intercession," *Theology 101* (1998): 270.

[14]Quoted in Tuomo Mannermaa, *Christ Present in Faith: Luther's View of Justification* (Philadelphia: Fortress, 2005), p. 311.

[15]A. Skevington Wood, "Spirit and Spirituality in Martin Luther," *Evangelical Quarterly* 61, no. 4 (1989): 311-33.

[16]Martin Luther, *The Complete Works of Martin Luther*, {St. Louis: Concordia), 1957 CD-ROM, 41:114.

[17]Ibid., 48:334.

[18]Ibid., 40:29.

[19]Ibid., 21:304

[20]Ibid., 22:303.

[21]Ibid., 36:301.

[22]Ibid., 26:387.

[23]Ibid., 41:143.

[24]Ibid., 41:144.

[25]Paul Althaus, *The Theology of Martin Luther*, trans. Robert C. Schultz (Philadelphia: Fortress, 1966).

[26]Mannermaa, *Christ Present in Faith*.

[27]Martin Luther, *A Simple Way to Pray* (Louisville: Westminster/John Knox, 2000), p. 17.

[28]Martin Luther, "Of God's Word, XX," *Table Talk* (Philadelphia: Lutheran Publication Society, 1997).

[29]It is often thought that Luther wrote "Away in a Manger." While this is not the case (it is an English Christmas carol) the spirit and message of the hymn fits him well.

[30]Samuel Taylor Coleridge, accessed at <http://www.theologywebsite.com/etext/luther_hymns.shtml>.

[31]John Calvin, *Institutes of the Christian Religion* (1536 edition) (Grand Rapids: Eerdmans, 1995), pp. 18-19.

[32]Ibid., p. 19.

[33]Ibid., p. 28.

[34]Ibid., p. 68.

[35]Ibid., p. 69.

[36]Ibid.

Chapter 4: Path Four

[1]See Bruce Metzger, *Lexical Aids for Students of New Testament Greek* (Grand Rapids: Baker, 1998). Metzger notes 164 different times that Paul uses the term "in Christ" to demonstrate that this life with God can only be realized by imitating Christ. See also Bruce Metzger, *The Text of the New Testament* (Oxford: Oxford University Press, 1968).

[2]See Ernst Troeltsch, *The Social Teaching of the Christian Churches* (Louisville: Westminster/John Knox, 1992), H. Richard Niebuhr, *Christ and Culture* (San Francisco: Harper & Row, 1951), and Richard Fox, *Jesus in America* (San Francisco: HarperSanFrancisco, 2004), as three classic examples. Of course, Jaroslav Pelikan's *Jesus Through the Centuries* (San Francisco: HarperSanFrancisco, 1985) remains the most focused and classic statement on the subject. In this latter text Pelikan creates a kaleidoscope of insight into the life of Jesus by identifying eighteen different archetypes that represent the way in which Jesus has been depicted throughout Christian history.

[3]Six key shifts occurred in the thirteenth century that opened the way for a new approach to our life with God. First, a new wave of urbanization was triggered as a significant and growing influx of people flocked to the cities. Second, this population migration stimulated a whole new wave of economic growth and expansion. Next, this expansion created organic pressure that forced European societies to create reliable infrastructures. The development of reliable infrastructures and the growing influx of populations gathering in cities increased legal disputes requiring innovations and adaptations that gave rise to our highly sophisticated and complex legal and court systems. Then, the rise of the population stimulated renewed interest and commitment to universal education, and this interest renewed a call for vernacular theology, a theology typified by its availability and accessibility to the masses. Finally, this rising population without class title or distinction led to an explosion of interest in trade and commerce,

launching one of the most profound quests to understand and exploit the vast resources of an emerging global economy. This is the context in which Christianity found itself as the thirteenth century opened, and this rapid expansion and change required a new expression of life with God.

[4]Francis of Assisi, *Francis and Clare: The Complete Works*, trans. Regis J. Armstrong and Ignatius C. Brady (New York: Paulist, 1982), p. 3.

[5]See Bonaventure, *Life of St. Francis,* trans. Ewert Cousins (New York: Paulist, 1978), pp. 177-333.

[6]See Bernard McGinn, *The Flowering of Mysticism* (New York: Crossroad, 1998).

[7]Bonaventure, *Life of St. Francis*, p. 216.

[8]Ibid., pp. 262-63.

[9]Francis of Assisi, "Later Rule" 10.8, in *Francis and Clare,* p. 144.

[10]Francis of Assisi, "The Earlier Rule" 16.1, in ibid., p. 121.

[11]Francis of Assisi, "Later Rule" 10.8, in ibid.

[12]Francis of Assisi, *Francis and Clare,* p. 4.

[13]Ibid., p. 31-34.

[14]Francis of Assisi, *The Little Flowers of St. Francis,* trans. Raphael Brown (Garden City, N.Y.: Doubleday, 1958), pp. 42-43.

[15]Ibid., p. 68.

[16]Paul Sabatier, *Life of St. Francis of Assisi* (New York: Charles Scribner's, 1894), p. 307.

[17]Ibid., p. 83.

[18]Francis of Assisi, *Francis and Clare,* p. 103.

[19]See Bonaventure's thirteen-volume work for an extensive treatment of his bibliography.

[20]Bonaventure, *Life of St. Francis,* pp. 182-83.

[21]Bonaventure, *The Soul's Journey to God,* trans. Ewert Cousins. (New York: Paulist, 1978). His best-known work is also his finest contribution, *The Journey of the Soul to God.* Originally published in 1259, it is a wonderful integration of his philosophical writings, his deeply held spiritual beliefs, his theories of human knowledge and his fidelity to St. Francis.

[22]See Jean Leclercq, *The Love of Learning and the Desire for God* (New York: Fordham University Press, 1961). This book provides an excellent resource for understanding the six basic steps in *lectio divina* and provides a wonderful guide to the way in which Scripture is used in our life with God.

[23]The phrase "the book of experience" was pioneered by Bernard and popularized by Bonaventure. In essence, it recovers an emphasis from the early church on our spiritual experiences of God providing help and confirmation for our spiritual life when understood properly.

[24]Bonaventure, *Soul's Journey to God,* p. 70

[25]Ibid., p. 81.

[26]Ibid., p. 82.

[27]Ibid., pp. 84ff.

[28]Ibid., p. 89.

[29]Ibid., pp. 92-93.

[30]Ibid., pp. 94-101.

[31]Ibid., pp. 102-9.

[32]Bonaventure, *The Life of St. Francis*, pp. 179-327.

[33]Bonaventure, "Prayer of St. Bonaventure," found at External Word Television Network, <www.ewtn.com/Devotionals/prayers/Bonaventure.htm>.

[34]Thomas à Kempis, *The Imitation of Christ*, trans. William C. Creasy (Macon, Ga.: Mercer University Press, 1989), p. 8.

[35]Ibid., pp. 150-54.

[36]Ibid., p. 21.

[37]Ibid., p. 26.

[38]Ibid., p. 23.

[39]Ibid., p. 78.

[40]Ignatius of Loyola *Personal Writings,* trans. Joseph A. Munitz and Philip Endean (New York: Penguin, 1996), p. 13.

[41]Ibid., p. 113.

[42]Ibid., p. 139.

[43]Abraham Black and William F. Prokas, *Classical Conditioning II* (New York: Appleton-Century-Crafts, 1972), pp. 422-23. See also Leland C. Swenson, *Theories of Learning* (Belmont, Calif.: Wadsworth, 1980), pp. 367-72.

[44]Ignatius of Loyola *Spiritual Exercises* (Boston: Daughters of St. Paul, 1978), pp. 41-59.

[45]Ibid., pp. 61-90.

[46]Ibid., pp. 102-114.

[47]Ibid., pp. 115-122.

[48]Ignatius of Loyola, *Personal Writings* (New York: Penguin, 1996) pp. 226-31.

[49]Ibid., pp. 232-37.

Chapter 5: Path Five

[1]William Ralph Inge, *Christian Mysticism* (London: Menthuen, 1899), p. 335.

[2]Rufus Jones, *Studies in Mystical Religion* (New York: Macmillan, 1923), p. xv. See also Evelyn Underhill, *Mysticism* (New York: Image/Doubleday, 1911); Ernst Troeltsch, *The Social Teaching of the Christian Churches,* vols. 1-2, trans. Olive Wyon (London: Allen & Unwin, 1931); and *Mysticism and Religious Traditions,* ed. Stephen Katz (New York: Oxford University Press, 1983); for a specific, comprehensive consideration see my chapter in *Truth's Bright Embrace,* ed. Paul N. Anderson and Howard R. Macy (Newberg, Ore.: Barclay, 1996), pp. 137-44.

[3]Julian of Norwich, *Showings* (New York: Paulist, 1978), p. xix.

4Julian of Norwich, *Revelations of Divine Love*, trans. Elizabeth Spearing (London: Penguin, 1998).

5Ibid., p. 11.

6Ibid., chap. 8, p. 12.

7Ibid.

8Ibid., p. 13.

9Ibid.

10Ibid., p. 14.

11Ibid.

12Ibid., p. 15.

13Ibid., pp. 15-18.

14Ibid., pp. 18-19.

15Ibid., p. 20.

16Ibid.

17Ibid.

18Ibid., pp. 22-27.

19Ibid., pp. 28-30.

20Ibid., pp. 30-32.

21Ibid., pp. 153-55.

22Ibid., p. 36.

23Julian of Norwich *Showings*, p. 186.

24Ibid., p. 199.

25Ibid., p. 181.

26Abba Anthony *Vitae Patrum* 7.38; PL 73:1055C, as quoted in Irénée Hausherr, *Penthos* (Rome: Pont. Institutum Orientalium Studiorum, 1944), p. 41.

27Julian of Norwich, *Showings*, p. 178.

28Ibid., pp. 184-86.

29Ibid., p. 249.

30Ibid., p. 248.

31Ibid., p. 253.

32*Enfolded in Love: Daily Readings with Julian of Norwich* (New York: Seabury, 1980), p. 15.

33John Punshon, *Portrait in Grey: A Short History of the Quakers* (London: Quaker Home Service, 1984).

34As noted earlier, Francis made a sustained effort to cultivate a devotion to the earthly, human example of Jesus Christ. Francis did not comment on Augustine's understanding of the inner Christ as teacher, but instead, amplified this teaching by focusing on Jesus' life as recorded in the Gospels.

35Augustine of Hippo, "The Teacher," in *Philosophy in the Middle Ages,* trans. Arthur Hyman and James J. Walsh (Indianapolis: Hackett, 1973), p. 31.

[36]George Fox, *The Journal of George Fox*, ed. John L. Nickalls (Philadelphia: Religious Society of Friends, 1985), p. 69.

[37]Ibid., pp. 1-100.

[38]Ibid., p. 14.

[39]Ibid., p. 40.

[40]John Locke, *An Essay Concerning Human Understanding* (Garden City, N.Y.: Anchor, 1974).

[41]René Descartes, *Meditations on First Philosophy,* trans. Laurence J. Lafleur (Indianapolis: Bobbs-Merrill, 1960).

[42]Fox, *Journal of George Fox*, p. 20.

[43]Ibid., p. 35.

[44]Ibid., p. 149.

[45]Ibid., p. 24.

[46]Ibid., p. 197.

[47]Ibid., pp. 169-70.

[48]As quoted in Lewis Benson, *What Did George Fox Teach About Christ?* (Gloucester, U.K.: Fellowship, 1976), p. 29.

[49]George Fox, *The Works of George Fox,* 8 vols. (New York: Isaac T. Hopper, 1831), 8:153.

[50]Benson, *What Did George Fox Teach?* p. 1.

[51]John Wesley, *The Works of John Wesley,* ed. Albert C. Outler (Nashville: Abingdon, 1984-).

[52]Samuel Johnson, *A Dictionary of the English Language,* s.v. "experimental."

[53]John Wesley, "Sermons on Several Occasions," *The Works of John Wesley,* 1:106.

[54]The phrase "the Wesleyan quadrilateral," was coined initially in the 1960s by Albert "Sandy" Outler.

[55]Blaise Pascal, *Pensées,* frag. 173, trans. Thomas Krailsheimer (Middlesex, U.K.: Penguin, 1966), p. 83.

[56]John Wesley, *The Works of John Wesley* (Oxford: Clarendon, 1975-1983), 2:599.

[57]See Robert Barclay, *Barclay's Apology,* ed. Dean Freiday (Elberson, N.J.: Sowers, 1967).

[58]John Wesley, "The Witness of the Spirit, I-II," *The Works of John Wesley,* 1:299-313.

[59]*The Journal of the Rev. John Wesley,* ed. Nehemiah Curnock (London: R. Culley, 1909-1916), entry dated August 25, 1763.

[60]Friedrich Schleiermacher, *On Religion: Speeches to the Cultured Among Its Despisers,* trans. Richard Crouter (New York: Cambridge University Press, 1988).

[61]Ibid., p. 162.

[62]Ibid., pp. 162-88.

[63]Ibid., pp. 189-223.

[64]John Calvin, *Institutes of the Christian Religion,* trans. Henry Beveridge (Grand Rapids: Eerdmans, 1989).

[65]A. Gerrish, *A Prince of the Church: Schleiermacher and the Beginnings of Modern Theology* (Philadelphia: Fortress, 1984), p. 25.

Chapter 6: Path Six

[1]John Cassian *Conferences* 14.1, trans. Colm Luibheid, Classics of Western Spirituality (Mahweh, N.J.: Paulist, 1985).

[2]Gregory the Great *Forty Gospel Homilies* (Kalamazoo, Mich.: Cistercian, 1990).

[3]John Cassian *Conferences* 1.2.

[4]Ibid., 10.6.

[5]Ibid., 14.1.

[6]Ibid., 14.2-3.

[7]For an expanded treatment of action and contemplation see Bernard McGinn and Patricia Ferris McGinn, *Early Christian Mystics* (New York: Crossroad, 2003), pp. 59-75.

[8]James Walsh, *Spirituality Through the Centuries* (New York: P. J. Kenedy, 1964). See Bede Griffiths, "John Cassian," in *Spirituality Through the Centuries,* ed. James Walsh (New York: P. J. Kenedy, 1964), pp. 25-41.

[9]John Cassian *Conferences* 2 (esp. 2.4). For an excellent secondary source treatment of "discernment" in Cassian see John Levko, "The Relationship of Prayer to Discretion and Spiritual Direction for John Cassian," *St. Vladimir's Theological Quarterly* 40, no. 3 (1996): 155-71.

[10]John Cassian *Conferences* 3.7.

[11]Ibid., 9.

[12]Ibid., 9.9

[13]Ibid., 9.16–9.26

[14]See John J. Levko, "Prayer in a Culture of Excess," *Diakonia* 33, no. 3 (Bronx, N.Y.: Fordham University Press, 1966), pp. 275-82.

[15]John Cassian *Conferences* 14.6.

[16]Ibid., 14.1.

[17]Ibid., 14.8.

[18]See Rebecca Harden Weaver, "Access to Scripture: Experiencing the Text," *Interpretation* 54, no. 4 (1998): 367-79.

[19]See Gregory the Great *Dialogues.* Gregory wrote the most extensive biography of Benedict. It is from his original pen that we derive much of our understanding of Benedict's work and much of our access to Benedict's life.

[20]Below are the 72 instruments of good works from *The Rule of St. Benedict in English* ([Collegeville, Minn.: Liturgical Press, 1982], RB#4, pp. 26-27) that create a balanced love of God and neighbor.

　1. Love God with all one's heart, soul and strength.

　2. Love one's neighbor as oneself.

　3. Do not kill.

4. Do not commit adultery.

5. Do not steal.

6. Do not covet.

7. Do not bear false witness.

8. Honor all persons.

9. Do unto others, as you would have them do unto you.

10. Deny yourself in order to follow Christ.

11. Chastise the body.

12. Do not seek delicate living.

13. Love fasting.

14. Relieve the poor.

15. Clothe the naked.

16. Visit the sick.

17. Bury the dead.

18. Help the afflicted.

19. Console the sorrowing.

20. Keep away from the things of the world.

21. Prefer nothing except to love Christ.

The second part, which deals with what person we are to become, is summarized in 22 through 72. Here they are in brief outline.

22. Do not give way to anger.

23. Do not harbor a desire for revenge.

24. Do not foster guile in one's heart.

25. Do not make a fake peace, but a real one.

26. Maintain charity.

27. Do not swear.

28. Always utter the truth from your heart and mouth.

29. Do not return evil for evil.

30. Do no wrong to anyone and patiently bear a wrong done to you.

31. Love our enemies.

32. Always extend a blessing.

33. Bear persecution for the sake of justice.

34. Do not be proud.

35. Do not be given to much wine.

36. Do not be a glutton.

37. Do not become drowsy.

38. Do not be slothful.

39. Do not become a murmurer.

40. Do not be a detractor.

41. Put your hope in God.

42. Always attribute any good to God alone.

43. Recognize and always impute to oneself the evil that one does.

44. To fear the day of judgment.

45. To be in dread of hell.

46. To desire with a special longing everlasting life.

47. To keep death daily before one's eyes.

48. To keep guard at all times over the actions of one's life.

49. To know for certain that God sees one everywhere.

50. To dash down on the rock Christ one's evil thoughts the instant that they come into the heart.

51. Lay your thoughts and faults open to your spiritual director.

52. Keep your mouth from evil and wicked words.

53. Do not love much speaking.

54. Do not speak vain words or such as move to laughter.

55. Do not love to laugh or engage in excessive laughter.

56. Listen willingly to holy reading.

57. To apply oneself frequently to prayer.

58. Daily confess your sins with tears and sighs to God, and to amend them for the time to come.

59. Do not fulfill the desires of the flesh.

60. Obey in all things the commands of the abbot, even though he himself should act otherwise; being mindful of that precept of the Lord.

61. Do not wish to be called holy before one is so; but first to be holy, that one may be truly so called.

62. Daily fulfill by one's deeds the commandments.

63. Love chastity.

64. Hate no one.

65. Do not be overcome with envy or jealousy.

66. Do not love strife.

67. Fly away from vainglory.

68. Reverence your seniors.

69. Love the juniors.

70. Pray for one's enemies in the love of Christ.

71. Make peace with an adversary before sunset.

72. Never despair of God's mercy.

[21]Rule 2.

[22]Rule 3.

[23]Rule 64, for this one and all the rest.

[24]Timothy Fry, ed., *The Rule of St. Benedict in English* (Collegeville, Minn.: Liturgical Press, 1982), p. 20.

²⁵Ibid., p. 21.

²⁶For the specific texts that pertain to the spiritual life see *Moralia on Job* 5.52-66; 6.55-61; 8.49-50; 10.31; 18.88-90; 23.37-43; 24.11-12; 31.99-102; *Homilies on Ezekiel* 1.3.9-14; 1.5.12-13; 2.1.16-18; 2.2.7-15; 2.5.8-29; *Pastoral Rule* 1.5-7; 2.5, 7. *Dialogues.*

²⁷Gregory the Great *Homilies on Ezekiel* 2.2.12.

²⁸Ibid., 2.2.14.

²⁹Gregory the Great *Homilies on Ezekiel* 1.3.14; *Homilies on the Gospels* 26.12.

³⁰See G. R. Evans, *The Thought of Gregory the Great* (Cambridge: Cambridge University Press, 1986); Gregory the Great *Homilies on the Gospel;* cf. with *Isaiah.*

³¹Gregory *Homilies on Ezekiel* 2.5.8.

³²Ibid., 2.5.9.

³³Gregory the Great *The Homilies of St. Gregory the Great on the Book of the Prophet Ezekiel* 2.2.7, trans. Theodosia Gray (Etna, Calif.: Center for Traditionalist Orthodox Studies, 1990).

³⁴Ibid., 2.2.9.

³⁵Ibid., 2.2.10.

³⁶Ibid., 2.2.11.

³⁷Ibid., 2.2.12.

³⁸Gregory the Great *Moralia on Job* 8.10.19.

³⁹Gregory the Great *Homilies on Ezekiel.*

⁴⁰Gregory the Great *Moralia on Job* 32.3.4; additional references and emphasis communicated throughout other writings, but especially in *Homilies on Ezekiel* 2.2.7-15.

⁴¹Ibid., 32.3.4.

⁴²Ibid., 28.

⁴³Ibid., 39.

Chapter 7: Path Seven

¹For an extensive treatment of this discovery see Paul Rorem, *Pseudo-Dionysius: A Commentary on the Texts and an Introduction to their Influence* (New York: Oxford University Press, 1993).

²*Pseudo-Dionysius: The Complete Works*, trans. Colm Luibheid, Classics of Western Spirituality (New York: Paulist, 1987).

³We have four extant works by Pseudo-Dionysius and ten articles or letters. Throughout his known works he makes reference to two additional books that are lost or destroyed: *Symbolic Theology* and *Theological Representations.*

⁴James McEvoy, ed. and trans., *Mystical Theology* (Dudley, Mass.: Peeters, 2003), 3.

⁵Ibid., 4.

⁶See Pseudo-Dionysius, *The Divine Names and Mystical Theology,* trans. John D. Jones (Milwaukee: Marquette University Press, 1980).

⁷*The Cloud of Unknowing* (San Francisco: HarperSanFrancisco, 2001), p. 21. Originally

translated by Paulist Press, 1981.

[8]Ibid., p. 30.

[9]Ibid., pp. 50-56.

[10]Ibid., pp. 35-36.

[11]Ibid., pp. 38, 84.

[12]Ibid., pp. 74-75.

[13]See Everett Cattell, *The Spirit of Holiness* (Kansas City: Beacon Hill, 1965).

[14]See also ibid., p. 56.

[15]Ibid., p. 108.

[16]Quoted from "The Cloud of Unknowing," Wikipedia <http://en.wikipedia.org/wiki/The_Cloud_of_Unknowing>.

[17]Quoted at <http://frimmin.com/books/cloudunknow.php>.

[18]Ibid.

[19]Ibid.

[20]*The Cloud of Unknowing,* ed. Emilie Griffin (San Francisco: HarperSanFrancisco, 1981), p. 66.

[21]Ibid.

[22]Ibid.

[23]Teresa also has a fourth book, *The Book of Foundations.* It is not as well known, but consists of several aphorisms that speak of the nature of the spiritual life.

[24]Teresa of Avila, *The Interior Castle,* trans. Kieran Kavanaugh (San Francisco: HarperSanFrancisco, 2004), p. x.

[25]Ibid., p. 3.

[26]Ibid., pp. 5-6.

[27]Ibid., p. 7.

[28]Ibid., p. 10.

[29]Ibid., p. 11.

[30]Ibid., pp. 18-20.

[31]Ibid., p. 30.

[32]Ibid., pp. 42-44.

[33]Ibid., p. 50.

[34]Ibid., p. 54.

[35]Ibid., p. 72.

[36]Ibid., p. 79.

[37]Ibid., p. 83.

[38]Ibid., p. 85.

[39]Ibid., pp. 89-92.

[40]Ibid., p. 104.

[41]Ibid., p. 121.

[42]Ibid., pp. 128-29.

[43]Teresa of Avila, *The Interior Castle* (Mahweh, N.J.: Paulist, 1979), p. 130.

[44]Ibid., p. 35.

[45]Ibid., p. 179.

[46]Ibid., p. 196.

[47]Ibid., pp. 132-33.

[48]John has a fourth major work, *The Spiritual Canticle*, which is a complement to *The Living Flame of Love*.

[49]John of the Cross, *The Dark Night*, trans. Kieran Kavanaugh (San Francisco: Harper-SanFrancisco, 2004), p. 1.

[50]Ibid., p. 3.

[51]Ibid., p. 5.

[52]Ibid., p. 7.

[53]Ibid., chap. 8.

[54]Ibid., chap. 10.

[55]Ibid., p. 14.

[56]John of the Cross, *Selected Writings (The Dark Night)*, ed. Kieran Kavanaugh, Classics of Western Spirituality (New York: Paulist, 1978), p. 162.

[57]John of the Cross, *Selected Writings (The Living Flame of Love)*, ed. Kieran Kavanaugh, Classics of Western Spirituality (New York: Paulist, 1978), pp. 293-94.

[58]Ibid., p. 143.

[59]John of the Cross, *Dark Night*, p. 208.

Appendix 1

[1]Evagrius of Ponticus, *The Praktikos,* trans. John Eudes Bamberger (Kalamazoo, Mich.: Cistercian, 1981), chap. 9.

[2]Plato *Phaedrus* 256b.

[3]Ibid., 253d.

[4]Ibid., 516a.

[5]Aristotle, *Nichomachean Ethics*, trans. W. D. Ross, The Complete Works of Aristotle (Princeton, N.J.: Princeton University Press, 1984), 2:1729-1867.

[6]Michael Stone, *Scriptures, Sects and Visions: A Profile of Judaism from Ezra to Jewish Revolts* (Philadelphia: Fortress Press, 1980).

[7]Louis Bouyer, *The Spirituality of the New Testament and the Fathers* (New York: Seabury, 1982), pp. 3-20.

[8]*The Works of Philo*, trans. C. D. Yonge (Peabody, Mass.: Hendrickson, 1993).

[9]Although there are numerous primary and secondary sources that assist our understanding on this point, two stand out. First, Robert Grant and David Tracy's fine book *A Short History of the Interpretation of the Bible* (Philadelphia: Fortress, 1984), covers this period succinctly and clearly. A second resource, *The Cambridge History of the Bible* (Cambridge: Cambridge University Press, 1970), amplifies Tracy's findings and pro-

vides an enormous bibliography of primary sources.

[10]Bruce Metzger, *Lexical Aids for Students of New Testament Greek* (Grand Rapids: Baker, 1998); Bruce Metzger, *The Text of the New Testament* (Oxford: Oxford University Press, 1968).

[11]Henry Chadwick, *The Early Church* (Middlesex, U.K.: Penguin, 1967), esp. pp. 125-59.

Appendix 2

[1]Madame Guyon, *An Autobiography* (Chicago: Moody Press, 1988).

[2]Madame Guyon, *Experiencing the Depths of Jesus Christ* (Auburn, Maine: Seed Sowers, 1975), p. 4.

[3]Jim Forest, *Love Is the Measure: A Biography of Dorothy Day* (Maryknoll, N.Y.: Orbis, 1994), p. 32.

[4]Ibid., p. 55.

[5]*Noble Lectures, Peace 1971-1980*, ed. Irwin Abrams (Singapore: World Scientific, 1997).

Index

Abba Anthony, 173
accountability, 224
Act of Toleration (British), 180
action
    in "Allegory of the Cave" (Plato), 290
    Cassian on, 207-9, 213-14
    in Gregory the Great's ordering, 228,
        229-30
    See also balance between action and
        contemplation
Adam (first man), 92-93, 233
"Affliction (III)" (Herbert), 67-68
agapé love, 143
"Allegory of the Cave" (Plato), 290
Allen, Diogenes, 9, 10
"Altar, The" (Herbert), 67
Anabaptists, 105
anfechtung, 102
anger, 58-59, 253, 333n. 5
Anglicanism, 184
Anthony the Great, 316-17, 318, 320
apatheia
    Bonaventure on, 137
    Evagrius of Ponticus on, 55, 61-62
    impossibility of, 139-40
    Origen on, 23
    rhythms of spiritual life and, 276-77
    Stoicism and, 287-88
    Teresa of Avila's dwelling places and,
        268
Apologetic Treatises Against Those Decrying
   the Holy Images (John of Damascus),
   323
appetites, 274
Arena, The (Brianchaninov), 328
Arianism, 317, 318, 319
Aristotle
    Athens academy and, 176
    influence of, 291-92, 315
    Thomas Aquinas and, 91, 97, 291
    worldview of, 65

Ascent of Mount Carmel, The (John of the
   Cross), 274, 278
"Ascetic Treatises" (Macarius), 321
Ascetica, 317
asceticism
    in Eastern Orthodoxy, 316-18, 323-24,
        327-28
    women and spirituality and, 298-99,
        301-2, 304, 307
Athanasius of Alexandria, 316, 317, 318
Augustine of Hippo, 26-33
    Blaise Pascal and, 42, 45
    on body and soul, 26-27
    Bonaventure and, 135
    Calvin and, 113-14
    Cassian and, 206-7
    on Christ as inward Teacher, 32, 113-
        14, 177, 179, 339n. 34
    conversion of, 31
    on correct doctrine, 28-29
    on disordered love, 31
    God-shaped vacuum and, 198
    Gregory the Great and, 227
    on heart's restlessness, 11
    on human will, 28-30, 32, 206-7
    Jansenism and, 333n. 38
    on knowing God, 27-29
    on longing for God, 14-15
    on loving God, 26-33
    on nature of faith, 28-29, 30
    Neoplatonism and, 176-77
    on reason, 27, 28, 32
    on sin, 45
    on temptation, 27-28
    Thomas Aquinas and, 91
    Thomas Merton and, 83
authority, 191, 220, 221-23, 256
"Away in a Manger," 336n. 29
balance between action and
   contemplation
    Benedict and, 203-4

Gudmarson, Ulf, 303-4
Guyon, Jacques, 306
Guyon, Madame (Jeanne-Marie Bouvier
  de la Mothe), 306-7
habit, 98, 151, 291-92
Hadewijch of Antwerp, 303
happiness, 53, 59, 92-93, 143, 275
heart
  body and mind and, 30, 45
  purity of, 127, 212, 242, 245, 259, 288
  true home of, 283-84
Helim, 21
Herbert, George, 65-74
Hildegard of Bingen, 89, 299-300
Hillel, 20
Hilton, Walter, 249
holiness, 45-46, 106, 116, 128-29, 190
"Holy Scriptures (II)" (Herbert), 69-70
Holy Spirit
  assurance of salvation and, 189
  cultivation of virtue and, 230
  dark night of the soul and, 274, 278
  double motion of spiritual life and, 74
  dual agency of Word and Spirit and,
    103-6
  eight deadly thoughts and, 288
  Fox on, 179
  imitation of Christ and, 126
  inward testimony of, 113-14
  mystical experiences and, 162, 167
  Pentecostals and, 202
  redemption and sanctification and,
    101-2, 106
  Scripture interpretation and, 188
  Teresa of Avila's dwelling places and,
    266
  union with God and, 258
  work of, 103-4
Homily 27 on Numbers (Origen), 21
honesty, 180
hope, 209
hopelessness, 102
Hopkins, Gerard Manley, 139

human condition, 43
human nature, 44-45, 49-50
humility
  in Benedictine spirituality, 219-21,
    224-25
  Bernard of Clairvaux on, 40
  Blaise Pascal on, 45-46
  in *Cloud of Unknowing*, 254-56
  discernment and, 210
  Ephraim the Syrian and, 318
  Evagrius of Ponticus on, 59-60
  Francis of Assisi and, 130, 132
  in Gregory's ordering, 229
  imitation of Christ and, 142-43, 147
  knowledge of God and, 213
  pride and, 59-60
  spiritual growth and, 212
  struggle and, 323
  Teresa of Avila's dwelling places and,
    264-65, 268
  twelve degrees of, 219-21
Hundred Years War, 249
Huxley, Aldous, 83
hymns, 130
Hymns of Divine Love (Symeon the New
  Theologian), 324
Ignatius of Loyola, 144, 146, 149-57, 261
illness, 50
illumination
  dark night of the soul and, 276, 277
  divine ascent and, 237, 241-43, 245, 247
  Teresa of Avila's dwelling places and,
    262, 265
image of God, 55-56, 112
imagination, 135-36, 152-53, 156, 166
imitation of Christ
  apostles on, 122, 336n. 1
  in Benedictine spirituality, 219
  Bonaventure's stages and, 137
  Francis of Assisi and, 121-22, 126-27
  historical expressions of, 122-23
  nature versus grace and, 142, 144-46, 148
  Origen on, 23

For more information about

Richard J. Foster

visit www.richardjfoster.com

For more information about

Gayle D. Beebe

visit www.westmont.edu

For more information about

RENOVARÉ

visit www.renovare.org

For a selected bibliography of the writings

of each figure covered in this book

visit the book's webpage at www.ivpress.com.

∫ormatio
TRADITION. EXPERIENCE.
TRANSFORMATION.

Formatio books from InterVarsity Press follow the rich tradition of the church in the journey of spiritual formation. These books are not merely about being informed, but about being transformed by Christ and conformed to his image. Formatio stands in InterVarsity Press's evangelical publishing tradition by integrating God's Word with spiritual practice and by prompting readers to move from inward change to outward witness. InterVarsity Press uses the chambered nautilus for Formatio, a symbol of spiritual formation because of its continual spiral journey outward as it moves from its center. We believe that each of us is made with a deep desire to be in God's presence. Formatio books help us to fulfill our deepest desires and to become our true selves in light of God's grace.